Vienna

A CITY GUIDE

by
Annabel Barber

SOMERSET LIMITED

© 2002 Somerset Kft.
Vörösmarty tér 1, Pf. 71
1051 Budapest, Hungary
Felelős kiadó: Ruszin Zsolt, a Somerset Kft. igazgatója
office@visiblecities.net
www.visiblecities.net
Visible Cities is a registered trademark.

Layout & Design: *Regina Rácz*
Photographs: *Annabel Barber, Thomas Howells, Sebastian Stachowski,
Historisches Museum der Stadt Wien, Kunsthistorisches Museum, MAK,
Oesterreichische Galerie Belvedere Vienna (pp. 17, 25, 38, 58, 59, 60, 61,
62, 96, 99, 100, 101, 135), Hotel Imperial Vienna*
Diagrams: *Imre Bába*
Architectural Drawings: *Michael Mansell RIBA*
Maps: *Dimap Bt.*
Repro Studio: *Overprint Kft.*
Printed by: *Novoprint Rt. Attila Miseje, Director*

Acknowledgements:

With special thanks to Christopher Wentworth-Stanley
Thanks also to: *Tabitha Barber, István Barkóczi, Darrel Joseph,
Robert Kenedi, Mónika Papp, Anna Mansel-Pleydell, Prof. H.D. Purcell,
Norah Purcell, Emma Roper-Evans, Jeremy Scott*

This is the first edition of **Visible Cities Vienna**:
corrections and general comments will be welcomed.

Other titles in the **Visible Cities** series:
· **Visible Cities Budapest** (2nd edition)
Visible Cities Dubrovnik
Visible Cities Krakow
Further titles are in preparation.

Cover illustration: *Detail from the Engel Apotheke in Bognergasse*
Previous page: *Detail from the courtyard of the Altes Rathaus*
Page headers: *Stylised lizards from the Secession Building*

Annabel Barber has lived in Budapest since 1992. A former editor at
Budapest Magazines and food and wine columnist for the *Budapest Business
Journal*, she works as a freelance writer and translator.

ISBN 963 00 9031 7
ISSN 1587-6403

CONTENTS

INTRODUCTION	7
Ten things to do in Vienna	8
How to use this guide	9
A handful of characters	9
HISTORY	10
The rise of the house of Habsburg	12
The Siege of Vienna	15
The War of the Spanish Succession	16
The end of the Holy Roman Empire	18
The 'pre-March' or Biedermeier age	20
Franz Joseph	21
Central Europe in the mid 19th century	24
Twilight of the Habsburgs	25
Central Europe after the First World War	27
Vienna in the twentieth century	28
Lead-up to the Anschluss	30
The Second World War and its aftermath	31
A Handful of Dates	33
The Holy Roman Empire	34
MAJOR SIGHTS	37
The Stephansdom	37
The Hofburg	42
The Belvedere	53
Gustav Klimt	62
The Ringstrasse	62
ARCHITECTURE	73
Gothic	74
Renaissance	75
Vienna Baroque	75
Rococo	78
Historicism or Ringstrassenstil	78
Jugendstil	79
Modernism & Functionalism	83
A handful of architects	85
ART GALLERIES & MUSEUMS	91
Kunsthistorisches	91
Jugendstil & the Secession Building	95
Other art galleries	97
Major temporary exhibition venues	99
Craft movements	99
Biedermeier	99
Wiener Werkstätte	103
Other major museums	104
COFFEE HOUSES	105
A selection of coffee houses	106
Sachertorte & Imperialtorte	111
Literary Vienna	112
MUSIC	113
Major musical venues	114
Classic Vienna music	116
The Waltz	118
A handful of composers	119
Metternich and the Congress of Vienna	125
RELIGIOUS MONUMENTS	126
The Jews in Vienna	129
The Edict of Tolerance	132
Churches	134
Doctors & philosophers	139
GUIDED WALKS	140
Walk One – *South from the Graben*	141
Walk Two – *Around the Freyung*	149
Walk Three – *From Am Hof*	157
An Officer and a Gentleman	166
Walk Four – *East of the Stephansdom*	167
Walk Five – *Between Wollzeile and Fleischmarkt*	173
Silverscreen Wien – A Selection	181
PLACES TO GO	182
Schönbrunn	183
Grinzing	198
A good day trip	200
PRACTICALITIES	204
Food and restaurants	205
Wine	211
Hotels & pensions	216
Practical tips	220
Index	222
MAPS	234
Walks in context	234
Map references	236
Central Vienna	238

PART I

PART II

PART III

PART IV

PART V

INTRODUCTION

There are two Viennas. Vienna the outpost: the last bastion of the West jutting into Eastern Europe, and Vienna the centrepiece: the hub of an empire and heart of a continent. Both identities have shaped the city's history and character.

Antonio Bonfini, the chronicler of the late 15th-century Hungarian king Matthias Corvinus, was impressed by what he saw. "The city stands like a palace amid its encircling suburbs," he wrote, "The streets and market places bustle with life. A great deal of money is made here, and all of it is spent on food, personal adornments and beautiful buildings." In some ways that view is as true today as it ever was. But Vienna is not that easy to pin down, perhaps because of the diverse mix of peoples who have formed it. Until the creation of the Iron Curtain, which left the city standing isolated and alone at the very dead end of the western world, Vienna lay at the crossroads of Europe. Its population united Latin elements from the south, Slavs and Magyars from the north, south and east, and Germans from the north and west. In the early 18th century it was much too small for the number of people crowding to live there. Two hundred years later, the reverse was true. In 1918 the imperial balloon burst, and suddenly a grandiose capital was left at the head of a tiny, truncated country.

Vienna owes its existence to the Danube, although the river does not flow through the centre of town, and it is possible to go for days without even seeing it. The Romans had patrol boats on it, and Vindobona - modern Vienna - was the base of their Danube fleet. In the year 180, the Roman emperor and philosopher Marcus Aurelius died at Vindobona, after a succession of freezing winter campaigns against barbarian incursion. Then - as now - there was nothing blue about the Danube. Its floodplain was an inhospitable land of icy marshes in winter and fly-blown swamps in summer; but it was eventually tamed. The marshes were drained, the many-armed river was confined to two single streams, and the city turned itself into one of Europe's most elegant and graceful metropolises, a symbol for intrigue and fleeting romance, all conducted in glittering style against a backdrop of some of Europe's greatest art and to the tune of some of its most enduring music.

The spire of the Michaelerkirche towering above tiled roofs, with tall 19th-century façades on either side. A typical central Vienna street scene.

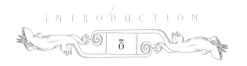
TEN THINGS TO DO IN VIENNA
There are a thousand things to do in Vienna: here is a selection.

1. Visit the Kunsthistorisches Museum, one of the finest art galleries in the world - *p. 91*.

2. See the Belvedere, Eugene of Savoy's Baroque palace, now housing five centuries of Austrian painting with many of Klimt's masterpieces - *p. 53*.

3. Visit the Leopold Museum, home to the best collection of Schiele's tortured works - *p. 97*.

4. Meditate in the Gothic Stephansdom - *p. 37*.

5. Enjoy cheap wine and song at a *Heuriger*. "Extraordinary the potency of cheap music," Noel Coward noted. Find out for yourself - *p. 198*.

6. Wax philosophical over coffee. Adopt your own coffee house: sumptuous or minimalist, fogey or trendy - *p. 105*.

7. Go on a Third Man tour. *De-dum-de-dum, de-dum, de-dum...* - *p. 181*.

8. Have a cocktail. Functionalist Albert Loos' American Bar is the place - *p. 88*.

9. Visit the Hofburg, the Habsburg palace in the heart of Vienna, where the Emperor Franz Joseph ate boiled beef and his beautiful wife Sisi worked out - *p. 43*.

10. Listen to music. The Opera House and the Musikverein are two of Europe's loveliest concert venues - *pp. 114 & 115*.

HOW TO USE THIS GUIDE

This book is organised into five sections. Part I contains the history of Vienna, Austria and the Holy Roman Empire. Part II is the guide to the city, beginning with a section on all the main sights, and including further sections on aspects of culture and entertainment for which Vienna is especially famed - art, architecture, music and coffee houses. Part III comprises five short, guided walks around the inner city. Each walk is designed to take no longer than an hour, and the route is clearly marked on an accompanying map. Part IV covers the palace of Schönbrunn and the vineyards and taverns of Grinzing, both outside the city centre. Part V contains information on food and wine, practical tips about how to get around town, and includes a short, selective listing of restaurants and hotels.

A HANDFUL OF CHARACTERS

Some of the names from Vienna's history which occur and recur in this book.

JOHANN BERNHARD FISCHER VON ERLACH (1656-1723) - Architect who created most of Baroque Vienna.

EUGENE OF SAVOY (1663-1736) - Soldier and statesman who won victories for Austria against France and the Ottomans.

JOSEPH II (1741-1790) - Reforming emperor famous for his Edict of Tolerance, which gave new freedoms to Protestants and Jews.

FRANZ I (1768-1835) - The last Holy Roman Emperor and first

Emperor of Austria. His daughter Marie Louise married Napoleon.

FRANZ JOSEPH (1830-1916) - The man who stood at the end of an era, and whose empire dissolved in the First World War.

OTTO WAGNER (1841-1918) - Vienna's most important Jugendstil architect.

ADOLF LOOS (1870-1933) - Architect who brought a new philosophy to cluttered, over-ornamented Vienna: Functionalism.

Opposite: View across Vienna from the Belvedere (c. 1760) by Bernardo Bellotto.

HISTORY

The city that is Vienna today sits on an inauspicious patch of flat, marshy ground beside the Danube river. Not an obvious site for the capital of a once-mighty realm. Vienna began life as the garrison town of Vindobona, an outpost of the Roman Empire, set up to guard the Danube, which was an important trading waterway between the provinces of east and west. When the Roman Empire fell, Vindobona fell too, and the territory around it was fought over by a marauding maelstrom of barbarian tribes until at last Charlemagne tamed it and included it in his Kingdom of the Romans and Franks, making it his Eastern March or Ostmark, the uttermost fringe of his domains, a bulwark against barbarian incursion. It was always rather a shaky bulwark. The region was constantly harried by the Magyars, until at last they were conclusively defeated by Otto the Great. When Otto was crowned by the Pope in 962, he became the first Holy Roman Emperor of the Saxon dynasty (see p. 34).

In 1156 another Holy Roman Emperor, Frederick Barbarossa, made Austria a hereditary duchy within the Holy Roman Empire. The Duke of Austria at the time, Heinrich II, made Vienna his capital, and a prosperous new city grew up on the remains of the old Roman camp. Heinrich and his successors, members of the Babenberg dynasty, increased their territory by means of astute marriages. The early 13th century was a time of prosperity and boom for Vienna, but also a time of threat from outside, with Magyars and Mongols invading from the east. When the last Babenberg died in 1246, a period of anarchy followed. King Ottokar of Bohemia entered Vienna and seized the crown. In 1273, a German duke by the name of Rudolf von Habsburg was crowned Holy Roman Emperor, and within three years he had thrown Ottokar out of Vienna. The long dominion of the House of Habsburg had begun.

Archduchess Marie Louise, daughter of the last Holy Roman Emperor, who was married to Napoleon in 1810 as a way of concluding peace between Austria and France. As Empress of France she wears an empire line gown embroidered with bees, an ancient Frankish emblem which Napoleon adopted instead of the Bourbon fleur de lys.

THE RISE OF THE
HOUSE OF HABSBURG

The Habsburgs were not popular overlords at first. More than once the citizens of Vienna rose up against them, protesting at the suppression of old privileges and against curbs on the city's powers of self-government. Throughout the early 14th century the Habsburgs responded by beheading Vienna's mayors. After one uprising had been particularly brutally quelled, the chronicles record a string of natural disasters of Biblical proportions: floods, earthquakes, plague, famine and swarms of locusts. It was Rudolf IV (the Founder) who brought all this to an end. He began work on the new Stephansdom in 1359, founded Vienna University in 1365, and generally paid the city some of the attention it felt it had been denied.

On the dynastic front the Habsburgs were even better at the marriage game than the Babenbergs had been, and soon their dominion over Central Europe was established - from 1437 onwards, right up until the 19th century, the Holy

Turkish plan of Vienna from 1683, made at the time of the siege (see p. 15), showing the cannon positions of the Ottoman army relative to the city walls, the Wien and Danube rivers and the outlying suburbs with their summer lodges.

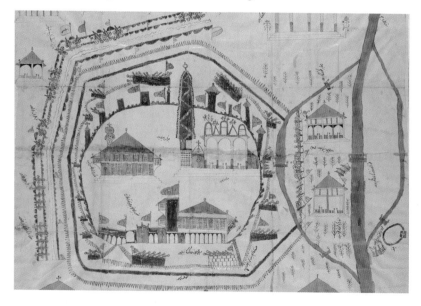

Roman Emperor and the head of the House of Austria were one and the same person. Control of Vienna was briefly lost in 1485, when the Hungarian king Matthias Corvinus conquered the city and made it his capital. Five years later, however, when Matthias died, the Hungarians were beaten back again. No one is sure who was responsible for the famous line about Austria: "You receive from Venus (goddess of love) what others receive from Mars (god of war)". Was it Matthias Corvinus in a moment of vexation? Or was it Austria's own monarch, Maximilian I, in a moment of self-congratulation? Certainly every inch of land that Matthias gained he had to fight for, while Austria simply married her territories in Burgundy, the Netherlands and what is now Switzerland. Maximilian (1493-1519) was one of the greatest rulers that Austria ever had. Like Matthias Corvinus before him, he was both a knight and a humanist, a bridge between two worlds, the man who took his country from the Middle Ages into the Renaissance. He made his court a centre not only of government but also of culture and learning, founding the Vienna Boys' Choir and what is now the Austrian National Library. The double marriage of his grandchildren to the thrones of Bohemia and Hungary secured those two kingdoms for Austria. His son married Juana the Mad of Spain, and the son of that union, the Emperor Karl V, ruled over more of Europe than any other monarch before or since, as well as over Spain's holdings in the New World.

Karl V was an austere man, more interested in stamping out heresy than in glorying in his temporal power, and he decided, after a mere two years, to split his vast and unwieldy domains in two. Retaining the Spanish lands for himself, as well as the title of Holy Roman Emperor, he bequeathed Austria and her dominions (which stretched right across Europe from the Netherlands through Alsace to Hungary) to his brother Ferdinand. Most of Ferdinand's reign was taken up with battles against the expansionist thirst of France on the one hand and of Ottoman Turkey on the other, and by 1541 the Turks had taken Hungary as far west as Buda. Ferdinand was also a devout Catholic, and it was he who asked Ignatius Loyola to send some Jesuits to Vienna to help stamp out Protestantism. For a full century the Counter Reformation rumbled on, eventually escalating into the Thirty Years War after the Defenestration of Prague in 1618 (*see p. 128*). Ostensibly a religious conflict pitting Catholic against Protestant, this war was in fact deeply political, and had a lot to do with France's own territorial ambitions at Austria's expense. The fact that Catholic France allied herself with Protestant Sweden under Gustavus Adolphus makes a nonsense of any notion that the Thirty Years War was entirely a religious affair. For Austria, the war was not a success. It ended, in 1648, with the French taking Alsace and yet remaining entirely unappeased. One bite of the cherry and they wanted more. Meanwhile the machinations of anti-Habsburg Hungarian princes on behalf of the Ottomans meant that the Turkish threat had far from receded. In 1683 the Ottoman forces reached the gates of Vienna, and France, seeing an opportunity to corral her quarry, sided with the Ottomans - or at least professed neutrality. In her hour of need, Austria turned to Poland. The dashing Polish king, Jan Sobieski, had enjoyed a victory over the Turks on his own soil ten years previously, and was more than happy to repeat the performance. Besieged for almost three months, Vienna was almost on the brink of despair when Sobieski's troops, together with another relieving army led by Charles of Lorraine, streamed down from the Kahlenberg mountain and stilled the "red wind" of the Turkish scimitars for ever. Throughout the long battle, Sobieski still found the time to write tenderly erotic letters home to his wife.

The imperial state carriage in front of the Stephansdom.

THE SIEGE OF VIENNA

In 1683 Kara Mustapha, Grand Vizier of the Ottoman Empire and lord of three thousand concubines, advanced on Vienna in a chariot of silver, with an army of 300,000 men, and with provisions and ammunition borne by 5,000 camels and 10,000 oxen. The Turkish Sultan, Mehmed IV, had not ordered Kara Mustapha to take Vienna. His mission was to secure positions on the Hungarian-Austrian frontier. But the Grand Vizier had other ideas. Knowing that his army was immense, and that Vienna's civilians numbered a mere 60,000, he intended to surround the city and force a surrender - a move which would allow him to keep all the booty for himself. If he conquered the city by force, he would, as custom dictated, have to allow his janissaries and the rag-bag crew of Habsburg-hating

Jan Sobieski.

Hungarians, Transylvanians and Wallachians who had joined his troops, to sack and pillage their fill. His army pitched its pointed tents on the glacis, the green belt around the outside of Vienna's city walls. The suburbs beyond these were instantly torched on the orders of Count Starhemberg, commander of the city garrison, the aim being to deprive the besieging army of any source of food or shelter. Everything was burned, including the lush vineyards on the site of what later became the Belvedere gardens. The emperor, Leopold I, left the city, taking refuge in Starhemberg's country castle at Dürnstein on the Danube. For fifty-nine days Starhemberg and his belea-guered city held out against the Turkish cannon fire. Food began to run low, and people found themselves forced to eat cats to survive. And then at last, on 12th September, liberation came, in the form of a united Christian army led by Charles of Lorraine and the Polish king Jan Sobieski. After hearing mass in the chapel on top of the Leopoldsberg, their troops grouped for battle. The fighting, on the slopes of the Kahlenberg, lasted late into the evening, when a lightning charge of Polish Hussars routed the Turkish troops, whose advance had been hampered by the difficult oak and vine-covered terrain. In distant Dürnstein, Leopold received news of the victory, news that came too late for Vienna's mayor Andreas von Liebenberg. After struggling to keep his hunger and dysentery-ridden population's spirits up, the exhausted mayor had died just two days before victory was declared. Kara Mustapha survived the battle, but he never made it back to Constantinople. The Sultan, enraged at the disaster his disobedience had incurred, sent him a noose of black silk, an unspoken hint as to what he should do with himself.

THE WAR OF THE SPANISH SUCCESSION, MARIA THERESA & THE VOLKSKAISER

In the decades that followed 1683, Vienna blossomed. Whereas before it had been used as the seat of the court and of government only if the currently reigning Habsburg felt inclined to use it (Maximilian always preferred Innsbruck, for example), it now became the permanent capital of the Archduchy of Austria, and permanent seat of the Holy Roman Emperor. The next 40 years or so saw the city develop from an old-fashioned town of cramped mediaeval streets into a city of high Baroque splendour. Troubles were never far away, though. In 1700 Carlos II, the last Habsburg king of Spain, died. Deformed, a semi-invalid, and possessor of the worst Habsburg jaw in history, Carlos had been unable to consummate either of his two marriages, which meant that the Spanish Habsburg male line died with him. Immediately the European powers found themselves embroiled in the War of the Spanish Succession, a contest between two contenders for the Spanish throne. Austria's ruler, Leopold I, had a younger son, Karl (the elder son Joseph was being groomed to rule Austria), and it was Karl whom the Grand Alliance of England, Holland and Savoy supported, sending its armies under Marlborough and Eugene of Savoy (*see p. 166*) to fight at Blenheim, Ramillies and Malplaquet against the French and their Bourbon candidate Philip, grandson of Louis XIV. When Joseph, who had succeeded to his Austrian titles in 1705, died unexpectedly of smallpox in 1711, however, the Grand Alliance was thrown into disarray. Continuing to support an Austrian claimant to the throne of Spain meant supporting Karl, who was now Holy Roman Emperor and Archduke of Austria. It was too much. Perfidious Albion, always keen to maintain a balance of power in Europe, concluded the Treaty of Utrecht with France in 1713, and the Bourbon claimant took Spain. Though Karl had always expected to rule Spain, and though he never felt at home in Austria, he did his best, devoting much of his time to the Spanish Riding School, which survives as a monument to his memory to this day (*see p. 44*). He had no sons, and in order to allow his daughter, Maria Theresa, to succeed, he introduced the Law of Pragmatic Sanction, to which both England and France had to be signatories. Both countries agreed, but at a price. England demanded that Austria close down her competing East India Company, which operated out of Ostend. France demanded the cession of Lorraine as soon as its duke Franz Stephan, Maria Theresa's consort, died.

Maria Theresa succeeded to her vast estates (though not to the crown of the Holy Roman Empire) in 1740. A much-beloved monarch, her reign was not without its troubles, and she relied heavily on her chancellor, Kaunitz (*see p. 166*), to steer her through them. Though Austria continued to win important victories, they were less resounding than before, and she always had to cede some territory to offset them. Maria Theresa's first challenge was Prussia, whose unappetising ruler, Frederick the Great, was determined to wrest territory from the woman he contemptuously referred to as "the apostolic hag". He succeeded, snatching Silesia, and choosing a particularly misogynistic passage from St Paul to be read out at the thanksgiving service he held afterwards ("Let the woman learn in silence. I suffer not a woman to usurp authority over the man."). Maria Theresa reacted by appealing to the Hungarians, an unlikely choice, considering their instinctive hostility to the Habsburgs; but the image of a young woman in distress roused their natural gallantry. Maria Theresa's exhortation to the Hungarian nobility in Pressburg had them rallying behind her to beat the Prussians back, which they did, though Silesia was never regained.

When Franz Stephan died, in 1765, Maria Theresa elevated her eldest son Joseph, who had also been elected Holy Roman Emperor, to the rank of co-regent. Joseph, the Enlightened Despot, recognised

Maria Theresa (1740-1780) by her court painter van Meytens. It was after securing Hungarian support that she succeeded in stalling the territorial expansion of Prussia. The crown on the table beside her is the Hungarian crown of St Stephen.

that the empire was politically overstretched, that it lacked a coherent internal structure, and that it was a tinderbox of ethnic tensions waiting to go up in flames. He also saw that if Austria was to be spared the revolutionary rumblings that were threatening France, social reform was essential. When Joseph became sole ruler of Austria in 1780, following Maria Theresa's death, he abolished serfdom, introduced freedom of conscience and the right to worship as a non-Catholic without the accusation of heresy. He insisted on tolerance of the Jews, introduced German as the single official language of the empire, made the Church subservient to the State, and began to build up a civil service. His social reforms earned him the soubriquet *Volkskaiser* (People's Emperor) - not that he was by any means a democrat. He still envisaged himself firmly at the helm, and despite his good intentions, he was too overweeningly zealous in his approach. He managed to antagonise and patronise in equal measure, and though Thomas Jefferson held him up as a shining example of how reform could be carried out without revolution, Joseph himself recognised that his efforts had ultimately resulted in failure.

THE END OF THE HOLY ROMAN EMPIRE

The late 18th century was a time of increasing social unrest. Riots broke out among the artesan classes, who never had enough to eat nor the wherewithal to keep warm in winter. Hunger marches were frequent occurrences. In 1793 Joseph II's sister, Marie Antoinette, was dragged to the guillotine in Paris. Less than five years later, Napoleonic France declared war on the entire continent of Europe, and Austria, as she controlled so much of it, was necessarily implicated. A series of defeats and losses culminated in 1805, when Napoleon entirely crushed the inadequate Austrian army at the Battle of Austerlitz. Pressing his advantage, he then occupied Vienna and forced the Emperor Franz II to renounce the title of Holy Roman Emperor (he continued to rule as Emperor Franz I of Austria) and dissolve the institution altogether. A thousand-year-old empire went up in a puff of smoke. In 1809 Napoleon occupied Vienna again, and set himself up in the palace of Schönbrunn, from where he proceeded to help himself to most of Austria's coastal territories on the Adriatic. It was time for someone dashing to gallop onto the stage, and obligingly someone did: Count Metternich (*see p. 125*), who immediately brokered

Napoleon the conqueror, by David. Napoleon personally supervised the painting of this canvas, which symbolises his triumphal progress towards dominion of Europe. The name Charlemagne - Napoleon's role model - is carved in the rock below the horse's hoofs.

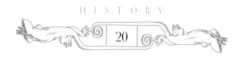

a marriage between Napoleon and the emperor's daughter Archduchess Marie Louise, then went behind Napoleon's back to form the Holy Alliance of Russia, Prussia and Austria against him. In 1814, after a series of humiliating defeats, Napoleon was exiled to Elba, and the Congress of Vienna, with Metternich as master of ceremonies, was convened to redraw the map of Europe. After 1815, when Napoleon was defeated once and for all at Waterloo, Austria settled down to 30 years of peace and prosperity.

THE "PRE-MARCH" OR BIEDERMEIER AGE

Metternich was a brilliant diplomat but a bad politician. A sworn enemy of nationalism, which he saw as Napoleon's dangerous legacy, he sought to prevent the middle and lower classes from ever having a say in anything, for fear they grow above themselves and threaten the established imperial order. In order to enforce the order he so loved, he introduced a system that was stiflingly repres-

Romantic Biedermeier-style scene of the emperor Franz Joseph and his fiancée Princess Elisabeth of Bavaria, out for the day in Bad Ischl.

sive, with a secret police force and ruthless censorship laws. The good-natured emperor Franz, and his simple son Ferdinand after him, were irresolute rulers, and both allowed Metternich to control the country. The people were for a time content to divert themselves with romantic music, literature, painting and rambles in the countryside, but the attractions of this soon began to pall, and serious dissent began to bubble under the surface. The country was full of able and educated people who simply did not have enough say in their own affairs. In March 1848 the cork flew out of the bottle. University students and staff demonstrated for freedom of the Press, and the hungry working classes went on the rampage. This sparked off nationalist feeling elsewhere in the empire, and soon there were uprisings in Prague, Hungary and the Italian provinces. Field Marshal Radetzky dealt with the Italians, while Prince Albert Windischgrätz sorted out the Czechs. The most difficult to contain were the Hungarians, who wanted not only independence for the Magyar people, but also to force Magyarisation on the many minorities who lived on Hungarian soil. Their political mouthpiece, Lajos Kossuth, baldly told a delegation of Hungarian Serbs that from now on they were to adopt the Hungarian language as their own. When the Serbs retorted that this was unacceptable, Kossuth announced that "the sword will decide". "The Serbs," he was coolly told, "have never feared the sword." It was a situation that required ruthless handling, and the man entrusted with the job was Prince Felix Schwarzenberg, who was later to become Austria's Prime Minister. Together with an army of a quarter of a million Russians, and with additional help from the Croats, who were only too happy to teach the Hungarians a lesson, he finally and bloodily put the Hungarian rebellion down in 1849. All this was too much for the feeble-minded emperor Ferdinand. He had already abdicated in favour of his 18 year-old nephew Franz Joseph.

FRANZ JOSEPH, FRANZ FERDINAND & THE FIRST WORLD WAR

Franz Joseph entered into his inheritance in the midst of battles and rebellion, and left it, when he died, plunged in the doomed *débâcle* of the First World War. Though he hung on to his throne for 68 years, longer than any European monarch has ever done, his reign was a long, slow disaster, full of personal losses and personal tragedy, as well as loss and disintegration for his empire. Hard-working, conscientious and keen to do his duty, Franz Joseph nevertheless lacked imagination, and he certainly lacked sparkle. Instead of working out a clear, progressive vision for the future, he plunged headlong into a desperate, losing battle to preserve the status quo. He also, fatally, relied too much on his own instincts. After the deaths of his canny and able prime minister Prince Schwarzenberg and his efficient - if ruthless - field marshal Radetzky, he tried to control too much himself. His entanglements with Napoleon III ended with defeat at the Battle of Solferino, with the resulting loss of Tuscany and Lombardy. When Russia appealed to him for help during the Crimean War, pointing out that she had helped Austria against Hungary in 1849 and that now it was up to Austria to return the favour, Franz Joseph refused to send troops, thus making an enemy of the Tsar - with dire consequences for the future. In Germany, Bismarck began to nourish thoughts about a German Empire with Prussia, and not Austria, as the mightiest state in the league. No sooner thought of than acted upon, Bismarck's army defeated Austria at Königgrätz (Sadowa) in 1866, and

then promised not to march on Vienna, but only on condition that Austria quit the German League altogether, leaving Prussia in command. In the following year, 1867, Franz Joseph was forced by continued and relentless Magyar agitation to enter into a Compromise Agreement with the Hungarians, whereby the Dual Monarchy of Austria-Hungary was set up. Franz Joseph was crowned Hungarian King, allowed Hungary to control her own domestic affairs, and swore an oath to protect Hungarian interests. This was all very well for the Magyars.

Otto von Bismarck, the Prussian leader who challenged Austrian hegemony in Europe.

For the Slavs within the empire it was a source of outrage. If Hungary had special privileges, then why not Slavs as well?

In 1879 Austria and Prussia signed a Dual Alliance whereby they pledged each other mutual support. In a clumsy attempt to kill Slav disaffection by depriving it of oxygen, Austria then announced the annexation of Bosnia and Herzegovina, knowing that Prussia was bound to support the move. Incensed at this treatment of fellow Slavs, Russia sided with Serbia. France, which lost no love on Prussia after Bismarck's behaviour during the Franco-Prussian War, was already on Russia's side anyway. Britain, with her mania for maintaining the balance of power, would step in to support whoever looked the weaker. The stage was set for war. All that remained to do was ignite the fuse, which Gavrilo Princip did when he shot the heir to the throne Franz Ferdinand at Sarajevo in 1914. Franz Ferdinand was a very different character from his uncle Franz Joseph. Franz Joseph had no time for him, but others in the imperial circle believed that he could actually have saved Austria-Hungary. His idea was to expand the Dual Monarchy into a Triple Monarchy composed of a federation of states: Austria, Hungary and the Slav regions as well, all on an equal footing. In principle it was a good idea, though Hungary was implacably opposed to letting the Slavs get so much as a toehold anywhere. Franz Joseph was reluctant to stand up to them; Franz Ferdinand might have managed it. He is more famous now for his morganatic marriage than for his political ideas. He was expected to marry the daughter of Archduke Friedrich, but he fell in love with a lady-in-waiting instead, Sophie Chotek, a minor countess who was not on the list of approved Habsburg consorts. Her lowly status meant that their children were debarred from succession. In the summer of 1914 Franz Ferdinand went to the Bosnian capital of Sarajevo to inspect military manoeuvres, and the anti-Austrian activists seized their chance. Gavrilo Princip, a member of the pan-Serbian Black Hand gang, shot Franz Ferdinand and his wife dead, though he was certainly not acting for the whole of Bosnia when he fired his pistol. Bosnian Serbs like Princip (just under 50% of the population) were opposed to Austrian rule and wanted to be part of Greater Serbia. The Croat and Muslim population in Bosnia, however, were almost certainly horrified by that prospect, and were happier under Austrian control. Austria reacted to the assassination by declaring war on Serbia, again knowing that under the terms of the Dual Alliance she could count on German support, and knowing too, that once Germany entered the fray, the rest of Europe would feel bound to enter it as well.

CENTRAL EUROPE IN THE MID 19TH CENTURY

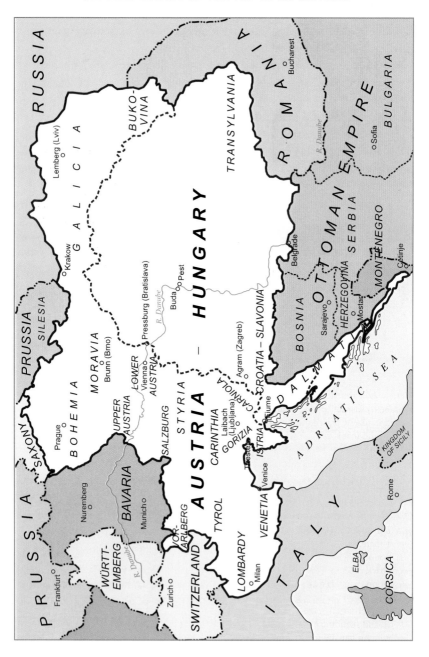

TWILIGHT OF THE HABSBURGS

FRANZ JOSEPH (1830-1916)

Old-fashioned in a swiftly changing age, Franz Joseph had a sublime belief in his role as God's deputy and in his mission as father of his people - an attitude which began to seem more and more out of touch and out of date. Dignified, conscientious, capable of iron self-control, he has had all the usual accusations volleyed at him: that he was heartless, repressed and had a mother complex. In fact he was a deeply passionate man, with genuine artistic leanings and a great love of parties and dancing, though he suppressed these when he became emperor in 1848. He spent his entire reign trying with all his might to keep at bay the forces of nationalism which were threatening not only to splinter his empire, but to plunge the whole of Europe into conflict, and it is an irony typical of his whole unhappy career that in the end it was his hand that signed the paper that sparked off that conflict - Austria's declaration of war on Serbia in 1914. Too stoic and stolid for his own good, Franz Joseph lacked vision, hated change, and was utterly unable to cope with the balance of power squabbles between Germany, Britain and Russia. Caught in the middle, he reacted like a rabbit dazzled by headlights: refusing to budge, and getting crushed as a result.

ELISABETH (1837-1898)

Passionate, romantic, obstinate and unforgiving, Elisabeth was not the girl Franz Joseph was supposed to marry. But she was wildly beautiful and poetic, and that is what caught his eye. Baroque Vienna, and particularly some of the Hofburg, has been described as "intolerably gorgeous". It - and the stifling lifestyle that went with it, along with a terrifying mother-in-law - were indeed intolerable to the dreamy, inexperienced, sixteen year-old empress, and in the end did drive Elisabeth stark, raving mad. She spent increasingly little time there, retiring to the country and spending days on end on horseback (her daredevil riding style caused consternation at hunting parties in England and Ireland) or taking off on restless, eccentric tours of the Mediterranean, obsessively reading the poetry of Heine, and spending enormous amounts of treasury money on building fanciful villas for herself, never seeming to remember that all this privilege came at a price: she was supposed to pay a certain amount of attention to Austria. When she did turn to politics, it was to throw herself into the Hungarian cause with a passion that was almost unhinged. Her lonely, questing, self-obsessed existence was brought to an abrupt end when she was stabbed by an Italian anarchist as she was boarding a steamer on Lake Geneva.

RUDOLF (1858-1889)

As a young man, Crown Prince Rudolf promised great things. He was dashing and intelligent, took a keen interest in politics and the army, and badly wanted to be given some responsibility by his father. His father wouldn't hear of it; he distrusted Rudolf's liberal ideas, didn't like his freethinking style, and considered his radicalism to be no more than iconoclasm with half-baked theories behind it. Once the Establishment had been destroyed, what was to come in its place? This paternal disapproval had the effect of making Rudolf more rebellious and anti-clerical than ever. It also turned him to drink, drugs and women. Desperate to break free from his dull wife, Stephanie of Belgium (whom he had made infertile by transmitting his syphilis to her), he wrote to the Pope asking for an annulment. When this reached the ears of Franz Joseph, a scene ensued behind closed doors. No one knows exactly what was said, but the next day Rudolf set off for his hunting lodge at Mayerling. His showgirl mistress Mitzi Kaspar had very sensibly refused to go with him, so he took the 17 year-old baroness Mary Vetsera instead. No doubt she was in love with him - how else could he have persuaded her to agree to his suicide pact? He shot her dead, scattered her body with flowers, and then turned his gun on himself. When the tragic pair were tracked down, Mary's body was bundled off in secret to the monastery of Heiligenkreuz, and Rudolf's - after furious wrangling with the Archbishop of Vienna (he was, after all, a murderer and a suicide) - was taken to the *Kaisergruft* (imperial burial vaults). The hunting lodge was converted into a tiny convent, with Carmelite nuns to pray daily for Rudolf's guilty soul.

KARL (1887-1922)

"Nothing has been spared me in this world!" exclaimed Franz Joseph when Elisabeth was murdered. It is probably a mercy that he died in 1916, before the end of the First World War, and was spared the spectacle of his empire in ruins. He was succeeded by his great-nephew, Archduke Karl. Karl spent his brief reign struggling to bring the war to an end without losing too much to Poincaré (who wanted Alsace-Lorraine), to Italy (who had only gone over to the Allies because she had been promised Trieste) and to Kaiser Wilhelm (who wanted Austria's very heart and soul). In the end he found himself handing the government of his country over to the Socialist Republic of Karl Renner, and renounced all political control. He refused to abdicate, however, and as a result was forced into exile in Switzerland. In 1921, when Hungary restored its monarchy under the regent Miklós Horthy, Karl attempted to reclaim the crown. It was a political act of the kind he had promised not to undertake. Switzerland refused to harbour him any longer, and he was sent to Madeira, where he lived in severe financial hardship until his early death.

In 1938, when Chancellor Schuschnigg was battling to keep Hitler from seizing power, Karl's son Otto offered to return to Austria as Chancellor. The offer was politely declined. In 1989, when Karl's wife, Empress Zita, died, Vienna saw its last state funeral. Zita is buried in the *Kaisergruft*.

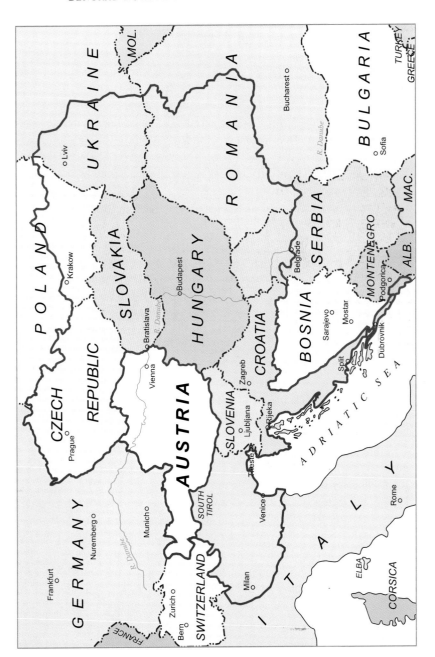

VIENNA IN THE TWENTIETH CENTURY

The Viennese lost no time mourning half a millennium of Habsburg rule. Almost as soon as Karl had been deposed, the Republic of German-Austria was proclaimed, the name chosen because "Austria" on its own was thought to have imperial, multi-national connotations. The Habsburg family was banished, their property was nationalised and the use of aristocratic titles was made illegal. In May 1919 Karl Renner, Austria's State Chancellor, went to Paris where the victorious Allies had convened for the Treaty of St Germain. Renner had a shock in store. After everyone else had helped themselves to territory, the "leftovers", as Clemenceau put it, were to constitute the new Austria, alone and without dependencies for the first time in her life. And her name was to be Austria. Not German-Austria. The new little country was a sorrowful place. Its people were divided between old monarchists whose world-view had been shattered, and pan-German nationalists, who sought to recoup some of the lost prestige by uniting Austria with Germany. When the Allies ruled out any possibility of this happening, it inevitably made the advocates of that union want it even more passionately. These were hard times for Vienna. Once the hub of a great empire, she was now the overblown capital of a tiny nation stranded on the wrong side of the Alps. She also failed as a capital in that she did not really represent her people. While provincial Austria remained staunchly conservative, Vienna became fiercely Socialist - and very poor. Her former agricultural and industrial supply-states in the north and east no longer belonged to her. No Polish coal meant that the freezing populace resorted to chopping down the Vienna Woods for fuel. Unemployment, tuberculosis and inflation ran riot. An enormous army of redundant imperial civil servants were left to fend for themselves, and found themselves begging for bread. In the 1930s the Depression hit hard. Growing hardship led to growing pro-Nazi sentiment, as people scrabbled to find an antidote for their malaise and scapegoats for their misery. The trend alarmed the Chancellor, Engelbert Dollfuss, so much that he over-reacted, outlawing both the Communist and the Nazi parties and trying to win support for the idea of an independent Austria, making her way in the world without Germany - an idea that appealed to almost no one. Dollfuss hated Hitler and was not a Fascist, but unfortunately he failed to get his people behind him. Pan-German nationalists disliked his anti-German stance, and Socialists found his conservative, authoritarian leadership style, with its reliance on armed force, distasteful. When police raided a workers' club in 1934, looking for a cache of weapons, members of the *Schutzbund*, the Social Democrats' defence league, panicked and opened fire: Three days of street fighting ensued, at the end of which the government out-lawed the Socialist Party. In response the Austrian Nazis - who represented perhaps 25% of the population - planned a coup, storming Dollfuss' office on the Ballhausplatz in July 1934, fatally wounding Dollfuss, and leaving him to die, ignoring his pleas for a doctor and a priest.

View of Am Hof after the Battle of Vienna in 1945, which raged between the occupying German troops and the Soviet army, who took Vienna for the Allies. On the former city arsenal building a proud double-headed eagle and two suits of Roman armour remain as tokens of Vienna's erstwhile might. Everything else lies in ruins.

THE LEAD-UP TO THE ANSCHLUSS

1934 (February)

The Vienna Socialists (and their self-defence league, the *Schutzbund*) organise a general strike, and heavy street fighting breaks out. The government mobilises the *Heimwehr*, the anti-Communist defence league, to disperse the rioters. Western Europe is shocked by the Austrian government's heavy-handedness.

1934 (July)

Nazi conspirators shoot Chancellor Dollfuss and leave him to bleed to death. Kurt Schuschnigg becomes Chancellor, and disbands the *Heimwehr*.

1935

Schuschnigg appeals to France, Britain and Italy to help stop Nazi infiltration of Austria. France is in political disarray, Mussolini smiles but does nothing, and the British Labour government is sniffy about Austria's treatment of the Socialist rioters the previous year. Schuschnigg negotiates with Hitler.

1936

Hitler recognises Austrian sovereignty and agrees not to interfere in Austrian affairs, but in exchange Schuschnigg is persuaded to include two Nazis in his cabinet.

1937

Further appeasement: the number of Nazis in the Austrian government increases to four.

1938 (February)

Schuschnigg goes to negotiate with Hitler at Berchtesgaden, enduring an eleven-hour lecture, a miserly vegetarian lunch and a smoking ban. Hitler threatens to crush Austria militarily unless Schuschnigg a) appoint a Nazi Vice Chancellor and a Nazi Foreign Minister; b) introduce anti-Semitic and anti-Czech legislation; c) leave the League of Nations.

Schuschnigg appeals to Britain once more. This time the Conservatives are in power, but are organising a reception for von Ribbentrop and have no time for Austria.

1938 (March)

Schuschnigg tries to defy Hitler on his own, rallying the Socialists to his cause, and announcing a referendum which would allow people to choose between a free and independent Austria or a German-"aided" Austria. Knowing that Schuschnigg would win the referendum with a comfortable majority, the German army prepares to invade. Recognising that his own army would be no match for the invaders, Schuschnigg resigns with the words "God save Austria".

Hitler enters Vienna, and the Gestapo begins its intimidation of Jews, Slavs and anti-Nazis. The only country to lodge an official diplomatic protest is Mexico.

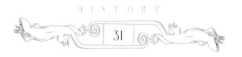
THE SECOND WORLD WAR & ITS AFTERMATH

Hitler's arrival in Vienna was cheered by around a quarter of a million people, who turned out in the Heldenplatz to hear him proclaim Austria's entry into the German Reich. Some were genuinely enthusiastic about the prospect of a united *deutsches Volk*; others saw this as the chance to redeem the loss of empire and regain power and prestige in the world. None of them can have known that the entire gold reserves of the Austrian National Bank had been transferred to Berlin to fund Hitler's war machine. A month after Schuschnigg's referendum was due to have taken place, Hitler organised one of his own. He registered a 99.7% vote in favour of the *Anschluss*, a result that is perhaps not surprising when one considers that a quarter of a million people supported him anyway, a further quarter of a million had been disqualified from voting because of their political or racial "undesirability", and the rest of the population were intimidated by the fact that the first cattle-waggons full of dissenting politicians and anti-Nazis had already left for Dachau. As soon as the referendum had been won, Vienna realised the mistake it had made. The iron hand of censorship came down over the arts, and scientists and intellectuals flocked to leave the country. There weren't even any top jobs for Austrian Nazis: Hitler

A relic of the Second World War. The letters LSK (Luftschutzkeller) were stencilled onto buildings that had air-raid shelters beneath them.

imported his own henchmen from Germany, which saved his Austrian supporters from the grisly reputations they no doubt deserved - with the notable exception of Adolf Eichmann, architect of the "Final Solution" which involved the deportation of Jews to the death camps of Belsen, Auschwitz and Buchenwald. When the Second World War broke out, Austria was inevitably dragged in on the German side.

In April 1945, after the Battle of Vienna, the Nazis were finally driven out by the Red Army, leaving the city in ruins. A free-for-all period of looting and rape followed, moving Viennese to remark that they "could survive another war, but not another liberation". The Allies then partitioned the country, leaving Vienna divided into four zones, one of them under Soviet control. In November 1945 Austria held its first free, democratic elections since 1930, and although the Communists gained only 5% of the vote, ten years of stalemate followed. The Soviet Union was reluctant to allow Austria to join the West; the West would not countenance any other solution. In 1955, the Austrian State Treaty was finally signed in Vienna's Belvedere. Under the terms of the treaty Soviet occupation ended and Austria became an independent sovereign republic, bound by a pledge of permanent neutrality.

A HANDFUL OF DATES

1156	Duke Heinrich II (Jasomirgott) makes Vienna his capital.	1848	Revolution in Vienna and across Europe.
1278	Rudolf von Habsburg begins 640 years of dynastic rule.	1867	The dual monarchy of Austria-Hungary is established. The monarch becomes Emperor of Austria and King of Hungary, hence the use of the adjective *k und k* (*kaiserlich und königlich*).
1485	Vienna captured by the Hungarian king Matthias Corvinus		
1521	Spanish and Austrian Habsburg lines split	1918-19	Emperor Karl I renounces political responsibility. Austria becomes a Socialist republic. The Treaty of St Germain defines the new republic's borders. The map of Europe is redrawn again.
1683	Turks defeated at the gates of Vienna		
1805-6	Napoleon occupies Vienna. End of the Holy Roman Empire		
1809	Napoleon occupies Vienna for the second time.	1938	Hitler enters Vienna and annexes Austria to his German Reich.
1814-15	Congress of Vienna follows Napoleon's defeat. The map of Europe is redrawn.	1955	Soviet troops leave Vienna. Austria proclaims permanent neutrality.

Left: Monument to Russian heroes of the liberation of Vienna. The Soviet troops freed Vienna from the Nazis after bloody street fighting in 1945. The city was not in turn freed from Soviet occupation until ten years later.

THE HOLY ROMAN EMPIRE

Franz I, last Holy Roman Emperor and first Emperor of Austria.

From its very inception the Holy Roman Empire was a symbolic creation. When the Frankish king Charlemagne was crowned in the year 800, he was crowned by the Pope - Leo III - as a symbol of his role as defender of Christendom. He was also crowned in ancient Roman garb, harking back to the golden age of the Roman Empire, with all its unifying and civilising might. He was crowned in Rome, too, the ancient cradle of that empire, and the seat of the Christian Church.

When Charlemagne conquered and christianised the Saxons, his empire acquired the Germanic element which in later centuries was to be its defining feature. When he died, the empire was divided among his heirs and became a broad federation of territories covering what is now most of France, Italy and Germany. Each dukedom or principality had its own ruler, and the symbolic role of the Holy Roman Empire became more marked than ever, representing a European federal ideal which has exercised the imagination of the continent's leaders ever since. The relationship between Holy Roman Emperor and Pope also became highly ambivalent. The Pope was the head of the Church, but the emperor was its defender - against pagan barbarians, the Arab infidel and the Byzantines, from whom the Roman church had split in 1054. Frequent quarrels broke out over which of them, emperor or Pope, had the better right to consider himself God's representative on earth.

Although by the mid 13th century the Holy Roman Emperor had almost no real power, his title remained a coveted one, and the symbolic image of Charlemagne began to exercise as much fascination as did the symbolic role as Catholicism's protector. Emperors did not inherit the crown; they were chosen by election, and then crowned either at Rome (seat of the Church), at Aix-la-Chapelle (where Charlemagne died) or at Frankfurt ("stronghold of the Franks"). The first meeting of the imperial diet was traditionally convened at Nuremberg, another of Charlemagne's key cities.

Though the title was not a hereditary one, ever since 1440, when the Habsburg duke Friedrich V was crowned Emperor Friedrich III at Rome, it might almost as well have been: from then until its demise in 1806, the Holy Roman Empire was presided over by the Habsburg ruler of Austria. Maria Theresa was the only exception. She never wore the crown, though her husband, Franz Stephan of Lorraine, did, and when he died it passed to his and Maria Theresa's eldest son, Joseph.

The empire's Frankish origins were swiftly diluted as the federation became more Germanic in its makeup. By the 15th century it was no longer Charlemagne's "Empire of the Romans and the Franks", but the "Holy Roman Empire of the German Nation", and before long it was being referred to as the "German Empire", a concept that put unholy ideas into the head of more than one modern despot. Napoleon wanted to reassert the empire's Frankishness. Seeing himself as the natural heir of Charlemagne, he instituted a plan of dividing to rule, systematically liquidating ecclesiastical foundations and inducing the German states within the empire to secede and form their own Rhenish League. As a reward for being so obliging, Napoleon turned many of the states (e.g. Bavaria and Württemberg) into kingdoms - under his protection, of course. In 1806 he effectively deposed the emperor Franz II, who then dissolved the Holy Roman Empire, and continued his reign as Emperor Franz I of Austria. Napoleon married Franz's daughter, and conferred the title "King of Rome" on the son that was born to them, the Duke of Reichstadt. Though Napoleon was doomed to be defeated, the spectre of the Holy Roman Empire refused to rest. Fired up by the idea of that once-glorious, late-mediaeval German Reich, Adolf Hitler set the countries of Europe at each other's throats to try to recreate it - the ultimate revenge of the Saxon on the conquering Charlemagne. In 1938 he had the imperial crown transferred from Vienna to Nuremberg, the ancient administrative city of Charlemagne's empire, and which he had chosen as the showplace for his infamous rallies. Today that crown is safely back in the Vienna Hofburg (*see p. 51*).

PART II

GUIDE TO THE CITY

p. 37   MAJOR SIGHTS

 The Stephansdom - p. 37

 The Hofburg - p. 42

 The Belvedere - p. 53

 The Ringstrasse - p. 63

p. 73   ARCHITECTURE

p. 91   ART GALLERIES & MUSEUMS

p. 105   COFFEE HOUSES

p. 113   MUSIC

p. 126   RELIGIOUS MONUMENTS

MAJOR SIGHTS

THE STEPHANSDOM
(The Cathedral)

Dedicated to the first Christian martyr, St Stephen, who was stoned to death in c. AD 35, the present-day Stephansdom stands on the site of a much earlier Romanesque basilica, which in turn stood on the site of who knows what prehistoric forest. When the foundations for the north tower were being dug in 1443, the builders unearthed a mammoth bone, which for many years afterwards the citizens of Vienna would come to gaze at in awe, believing, presumably, that it was a relic of Noah's flood.

The Gothic church we see today was begun in 1359, and took a hundred years to complete - if it can ever be said to have been completed. The planned north tower was never finished, some say because the money ran out, others because the master mason, Hans Puchsbaum, fell to his death from the scaffolding. Even today the building needs constant touching up, because the soft Burgenland sandstone from which its façades are carved weathers so easily. The mortar which holds the stones together is reputed to be particularly strong, for it was mixed not with water, but with astringent Austrian wine. The story goes that one year the harvest was so bad that the wine was undrinkable and had to be poured away. Shocked at the waste, the emperor Friedrich III ordered that it be used for the Stephansdom instead.

When the Hungarian king Matthias Corvinus conquered Vienna in 1485, he is said to have had the cathedral roof tiled in majolica which gleamed in the Hungarian colours of red, white and green. Old paintings of the Stephansdom seem to bear this out. Today the roof is tiled in glossy round tiddly-wink tiles in green and white, as well as the imperial livery colours of black and yellow. The cathedral was badly damaged by fire during the Second World War, a fire which blazed for three days - much longer than it need have done, because the retreating Nazis had stolen all the Vienna fire department's equipment, and the people had to do the best they could with a bucket chain.

Previous page: The august façade of the Hofburg on the Michaelerplatz.

19th-century view of the Stephansdom by the watercolour artist Rudolf von Alt. The roof is tiled in red, white and green, the Hungarian colours, said to be the legacy of King Matthias Corvinus, who conquered Vienna in 1485.

The spire, nicknamed the *Steffl*, is 137 metres high. As the Ottoman forces besieged the city in 1683 (*see p. 15*), Ernst Rüdiger von Starhemberg, the commander of the city garrison, climbed almost to the top to monitor the approach of the relieving armies of Charles of Lorraine and Jan Sobieski. When the Turks were finally routed their captured standard, a golden crescent, was fixed to the top of the *Steffl*. In place of that crescent now are the double-headed eagle and double-barred apostolic cross of the Holy Roman Empire.

The stumpy north tower, the *Adlerturm*, has an iron handle resembling a mini dumb-bell, embedded in one of the columns supporting its entrance portico. This is the so-called *Asylgriff*, so called because in the middle ages any outcast or criminal who managed to evade their pursuers and grasp the iron handle was granted instant asylum. The tower itself houses the Stephansdom's massive bell, the 20-ton Pummerin, cast from the iron of 180 Turkish cannon. When the cathedral caught fire in 1945 the wooden bell-yoke gave way and the Pummerin crashed to the ground, shattering into pieces which were gathered up, smelted down and re-cast.

To the right of the main cathedral entrance, behind a sheet of perspex, you will see the glyph O5 carved into the stone. O plus five, meaning the fifth letter of the alphabet, in other words E, makes OE, the first letter of the word Oesterreich when spelt without an *umlaut*. O5 was the symbol of the secret Austrian resistance movement during the Second World War.

INSIDE THE STEPHANSDOM

As soon as you enter the Stephansdom, through the elaborate Romanesque west portal, you find yourself in a lofty Gothic building of great beauty and grandeur, soaring above the busy crowds and over-ornate Baroque altars with which it is filled. *The selected sights listed below are all marked on the plan on p. 41.*

1 THE TOMB OF EUGENE OF SAVOY. To the left of the main entrance, behind heavy Baroque wrought iron doors, is the chapel of Prince Eugene (*see p. 166*), with his red marble tombstone let into the floor.

2 THE WEEPING MADONNA. In the south aisle. This miracle-working altarpiece was brought from a village church in what is now Slovakia, after members of the congregation reported seeing it shed tears. Hearing of its wondrous properties, Leopold I had it brought to Vienna, believing that it would offer him succour in his struggle against the Turks (1683), which it apparently did. The pews in front of the altar are still a popular place for prayer.

3 THE PULPIT. Amazingly intricate, this delicate piece of filigree-in-stone is the work of master stone-carver Anton Pilgram (1515), who left a portrait of himself to the right of the pulpit-stem, leaning out of a casement, with a pair of compasses in his hand. The pulpit's banister rail is infested with stone toads and lizards, symbols of evil, doing eternal battle with stone snakes, symbols of immortality.

4 THE PUCHSBAUM BALDACHIN. Across the church from the old organ loft is the Leopold Altar, above which hangs one of the oldest baldachins in the cathedral. It was carved in the mid-15th century by Hans Puchsbaum, the master mason

The self-portrait of master stone mason Anton Pilgram on the Stephansdom's early 16th-century pulpit.

enormous red marble tomb, made for Friedrich von Habsburg (ruled Austria 1457-1493) by a master carver from the Low Countries. Friedrich was the first member of his family to be crowned Holy Roman Emperor in Rome itself (1440), and succeeded to the Duchy of Austria 17 years later. He was not a particularly popular ruler with the Viennese. He was also a great gourmet and a heavy drinker - and his excesses told on his figure, which was immensely fat and unwieldy. In

who allegedly fell to his death from the incomplete north tower.

5 THE OLD ORGAN LOFT. Anton Pilgram's second self-portrait takes the form of a painted stone corbel at the base of the former organ loft (1513). Once again he appears as if leaning out of a window, set square and compasses in hand.

6 THE TOMB OF FRIEDRICH III. The high altarpiece shows the stoning of St Stephen, painted on tin (1640). To the right of the high altar, at the end of the south aisle, stands an

Interior of the Stephansdom, with the red marble tomb of Friedrich III.

1462 a furious mob surrounded him in his palace. He escaped unhurt, but didn't turn himself into a svelter, more vigorous or decisive ruler. When Matthias Corvinus led his Magyar hordes against Vienna in 1485, Friedrich let him capture it and retreated to Wiener Neustadt to wait for the storm to pass, re-emerging in 1490, when his son Maximilian beat the Hungarians back. However, Friedrich did achieve one great and lasting thing: he consolidated the power of his family and the extent of their influence in such a way that for the next three and a half centuries, right up until its demise in 1806, the crown of the Holy Roman Empire was always worn by a member of the House of Austria. Maximilian, who succeeded his father in 1493, was one of the greatest monarchs Austria ever had (*see p. 13*).

GROUND PLAN
OF THE STEPHANSDOM

1 TOMB OF EUGENE OF SAVOY

2 WEEPING MADONNA

3 PULPIT

4 PUCHSBAUM BALDACHIN

5 OLD ORGAN LOFT

6 TOMB OF FRIEDRICH III

7 LIFT TO THE PUMMERIN

8 BASE OF THE ADLERTURM

9 BASE OF THE STEFFL

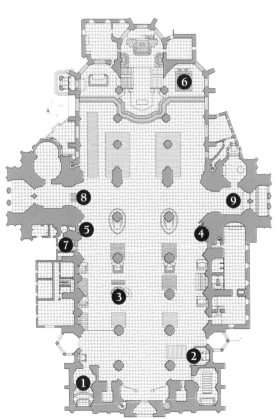

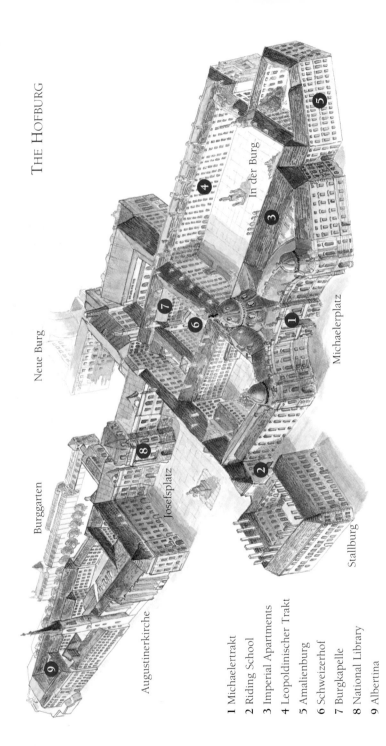

THE HOFBURG

In der Burg

Michaelerplatz

Neue Burg

Stallburg

Burggarten

Josefsplatz

Augustinerkirche

Albertina

1 Michaelertrakt
2 Riding School
3 Imperial Apartments
4 Leopoldinischer Trakt
5 Amalienburg
6 Schweizerhof
7 Burgkapelle
8 National Library
9 Albertina

THE HOFBURG
(The Imperial Court)

The enormous Hofburg complex, with its two and a half thousand rooms, is not so much a palace as an agglomeration of imperial residences constructed over several centuries according to a variety of different imperial tastes and architectural fashions. Though a fortified castle existed on the site as early as the 13th century, it was not until after 1683, when the Turks had been defeated once and for all, that it became the permanent seat of the Habsburg court.

The plan opposite marks the different sections of the Hofburg. Descriptions of each section and what to see where appear below.

❶ THE MICHAELERTRAKT. The entrance to the Hofburg complex takes the form of a triple gateway under a massive green dome adorned with a looped gold brocade effect, rising above the entrance rather like an enormous tasselled lampshade. Tall statues flank the entrance, each one symbolising power and dominion achieved by brute force, as does so much of the statuary of imperial Vienna. The building was designed by the younger Fischer von Erlach (*see p. 86*) in 1723, but not actually con-structed until 1889-93, by which time the Baroque spirit had become somewhat ponderous: grand, but without the exuberance. Once through the gateway, you will find an entrance to the **imperial apartments** (see over) to your right, and another to the **Spanish Riding School** on your left.

❷ THE REITSCHULTRAKT AND STALLBURG. The Winter Riding School was built on the site of the

Herculean feats of brute force are a favourite motif in Viennese architectural sculpture.

former court vegetable garden by the younger Fischer von Erlach (*see p. 86*). Commissioned by Karl VI, it was completed it 1735. Karl was not the founder of the Spanish Riding School, though he did much to cultivate it. He had been brought up in Spain, and had never expected to succeed to the throne of Austria. When he did, in 1711, he brought with him a great love of Baroque architecture and a profound homesickness. A portrait of Karl now hangs in the riding school's imperial box, and riders doff their hats to it as they enter. The cultivation of skilled and stylised horsemanship has a long tradition in Vienna. The Spanish Riding School was first founded, with Arab and Spanish cross-breed horses, in the second half of the 16th century, and in 1580 Archduke Karl, son of Ferdinand I, founded a stud at Lippiza (now Lipica in Slovenia), hence the name of the horses: Lippizaner. The Habsburgs have always loved horses. Empress Elisabeth was famous for treating her nags to marble drinking troughs. In the Spanish Riding School they get Venetian chandeliers. The Stallburg was originally the court stables, but since Karl VI's time has been used exclusively for the Lippizaners. Built in the mid 16th century, with its graceful arcades, it is a rare Renaissance survival. The first floor was used as living quarters by the emperor Matthias (reigned 1608-1619). The **Lippizaner Museum**, situated at Reitschulgasse 2, is open every day from 9am to 6pm. There is also a website at www.spanische-reitschule.com

3 THE REICHSKANZLEITRAKT AND IMPERIAL APARTMENTS (*Kaiserappartements*). The entrance to the imperial apartments is under the dome of the Michaelertrakt. A broad stairway takes you up to the **quarters occupied by Franz Joseph and Elisabeth** (Sisi), after Elisabeth insisted on separate bed-rooms following the death of her baby daughter in 1857. The long *enfilade* of rooms, opening one into the other with access from a continuous corridor running the length of the courtyard-facing side, is almost Elizabethan in its old-fashioned structure, and gives a vivid idea of the kind of lives the imperial couple led: surrounded by splendour, and always on public display, even in bed. Of course there were screens around the beds when they slept in them, and the corridor that visitors tramp today was not used as overtly as a corridor then - but even so, every move the imperial pair made was monitored, and it drove them both to distraction, though Franz Joseph was better able to cope with it. It was not only the tenor of Hofburg life that was not to Sisi's liking; it was the rooms themselves. Either painted white and decorated with gilt Rococo curlicues, or hung with oppressive red brocade, uniformly box-like in shape with windows all on one side, the effect is like living on a shelf or in a dolls' house. Franz Joseph didn't care for the Hofburg either, but instead of insisting on something more congenial, he grinned and bore it. Today the rooms contain portraits and furniture and personal effects of the imperial family, including Sisi's travelling cocaine syringe. Franz Joseph's study and bedroom (with his famous iron bedstead) are followed by Sisi's apartments, including her dressing room and gym, complete with her exercise bars. Elisabeth was proud of her slender figure, and as vain as any film star. All photographs had to be approved before release, and were painstakingly touched up if any hint of a wrinkle or slackening jaw was detected. Though complicit in the affair between Franz Joseph and the actress Katharina Schratt, Sisi could not prevent a kind of spiteful triumph when Katharina's *embonpoint* began to border on dumpiness. She even wrote a little poem in Hungarian about how

Kathi Schratt
Should shed her fat.

Sisi's gruelling routine on her wallbars meant that she herself hadn't a surplus ounce to shed. Though very partial to cakes and sweets, in order to keep slim, she would very often eat almost nothing at all, which caused her faithful, put-upon Hungarian ladies-in-waiting much concern.

The grand salon contains the famous Winterhalter portrait of Elisabeth, aged about twenty-six or twenty-seven, with diamond stars in her hair. Every morning she was subjected to the two-hour ritual of having her hair dressed. "My head aches the whole time," she complained, "and I know why. All my energy flies out through my hair and into my hairdresser."

The suite of rooms also includes a small **Memorial Room for the Emperor Maximilian** (1832-1867).

The Empress Elisabeth - Sisi - painted by Franz Winterhalter in 1865.

Maximilian, the bluff, good-hearted younger brother of Franz Joseph, was originally given the title of governor general of Lombardy. It was part of a deliberate strategy of Franz Joseph's to try and make the Italians warm to Austrian rule. It didn't work. The fever of nationalism was running too high, and despite the fact that Maximilian was a kind and benevolent overlord, Lombardy didn't want him. Instead they looked to France and to Napoleon III to liberate them. Austria went into battle against France, and lost Lombardy at the Battle of Solferino in 1859. Maximilian retreated to his castle above Trieste, and there he stayed until 1864, when a clerical minority faction in Mexico offered to make him their emperor. France supported the idea, no doubt imagining that Maximilian could more or less be controlled from Paris and that his appointment would increase French prestige in the New World. Maximilian's wife, the beautiful, ambitious Charlotte of Belgium, was agog with excitement. Franz Joseph was appalled - but no one listened to him; he was assumed to be jealous of his brother's popularity. Maximilian was never popular in Mexico. Despite the fact that his brief reign was liberal and humanitarian, he was as much loathed there as he had been in Italy. When the French withdrew from the region after the American Civil War, Maximilian was left without a single protector. He was killed by a Mexican rebel firing squad at the age of 34.

The imperial apartments are open 9am-5pm every day.

The façade of the Reichskanzleitrakt is in the high Baroque style, designed by von Hildebrandt (*see p. 86*) and completed by the younger Fischer von Erlach. It has three separate entrances. The central entrance, to the left of the Café Silberkammer, is the *Kaisertor*, where the Emperor would enter, going to his rooms up the *Kaiserstiege*. The entrance to the court cellars is also here, where Franz Joseph kept his stocks of Tokaj wine, one of the few luxuries he really enjoyed.

4 THE LEOPOLDINISCHER TRAKT. Opposite the Reichskanzleitrakt in the same courtyard (the courtyard known as In der Burg), this section of the Hofburg is named after Leopold I, the emperor during whose reign the Turks were finally and conclusively defeated (1683), and who was responsible for the rather plain, early Baroque building you see today. In the following century it was completely filled by Maria Theresa's 16 children, and even when Joseph II grew up and became emperor he saw no reason to move, and continued to have his apartments here. In subsequent reigns the various entrances were used by tradesmen, thus we have the Lackey's Gate and the Confectioners'

The main courtyard of the Hofburg is dominated by the statue of Emperor Franz I, crowned with bays and wearing a toga. Behind him are the gilded insignia of the Holy Roman Empire.

Gate. Confectioners had their work cut out for them purveying to the imperial and royal court. The Empress Elisabeth had a notoriously sweet tooth. In later life she never smiled in public, and it was whispered behind her back that it was because her teeth had gone completely rotten.

The **statue** in the centre of the square is of Franz I, guyed up as a Roman emperor, an ironic touch given that it was he who was forced by Napoleon to dissolve the Holy Roman Empire, though this was not an irony that was lost on the man who commissioned the statue, Franz's son Ferdinand I. The statue was made in Milan in 1846, and was so heavy that it took eight pairs of oxen and nine pairs of horses a total of 33 days to drag it to Vienna.

5 THE AMALIENBURG. Standing in In der Burg facing the sundial, the entrance to the Amalienburg is straight ahead of you. To your left is the archway through to the Neue Burg and Heldenplatz (*see p. 66*). Behind you is the Schweizertor (*see p. 48*). The Amalienburg is named after Amalia of Brunswick, widow of Joseph I, who lived here between 1711 and 1742. Since then the Amalienburg was always used as a residence for imperial dowagers. Above the clock, just below the tower, is a lunar clock which registers the phases of the moon, placed there by the astronomer-emperor Rudolf II. Outside the Amalienburg and facing it, at Ballhausplatz 2, is Johann Lukas von Hildebrandt's **Imperial Chancellery**. The Ballhausplatz is so named because an old ball court stood here in the 16th century, where courtiers would disport themselves at shuttlecock and battledore. The Chancellery building was subsequently where Maria Theresa's great adviser Kaunitz (*see p. 166*) held court, and later was where delegates of the Congress of Vienna met. Its huge council chamber only had three doors, so Metternich (*see p. 166*) had two more matching ones built in overnight (literally), so that the Emperor of Austria, the Russian Tsar, and the kings of Denmark, Prussia and Württemberg could enter the room at the same time. Metternich was holding a grand ball here in 1815 when a breathless messenger arrived and whispered the dread tidings that "the little man" had escaped from Elba. The party instantly went dead. In more recent times the building became so bound up with Austrian foreign policy that the mere word "Ballhausplatz" was used to mean the foreign ministry. It was in this building that Chancellor Dollfuss (*see p. 28*) was shot in 1934.

6 THE SCHWEIZERHOF & TREASURY. To enter the Schweizerhof, go through the black and russet striped Renaissance doorway, the **Schweizertor** (1553). This is the oldest part of the Hofburg. When the Hungarian king Matthias conquered Vienna in 1485 he took up residence here, and converted part of the Hofburg into a beautiful hanging garden. The name Schweizertor ("Swiss gate") derives from the Swiss mercenaries who briefly guarded it in the 18th century. Commonly bands of such mercenaries would perform similar services all over Europe. The only place where they still survive is the Vatican City. The

The Renaissance Schweizertor.

Schweizerhof contains the entrance to the **Temporal and Spiritual Treasury** (*Weltliche und Geistliche Schatzkammer*). This contains the orbs and sceptres wielded by Holy Roman Emperors, the tabards worn by their heralds, the robes of the Order of the Golden Fleece - and much more besides. The exhibits have captions in German only, but audio guides are available. If you want to get the most out of this superb collection, the illustrated guide (available in the museum shop) is excellent. It probably makes sense to buy it and read it before your visit. Trying to digest all the information as you stand before each show-case would be a cumbersome process.

A Selection of Exhibits in the Treasury

THE CROWN OF THE AUSTRIAN EMPIRE: Holy Roman Emperors did not keep their sacred coronation regalia in their possession; they remained in safekeeping in Nuremberg. Instead each emperor had his own personal crown made for use on state occasions. This crown, the personal crown of the emperor Rudolf II, was made in Prague in 1602. Half crown half mitre, it symbolises the blend of temporal and spiritual power which Holy Roman Emperors were meant to possess. When the emperor Franz, in response to Napoleon's declaring himself Emperor of the French, dissolved the Holy Roman Empire and declared himself Emperor of Austria in 1806, he chose this crown - the only personal crown that survives - as the crown of the House of Austria. A portrait by Friedrich Amerling (*see p. 58*) of a gruff-looking Franz wearing the crown is also held in the treasury.

THE CRADLE OF THE DUKE OF REICHSTADT: The emperor Franz's daughter Marie Louise married Napoleon in 1810, as a way of sealing the peace that had recently been declared, and preventing Napoleon from mounting any more campaigns to tear Europe apart. The son of that marriage, Napoleon Franz, was given the title King of Rome, an obvious allusion to the title of Holy Roman Emperor which his grandfather had renounced, and which his ambitious father so coveted. His gold and silver-gilt cradle, made in Paris in 1811, is thick with symbolism, as Napoleon scrambled to create a legitimacy for himself and to found a new and glorious dynasty. The hood resembles a kingly throne. The tops of the legs are made in the form of cornucopiae. Around the sides there are little golden bees, symbols of productivity. Napoleon chose the bee, ancient symbol of the Kingdom of the Franks, as his own emblem instead of the French *fleur de lys*. The winged figure hovering above the bed is the goddess of victory, holding aloft a crown of laurels (fame and renown) above which dances a circlet of stars, the heavens themselves. The central star is embossed with the letter N - Napoleon - the brightest star in the firmament (in his own estimation, anyway). At the foot of the bed sits a baby eagle, symbolising the boy king

himself, gazing upwards at his father's glory (*see p. 191*).

THE CORONATION REGALIA OF THE HOLY ROMAN EMPIRE: The Mantle - A perfect half-circle of scarlet samite embroidered with gold, it was made in Palermo in 1134. Sicily was at that time a Norman kingdom with a substantial Saracen population. Its ruler, Roger II, married his daughter to the future Holy Roman Emperor Henry VI, which is how these Sicilian vestments (the stockings, gloves and tunic are also Sicilian) came into the Holy Roman Emperors' possession. From the early 15th century the

Coronation mantle of the Holy Roman Emperors, on display in the Treasury. It was made in the 12th century by Islamic artists in the Kingdom of Sicily, hence the Arabic inscription around the hem.

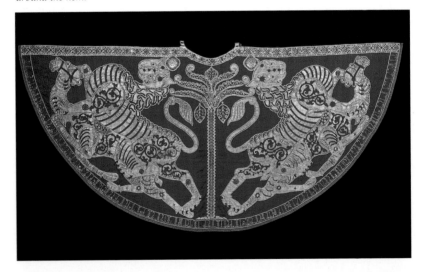

regalia were kept permanently at Nuremberg, and were only transferred to Vienna during the Napoleonic Wars, because it was known that Bonaparte was trying to get his hands on them. The design of the mantle is an exquisite symmetrical composition of twin lions attacking camels, with a stylised Tree of Life in the centre. The Arabic inscription around the hem points to the fact that the mantle was almost certainly worked by Islamic artists.

The Crown - German, late 10th century. Eight hinged gold plates are encrusted with precious stones and decorated with enamel plaques representing King David, King Solomon, the prophet Isaiah and Christ enthroned. The topmost jewel in the front plate of the crown, a pale, heart-shaped sapphire, clearly does not fit into its setting. This is because the original stone, a precious opal, symbolising Christ the universal, uniting all the colours of the spectrum and conferring a luminous wisdom on the wearer, was lost, stolen or strayed sometime in the 14th century. It is thought that the crown was made for the coronation of Otto the Great in 962. The arched band across the top is a later addition. The inscription on it, picked out in tiny pearls, refers to *Conradus, Romanorum Imperator* (ruled early 11th century).

The Treasury is open 10am-6pm every day except Tuesday.

7 THE BURGKAPELLE (IN THE SCHWEIZERHOF). This court chapel contains the only traces of Gothic architecture still remaining in the Hofburg, though most of what stands today was Baroque-ised by Maria Theresa. The chapel houses a miraculous crucifix which allegedly spoke to Ferdinand II when Vienna was under threat of siege during the Thirty Years War (1618-1648). Ferdinand was kneeling in prayer before it when it suddenly spoke, declaring "I will not forsake you!" Armies of Swedes who had been encamped outside the city ready to attack then abruptly turned round and went away again, as news opportunely reached them of an unfavourable turn of events in war-torn Bohemia. Today the chapel still functions as a place of worship. The **Vienna Boys' Choir** sings here on Sundays.

The chapel is open Mon-Thur 11am-3pm; Fri 11am-1pm. Sunday mass begins at 9.15am (no services July and August). Ticket office open Fri 11am-1pm; 3pm-5pm and Sun from 8.15am until mass begins. Telephone reservations on (43 1) 533 9927.

The bright white, late Baroque façade fronting the Josefsplatz.

8 THE NATIONAL LIBRARY. Go through the Schweizerhof and into the harmonious, white-façaded, cobbled **Josefsplatz**, its central roofline adorned by two huge golden globes, the sphere of the heavens and the sphere of the earth, borne by Atlas. In the centre of the square is the entrance to the former court library, now the Austrian National Library, which was built by the Fischer von Erlachs, father and son, and completed in 1735. The main attraction is the **Ceremonial Hall** (*Prunksaal*), which runs the whole length of the first floor, and has ceiling frescoes by Daniel Gran (*see picture on p. 73*). The main fresco (1730) shows figures engaged in the arts of Navigation, Music, Geography, Medicine, Warfare and Astronomy leaning over a *trompe l'oeil* balustrade. Above their heads other figures soar heavenwards amid a feast of symbols: hives teeming with bees, cornucopiae disgorging crowns and jewels, a tablet depicting Maximilian I, founder of the first court library, a medallion showing Karl VI, who commissioned this building, an owl symbolising wisdom, architectural motifs, and a banner bearing the vowels AEIOU, said to stand for *Austria Est Imperare Orbi Universo* (It is Austria's destiny to rule the world). When the dome showed signs of subsidence in 1769, it was shored up by Maria Theresa's court architect Nikolaus Pacassi, and the fresco restored by Maulbertsch (*see p. 55*).

The library is open every day except Thursday, 10am-4pm (winter) and 10am-7pm (summer).

9 THE ALBERTINA. At the corner of Augustinerstrasse, beyond the Augustinerkirche (*see p. 134*), this palace was originally given to Albert of Saxe Teschen by Maria Theresa as a way of tempting him to stay in Vienna (he had

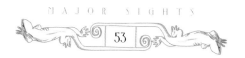
voluntarily renounced politics and statecraft and wanted to go home to Saxony). Maria Theresa was not so much interested in Albert himself as in her favourite daughter, Marie Christine, whom he had married. The palace now houses an exceptional graphics collection that was begun by Albert himself.

THE BELVEDERE
(Summer Palace of Eugene of Savoy
and home to the Austrian Art Gallery)
*District 3, Rennweg 6. Open Tues-Sun 9am-6pm (April-Oct)
and 9am-5pm (Nov-March)*

The peculiar-looking Palais Schwarzenberg, at Rennweg 2, looks peculiar for a reason. It was always intended to have a dome, and looking at the building head-on, it is clear where the dome was meant to go - it just never got there. The reason for this is said to be because the great soldier and statesman Prince Eugene of Savoy objected, and in modern parlance blocked planning permission, so that the views from his neighbouring Belvedere would remain unobscured. The Belvedere itself, summer residence of Prince Eugene, is the great-

View of the Lower Belvedere, which housed the summer living quarters of Prince Eugene.

Memorial to the Soviet heroes of World War Two, still standing although Soviet occupation ended in 1955. Behind the column to the left is the Palais Schwarzenberg. The dome that was meant to surmount the building was allegedly disallowed by Eugene of Savoy, who feared that it would spoil his views from the Belvedere.

est work of Fischer von Erlach's rival, Johann Lukas von Hildebrandt (*see p. 86*). Composed of a lower palace, an upper palace and an ornamental park, the effect of the whole is rather like an open-air Baroque church, with everything tending upwards and forwards to converge on the high altar - in this case the roofscape of the upper palace. The park was laid out between 1700 and 1725, with a landscape gardener and a hydro-engineer employed to make sure that it contained all the very best that Italian Renaissance and French Baroque garden design could provide. There is statuary everywhere: the nine muses, the four seasons, the twelve months of the year - every must-have group in the contemporary catalogue. There is no truth in the myth that the sphinxes are all modelled on Prince Eugene's mistresses. He wasn't that kind of man. The little hump-backed soldier's skills were martial not extra-marital.

LOWER BELVEDERE
(*Unteres Belvedere*)

The lower palace was completed in 1716, and is the building that Prince Eugene actually lived in when he was in residence. The decoration of the

marble hall was deliberately designed to flatter him, being full of images of war and victory. The ceiling fresco depicts Apollo in his triumphal chariot, and there are chained captive Turks looking mournfully down from above the fireplaces. The lead statues in the middle of the room are the originals from the Providentia Fountain in Neuer Markt (*see p. 146*). **Prince Eugene's former bedroom** also survives, although he would not recognise it if he saw it. It was transformed into a twinkling cabinet of gold in Maria Theresa's time.

THE COLLECTION

The Lower Belvedere contains the **Austrian Baroque collection**, with works by artists who were also commissioned to produce frescoes and altarpieces for the city's churches. The most noted of these are **Johann Rottmayr** (1654-1730), who trained in Venice, worked as court artist to the Prince-Bishop of Salzburg, and provided paintings for the Karlskirche (*see p. 136*), and **Franz Anton Maulbertsch** (1724-1796). For a long time Maulbertsch's genius was overlooked in Vienna, where he was considered to be just a little bit too bold and modern - his figures are sometimes strangely Mannerist, stylised and tending to the distorted: less idealised than was the norm. Most of his best work was carried out in Hungary and Bohemia, although after Joseph II came to the throne Maulbertsch's career picked up. Joseph, who aspired to be a true Enlightenment monarch, found Maulbertsch's style more to his liking.

The Lower Belvedere, Marble Hall. Note the sculpted Turkish captive above the fireplace, placed there to remind Prince Eugene of his many victories over the armies of the Sublime Porte.

The prize work in the collection is David's famous painting of **Napoleon on the St Bernard Pass** (1801), which shows Napoleon on horseback crossing the Alps. The fact that Hannibal had memorably done this before him was not lost on the little Corsican; Hannibal's name appears engraved on the rocks below his horse's feet. Napoleon is clearly not concentrating on crossing the Alps at all, but on being admired by an audi-ence. He personally supervised the progress of this painting, and his pose on the horse is fully intended to sym-bolise the onward and upward nature of his triumph. Note the inscription under his horse's back legs, too: *Karolus Magnus Imp.* As a Frenchman Napoleon saw himself as Charlemagne's legitimate heir, and he wanted to wrest the Holy Roman Empire away from the Germans and take it back for the Franks.

The Austrian mediaeval collection is housed in the Belvedere's former orangery.

UPPER BELVEDERE
(*Oberes Belvedere*)

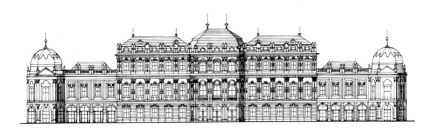

The upper palace was used by Prince Eugene for receptions and balls. Though essentially a private person, he had more than a trace of vanity, and loved pomp and partying. He is said to have received the envoys of the defeated Ottoman Sultan with such ceremony that he was mistaken for the emperor himself. In 1700 Eugene held a masked ball for 6,000 guests in the palace gardens. No matter that the palace was not yet built - he had a marquee erected, the walls and roof of which were painted to look like gardens. The palace was completed in 1723, again designed to remind Eugene of his heroic status, with a roofline meant to resemble an Ottoman tent. When Eugene died,

the lion in his menagerie died too, on the very same night. As Maria Theresa put it (though not in so many words), Austria ceased to roar. Eugene's niece sold the Belvedere to Maria Theresa, who held an enormous reception here to celebrate the engagement of her fourteen-year-old daughter Marie Antoinette to the French dauphin, the ill-starred future Louis XVI. The palace was last used as a residence by the Archduke Franz Ferdinand, who lived here from 1889 until his assassination in Bosnia, which triggered the First World War (*see p. 23*).

INSIDE THE UPPER BELVEDERE

It is tempting to wonder if Prince Eugene ever wearied of being reminded of his own glory. The ground floor **garden salon** (*sala terrena*), where the ticket office is, has a vaulted stucco ceiling supported by four enormous Atlases, with military paraphernalia and emblems of imperial might (expressly Roman) bristling above their heads. The low-ceilinged room to the right of this has a ceiling fresco of the forces of light triumphing over darkness by the Swiss-born artist Carlo Carlone. On the first floor is the grand **marble hall**, overlooked by gallery windows from the floor above. Its ceiling fresco is an allegory of fame. It was in this room, in May 1955, that the five foreign ministers Molotov (USSR), Dulles (USA), Macmillan (United Kingdom), Pinay (France) and Figl (Austria) signed the declaration giving sovereignty to the state of Austria. The document was then displayed to cheering crowds, who thronged the Belvedere gardens outside. The **palace chapel**, in the south-east corner pavilion (viewable from the glazed door to its first-floor gallery), has a ceiling fresco of God the Father and the Holy Ghost, also by Carlone.

THE COLLECTION

First Floor:
Historicism, Impressionism, Jugendstil, Expressionism.

Second Floor:
Classic, Romantic, Biedermeier.

The collection represents Austrian art almost exclusively, although there are a number of paintings by French Impressionist masters too. A selection of the major artists appears below:

A HANDFUL OF ARTISTS ON DISPLAY IN THE UPPER BELVEDERE

SECOND FLOOR

FERDINAND WALDMÜLLER (1793-1865) - To escape the importunate urging of his pious mother, who wanted him to join the priesthood, Waldmüller left home and eked out a living aquatinting engravings. He taught himself to paint by making copies of old masters. His work includes some technically highly adept portraits and pretty landscapes, as well as some soppy genre scenes of children and peasants: twee and moralising, like a lot of Biedermeier art.

FRIEDRICH VON AMERLING (1803-1887) - The most sought-after portrait painter of his day among the upper classes, the wealthy bourgeoisie and even the imperial court, Amerling was famed for his ability to create images that seemed to capture intimate family moments, rather than staged tableaux.

MORITZ VON SCHWIND (1804-1871) - Trained as a classical, monumental artist, von Schwind later came to reject this style in

The Arthaber Family by Friedrich Amerling. Mrs Arthaber, who had died not long before this was painted, is present in the scene in the form of a portrait held by her youngest child.

favour of something dreamier and more poetic. His works on display in the Belvedere seem derivative and slightly absurd, but it is easy to see how he made the transition to illustrating fairy stories, at which he made his name. Although today he is more famous as a friend of Schubert than as an artist in his own right, he is nevertheless an important exponent of the German late Romantic school. There are frescoes by him in the loggia of the Opera House (*see p. 114*).

Emperor Maximilian on the Martinswand, by Moritz von Schwind.

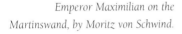

FIRST FLOOR

HANS MAKART (1840-1884) - A celebrated painter of large historical canvases, Makart designed the costumes and floats for the silver wedding procession of Franz Joseph and Elisabeth in 1879. Makart himself rode at the head of the procession, mounted on a white charger which almost threw him off. He painted allegorical friezes in the *piano nobile* apartments of Ringstrasse tycoons, a fashion set by the merchant and plutocrat Nikolaus Dumba, who was also a great patron of the arts and one of the founders of the *Gesellschaft der Musikfreunde*. Before

Makart set to work on Dumba's mansion, Dumba paid for him to go to Venice to study the Renaissance originals he was expected to imitate. Society gossiped non-stop about Makart's love life and about the orgies he was rumoured to have held - nevertheless ladies in the forefront of fashion were falling over themselves to be painted by him. It is easy to believe that the faces of his *Five Senses*, which are in effect portrait heads stuck onto the same stock body, could well have belonged to the wives and daughters of bankers and steel barons. The type of interior

The Triumph of Ariadne by Hans Makart, the man who dictated the artistic fashions of the Ringstrasse era.

OSKAR KOKOSCHKA (1886-1980) - Vienna's leading Expressionist artist was the son of an Austrian mother and a Czech father who came from a long line of goldsmiths, and from whom Kokoschka claimed to have learned that it is better to live in poverty than to do work one does not enjoy. Kokoschka began working for the Wiener Werkstätte (*see p. 103*) in 1907, but when his first paintings were exhibited a year later their violent mood caused such a stir that the Werkstätte disowned

decor that became all the rage among middle-class Viennese - heavy fabrics, oriental screens, arrangements of dried palm fronds and peacock feathers - was largely shaped by Makart. Despite his enormous fame, however, by the time he died Makart had begun to outlive it. When his paintings were auctioned after his death there were virtually no buyers - and soon enough the colours of his paintings, of which he had always been inordinately proud, began to fade. The chemicals he had mixed with his paints to make them dry quicker also turned out to hasten their deterioration.

Oskar Kokoschka: Mother and Child.

him and declined to give him further work. Kokoschka resorted to betting people that he could drink them under the table as a way of making ends meet. The only person prepared to champion him in Vienna was Adolf Loos (*see p. 87*). Kokoschka cut his losses and went to Berlin, where he enjoyed more success, returning to Vienna a few years later, even though on seeing his works the heir to the imperial throne, Franz Ferdinand, had denounced him as a scoundrel who deserved to have every bone in his body broken. The 1920s were good years for Kokoschka, but the rising tide of Fascism in the 30s made his life more difficult. He emigrated to England and became a British citizen. After the War he had a number of retrospective exhibitions, but somehow he had outlived his own daring, and he no longer seemed so shocking or so *avant garde* as he once had done. In the years before his death, though a known name, he was largely forgotten, and there were people who expressed amazement that he was still alive.

EGON SCHIELE (1890-1918) - The son of a station master who went mad and died when Schiele was still a young boy. Schiele had loved his father intensely. He was very hard on his mother, complaining that she didn't

Egon Schiele's portrait of his wife Edith.

understand him, nor love him sufficiently, nor make sufficient sacrifices. Clearly a problem character. He lavished affection on his sister, in a way that people whispered was hardly decent. He won a place at the Academy of Fine Art, where he showed his work to Klimt, who reportedly reacted by saying the problem with it was not that it displayed no talent but that it displayed much too much. Schiele's fascination with pubescent girls was notorious, and his studio flat was said to have been permanently full of them, in various degrees of undress. For some time he made a living by selling his works to collectors of pornography. Narcissistic, self-pitying and self-aggrandising, a portrait that he produced of himself in the guise of Saint Sebastian is utterly typical of his attitude: the wronged martyr. Nevertheless, Schiele's talent brought him the rewards he deserved. He enjoyed a reputation as one of Austria's leading artists and earned a reasonable living as a result, but still he insisted on dressing in rags to create an illusion of romantic artistic poverty. He died of Spanish flu at the age of 28, three days after his pregnant wife.

More works by Schiele can be seen in the Leopold Museum in the Museumsquartier (see p. 98).

GUSTAV KLIMT (1862-1918) Together with his brother Ernst, Klimt began his career producing frescoes and friezes for the Historicist buildings of the Ringstrasse (Burgtheater, Kunsthistorisches Museum). By the 1890s, however, he had left all that behind him and become the shining beacon of the new wave. As first president of the group of artists and architects who called themselves the Vienna Secession, he mounted an exhibition aimed at showing the public how behind-hand the arts world in Vienna was

View of the Schloss Kammer.

compared to Paris, which had long abandoned Historicism in favour of Impressionism and Symbolism. Klimt was interested in Japanese art, as many artists had been before him. His Jugendstil style, however, was something entirely new. It is largely thanks to Klimt that Vienna art and architecture took off in the new and inspired direction that they did. Klimt's own work, which is highly stylised and highly original, was perhaps too much even for some of the modernisers. In 1905 he and his disciples, the *Klimtgruppe*, seceded from the Secession and went their own way. Vienna society, usually thought of as highly conservative, nevertheless loved Klimt. The ladies of the *haute bourgeoisie* abandoned Makart and began queuing up to be painted by Klimt in the daring new style.

MAJOR WORKS BY KLIMT IN THE BELVEDERE

PORTRAIT OF SONJA KNIPS (1898): Superficially traditional, this work is in fact very interesting in the way the subject is not the centre of the canvas, but placed to one side, the armchair she sits in cropped by the frame. The arrangement of flowers behind her and the large black expanse in the top left-hand corner are reminiscent of Japanese prints.

THE KISS (1907/8): This oil painting with applied silver and gold leaf is almost iconic in the way the heads and arms of the figures emerge from a highly stylised golden cloak. This work completely blurs the division between art and design, ancient and modern, religious and secular, hallowed and profane. Other works in his famous "Golden Style", include *Judith I* (1901) and *Adele Bloch-Bauer I* (1907).

PLEIN-AIR PAINTINGS: Once again Klimt hovers on the boundary between faithfully rendering reality and creating design - see *Beech Wood* (1903) or *Apple Tree* (1912). His views of the Schloss Kammer on the Attersee (around 1910) begin to betray his interest in Van Gogh.

For other works by Klimt, see the Secession Building on p. 95 and the Kunsthistorisches Museum on p. 92.

THE RINGSTRASSE

"If the emperor found it proper to permit the gates of the town to be laid open, that the *faubourgs* might be joined to it," wrote Lady Mary Wortley Montagu when she visited Vienna in the early 18th century, "he would have one of the largest and best-built cities of Europe." Vienna when she saw it was an old town of tall narrow houses and winding narrow streets clustering within the encircling embrace of stout city walls, studded every so often with jutting bastions. Beyond this was an area of meadowland, the glacis, not built on for strategic reasons, so that any besieging enemy would have nowhere to run for cover. Beyond the glacis stretched Vienna's total of 34 suburbs. And that state of affairs remained unchanged right up until the middle of the 19th century, when, in December 1857, an imperial decree went out to the effect that the walls were to be torn down and a new, modern boulevard was to be created, linking the *Innere Stadt* to its suburbs. Military experts pulled long faces and tugged at their moustaches. In 1848 heated revolutionaries from the suburbs

Archive photograph of the Ringstrasse in 1908.

had been stopped dead in their tracks by the simple expedient of slamming the city gates on them. With no such gates to slam, how could future would-be insurgents be beaten back? Plenty of ordinary citizens opposed the proposals, too. They liked the glacis as a Sunday promenading place, and they were worried about how much the new buildings would all cost. Franz Joseph was adamant, however. He wanted a grand, modern city complete with a grand, modern boulevard that would lend it beauty and solemnity. He got his way, and thirty years of fevered construction work began.

As the Ringstrasse began to take shape, imposing - even palatial - residences began to spring up all along its length. The most fashionable stretch, popular with the haute bourgeoisie and new plutocrats, was the stretch near the Opera. The old aristocracy preferred the quieter, leafier environs of the Parkring. The owner of the building would have his apartment on the *piano nobile*, and rent out the rest of the house as flats. Street-facing apartments were the most prestigious (even having one street-facing room meant a lot), but if people could only afford a room or two facing the courtyard, dingy and poky though they were, a Ringstrasse address was still worth having.

The Ringstrasse's champions hailed it as a triumph of urban planning: solid, dignified and imposing, perfect for the imperial capital it served, a far better promenading place than the glacis for the city's well-to-do belles and swells, and also ideal for ceremonial parades. It hosted Franz Joseph's silver wedding pageant in 1879 and his funeral procession in 1916. John Stuart Mill was appalled at what he saw. "Outside the palaces on the Ring," he wrote, "loitered thousands of unemployed, and beneath this *Via Triumphalis* of old Austria dwelt the homeless in the gloom and mud of the canals. In hardly any German city could the social question have been studied better than in Vienna." Other critics of the Ringstrasse complained that the monumental, Historicist style of its buildings was just a hark-back to tired old ideas from the past, betraying a tragic lack of imagination and no concept of how to be modern. It was also, alas, perfect for rallies of a rather more sinister kind. When Hitler entered Vienna in 1938 and put himself up at the Hotel Imperial, he addressed massed crowds in the Heldenplatz from the balcony of the Neue Burg (*see p. 69*).

THE STADTPARK & PARKRING

PARKRING: This was the very smartest enclave of Ringstrasse society, with its high-ceilinged, chandeliered, fresco-covered first floor apartments overlooking the Stadtpark. Many of the house-owners were from the lesser nobility and gentry, but not all. Some were self-made men like Nikolaus Dumba, a Macedonian who settled in Vienna and amassed a huge fortune through trade with the Near East. Dumba was probably a typical example of the self-made men who populated the Ring. He was a prominent member of the Left Wingers' Club and got on well with the liberal-minded Crown Prince Rudolf. He was also a great patron of the arts: he commissioned Gustav Klimt and Hans Makart (*see p. 59*) to paint frescoes in his apartment, and was a founding member of the Musikverein.

The Stadtpark incorporates an above-ground section of the river Wien, flowing along a man-made trench - a very deep trench for such a little river. This area was once famous for its thermal springs. Water from them was said to be highly restorative, and was available by the glass in the park's Kursalon, a venue that was also used for concerts, which is its main function today.

Strauss the Elder conducted a performance of his Radetzky March here in July 1848. Field Marshal Radetzky, who had done so much to keep Franz Joseph's revolutionary subjects in check, was rewarded by the great favour of apartments in the Hofburg and the honour of not having to book a prior appointment when he wished to speak to the emperor.

MOVING WEST FROM THE NEUE BURG

NB: The Ringstrasse is not strictly speaking a "sight". It would be too much to walk from one end of it to the other. Nevertheless, it is an important monument in Vienna's development, and is flanked by a number of the city's major 19th-century buildings. These are given below, and are also shown on the map opposite.

NEUE BURG AND THE HELDENPLATZ: There are two equestrian statues in Vienna's "Heroes' Square". On the right as you enter from the Ring is **Eugene of Savoy** (*see p. 166*). On the left is **Archduke Carl** (1771-1847), brother of the emperor Franz. Carl led Austria to victory over Napoleon at Aspern in 1809. It was Napoleon's first ever defeat - but later the same year he turned the tables, and

defeated Austria at the battle of Wagram. Carl immediately entered into negotiations to cease hostilities, but this was against the wishes of the emperor, and he was forced to resign his post as Field Marshal as a result. The statue, which was erected in 1859, is dedicated to all "dogged fighters for Germany's honour", identifying Austria inextricably with the German peoples - an identification

The statue of Hans Makart in ruffled shirt and knee breeches stands in the Stadtpark, close to the mansions of those patrons whose portraits he painted and whose salons he decorated.

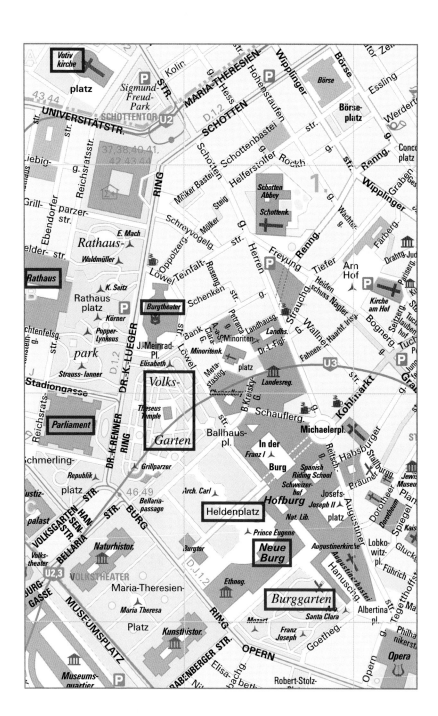

she was happy with until Bismarck began his work of chipping away at her empire. Carl's German wife Henriette is famous for having introduced the Christmas tree to Austria in 1816, an innovation which so took the emperor's fancy that he ordered a tree for the Hofburg as well.

The **Burggarten** to the rear of the Neue Burg was closed to the public, and kept exclusively for the use of the imperial family. In 1918 it was overrun by the angry revolutionary crowds, and the statue of Franz Joseph was shot to pieces. The statue has since been replaced, by a monument that makes him look like a stooping, shuffling, rather sad old *pantouffle*. The garden has been open to the public since 1919. The **Volksgarten**, which lies beyond the Heldenplatz, was - as its name suggests - always a public park.

Massive without being impressive and grand without being beautiful, the stodgy architecture of the **Neue Burg** (completed 1913) is largely the work of Ludwig Baumann. The original designs for the building were by Semper and von Hasenauer, the architects of the Kunsthistorisches Museum (*see p. 91*) and the Burgtheater (*see p. 70*). After their deaths the project was taken on by Emil Förster, but Baumann, who completed the building, tore down a lot of what

Equestrian statue of Eugene of Savoy on the Heldenplatz.

The Pallas Athene fountain outside Theophil Hansen's neo-Classical Parliament.

Förster had done and started again, maintaining that Förster's palace was not stately enough. Crowds gathered in their thousands under the Neue Burg balcony in 1938 to hear Hitler's fevered pronouncements. It was a sad moment for Vienna, although a triumphant one for Hitler himself, personally as well as politically. The struggling, unsuccessful, chippy little artist who had felt so humiliated in Vienna in 1906-1913 was now about to annexe it to his Thousand-year Reich. Vienna, he famously said, was a jewel, and a jewel that he intended to mount in an appropriate setting. What he brought to the city was ignominy and destitution. During the Second World War, the Heldenplatz was ploughed up and used as farmland to help feed the starving population.

PARLIAMENT: By Theophil Hansen (1813-1891), a Danish architect who had worked in Athens before settling in Vienna, where he married the sister of Emil Förster (see above), and was made a freeman of the city. The Parliament took Hansen 10 years to complete (1873-1883), but it was his crowning success and embodied his dearest architectural ideal: a monumental building in the Hellenistic style. The style was doubly appropriate for a parliament, he felt, as ancient Greece was the cradle of modern democracy. Not that Pericles and Franz Joseph had much in common. To the end of his days, despite his grand Hellenistic Parliament building, Franz Joseph remained an absolute monarch. A bas-relief of him, clad in a toga and with mutton-chop whiskers, appears on the tympanum above the main entrance. In front of the building is the Pallas Athene fountain. Athene was the patron goddess of Athens, hence her symbolic adoption here.

Night-time view of the Rathaus, Vienna's neo-Gothic Town Hall.

RATHAUS: Completed in 1883 by the architect Friedrich Schmidt, the neo-Netherlandish Gothic style of the Rathaus is highly unfashionable now, but at the time it was all the rage and the building was an instant success. Vienna was thrilled with it. It was in the Red Room here that, in 1945, the second Austrian republic formed its first government under Karl Renner, the Socialist leader who had first come to power in 1918, following Karl I's renunciation of all involvement in Austrian state affairs (*see p. 26*), and after whom this section of the Ring is named. The Rathaus is also famed for its collection of portraits of Vienna's mayors, where there is a conspicuous gap between 1938 and 1945. The puppet mayors installed by the Nazis were not deemed worthy of inclusion.

BURGTHEATER: Completed in 1888, the Burgtheater stands on the site of a bastion where the Turks finally broke through the city walls in 1683, after a 59-day siege. Looking at the area now, it is difficult to imagine it covered with a sea of 25,000 tents. One of the Burgtheater's architects was the Dresden-born Gottfried Semper. The other architect was an Austrian, Karl von Hasenauer, who collaborated with Semper on the Kunsthistorisches Museum (*see p. 91*). The last building to be completed on the Ringstrasse, the Burgtheater was equipped with electric light right from the beginning, and boasts ceiling frescoes by Klimt (*see p. 62*). Its auditorium was ventilated by shafts opening into the Volksgarten - the scent of lilac would waft in in the late spring. Franz Joseph's mistress Katharina Schratt was an actress here. The empress Elisabeth had always condoned the relationship between Katharina and her husband, and acted in some measure as Katharina's protector. After Elisabeth's death, however, the knives came out. It was not just the imperial family who was out to get Katharina, but also Franz Joseph's Court Chamberlain, Prince Montenuovo, a bitter and twisted character descended from the illegitimate son of an army officer and the Austrian Archduchess Marie Louise, wife of Napoleon and sometime Empress of France (*see p. 49*). Montenuovo's post gave him control over the court theatres, and he exercised it ruthlessly. When Elisabeth died he refused to renew Katharina Schratt's contract. Appealed to for help, Franz Joseph refused to intervene, feeling that it would be humiliating for Katharina as well as for him. Of course he could flatly insist that she be

The Burgtheater, where Franz Joseph's mistress Katharina Schratt was an actress.

given her job back - he was the emperor. But she was the emperor's mistress, and if he did insist it would compromise them both. It was the end. Katharina refused to see Franz Joseph again, leaving him heartbroken but adamant that he could not have acted any other way.

VOTIVKIRCHE: In 1853, while inspecting a military parade, the emperor Franz Joseph was attacked by a young Hungarian tailor's assistant. Seeking revenge, presumably, for Austria's crushing of the Magyar bid for independence in 1849, the boy rushed at Franz Joseph with a dagger, meaning to plunge it in his neck. Franz Joseph was lucky: he escaped with a shallow scratch. The idea to build a votive church on the site of the attack, to give thanks for the emperor's life, came from Franz Joseph's brother Maximilian (*see p. 46*), who had the foundation stone specially shipped over from the Mount of Olives. The resulting Church of the Holy Saviour, built in the neo-Gothic style by Heinrich Ferstel, was completed in 1879. At that time it would have been quite a magnificent sight, standing alone in a part of town that was largely undeveloped. Contemporary engravings show it looking almost as graceful and slender as a true Norman Gothic cathedral. The church contains a famous 19th-century organ which Anton Bruckner often played. The modern stained glass uses motifs from Austrian history fused with Christianity. One window is called "Christ at Mauthausen" (a concentration camp near Linz). Another shows a peasant destroying a swastika. The peasant was a real person: Franz Jägerstetter, executed by the Nazis for refusing to join the army and fight for them. A third window shows pilgrims on their way to Mariazell. One of the men in the procession is Chancellor Dollfuss (*see p. 28*).

ARCHITECTURE

There are three main architectural styles that typify Vienna. The Baroque: the triumphal style that was adopted during the half century after the defeat of the Ottoman army in 1683 (*see p. 15*), and which continued throughout the glorious period of Eugene of Savoy's military victories; Historicism: the grand and stately swansong style of Vienna's last decades of empire; and Jugendstil: the style through which Vienna was reborn as a vibrant and modern cultural capital.

The chronological list below outlines these major architectural styles, as well as others which came before and between them, giving examples of buildings in each style. These buildings are all as far as possible in central Vienna.

To locate the buildings and streets mentioned in this section, see the Map References on p. 236.

Allegory of architecture and the other liberal arts. Ceiling fresco by Daniel Gran (1730) in the ceremonial hall (Prunksaal) of the National Library.

GOTHIC

Gothic lace spire of Maria am Gestade.

The best Gothic survival in Vienna is the Stephansdom (*see p. 37*). Another is the church of Maria am Gestade (Salvatorgasse 12). Built on a stepped platform to preserve it from the waters of the Danube, an arm of which once ran past it, the present Gothic structure was completed around 1408. The emperor Joseph II had plans to demolish it, but shelved them when no firm of contractors could be found willing to haul away the rubble. When Napoleon occupied Vienna in 1809 (*see p. 18*), he used the church as an arsenal and stables, and the interior was badly damaged as a result. The exterior, however, particularly the tracery-work spire, is graceful and beautiful.

RENAISSANCE

There is very little Renaissance architecture in Vienna. The reason usually given is that the contents of the city's coffers were being poured into strengthening the mediaeval walls against the Ottoman threat, leaving nothing behind for either sacred or secular building. Another reason, and perhaps a more convincing one, is that during the Renaissance period the money was never in Vienna anyway. Although Maximilian I, the great humanist monarch (reigned 1493-1519), took Austria away from the mediaeval and the Gothic and into the Renaissance, he didn't concentrate his efforts in Vienna. The Vienna Boys' Choir and the National Library are his main Viennese legacies - but these are institutions, not buildings. It seems that he never quite forgave the Viennese for besieging his father in the Hofburg (*see p. 41*), and most of his time and

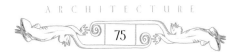
money was spent on Innsbruck instead. In fact no monarch lived permanent-ly in Vienna until after 1683, and wherever the court went, the aristocracy and the money followed. What Renaissance architecture there is in Vienna includes the Stallburg in the Spanish Riding School (1565), the Schweizertor entrance to the Hofburg (1553) and the pretty little arcaded courtyard at Bäckerstrasse 7 (1580s, *picture below, see also p. 176*).

THE VIENNA BAROQUE

Just as the Renaissance belongs to Florence, so the Baroque belongs to Vienna, as the most characteristic architecture of her imperial heyday. After 1683, when the Ottoman threat had been resoundingly seen off, Vienna began to spend money on herself again. Not only that, but having convincingly driven out the infidel, her rulers now wanted to drive out heresy, asserting once and for all the authority of the Roman Catholic Church. Baroque architecture sets out to do this magnificently. It is a style designed to ensnare the senses with its pomp and theatricality. It has no time for reposeful white walls which allow for

Renaissance courtyard in Bäckerstrasse, with an old iron manger still in place.

individual reflection and encourage introspection and thought. The aim instead is to fill all the available space, to enslave the imagination with flamboyant sensuality, and to draw a clear parallel between God, the father of all mankind, and the Emperor, God's ambassador on earth, and father of all his peoples. The conflation of worldliness and godliness leads to an almost stifling level of gaudy pomp and ceremonial, both in the churches and in the palaces.

Trompe l'oeil dome of the Jesuit Church.

Major Examples of the Baroque

Sacred Architecture

The Jesuit Church - The basic exterior was completed in 1627 (architect unknown).

Between 1703 and 1707 the Jesuit father and architect Andrea Pozzo remodelled the façade, built the two towers, and provided the magnificent, high Baroque decoration of the interior (*this is described in more detail on p. 135*).
District 1, Dr Ignaz Seipel-Platz.

The Karlskirche - The last and finest work of Vienna's greatest Baroque architect, Johann Bernhard Fischer von Erlach, completed posthumously in 1737. The exterior, with its twin columns and enormous dome, is truly original. The columns are usually described as being modelled on Trajan's column in Rome. Because there are two of them, however, and because of the ribbon motif that spirals round them, they also resemble the double-column-and-scroll motif of the

Spanish Habsburgs, from whom Karl VI - at whose behest the church was built - was descended. This device, the originator of the modern dollar sign, is still used on the Spanish royal insignia. *For more detail on the church see p. 136. District 4, Karlsplatz.*

SECULAR ARCHITECTURE

THE CEREMONIAL HALL (PRUNKSAAL) OF THE NATIONAL LIBRARY - Designed by Fischer von Erlach and completed by his son in 1726. It is magnificent in a dignified sort of way, without ever really arresting the attention - appropriate for a library, where people want to

read and study and not be distracted by naked angels. Fischer von Erlach is said to have based his theories of architectural proportion on the intervals of the musical scale - an idea which must have come to him from Palladio, whose work he admired and often imitated (*see p. 52*). *District 1, Josefsplatz.*

THE BELVEDERE - Part palace part pleasure dome part ornamental park, this exquisite building is probably the finest Baroque palace in the world (*see p. 53*). It is the work of Fischer von Erlach's great contemporary Johann Lukas von Hildebrandt. *District 3, Rennweg 6.*

The Palais Kinsky (Freyung 4), typical of von Hildebrandt's domestic architecture.

ROCOCO

A mid to late 18th century offshoot of the Baroque, but daintier and less unsubtle, and - perhaps because it is so associated with Maria Theresa and the age of the Rosenkavalier (*see p. 116*) - more feminine. The Vienna Rococo is exemplified par excellence by the palace of Schönbrunn. Although the original design was by the great master of the Baroque Fischer von Erlach, what you see today is largely the result of alterations carried out by Maria Theresa's court architect, the Wiener Neustadt-born Nikolaus Pacassi.

For a detailed description of the Schönbrunn palace and gardens, see p. 183.

HISTORICISM OR RINGSTRASSENSTIL

Historicism is the style of the late 19th century, and can be seen all over the former Austro-Hungarian empire. Solid, well-proportioned, imposing but never daring, Historicist buildings borrow architectural precepts first and fore-

Marble hall of the Hotel Imperial, former Palais Württemberg, a grand example of a Historicist Ringstrasse interior.

most from the Renaissance (sometimes entire buildings are copied), with the Gothic, the Baroque and the Classical also making an appearance. Sometimes several styles will appear at once on a single building. None of the styles, when Historicised, is ever quite the same as in its original incarnation. The neo-Renaissance buildings lack the whiff of cutting-edge engineering and the genius of craftsmanship that are stamped on their Florentine prototypes. The neo-Gothic buildings lack the solemnity and serene spirituality of a genuine mediaeval cathedral, and the neo-Baroque lacks the sheer naïve exuberance of bad taste. The shadow of *memento mori* also tends to be absent - the late 19th century, after all, was an age when people had an eye much more on this world than the next. Historicist building is solidly complacent rather than aesthetically inspired. From an intellectual point of view it is easy to criticise. From an aesthetic point of view it may not enthral, but it seldom offends.

Begun in 1875, Vienna's Ringstrasse is a masterpiece of late 19th-century Historicism. Fundamentally neo-Renaissance in spirit, elements of Classicism and the neo-Gothic are also thrown in, making for an overall eclectic effect radiating wealth, confidence and self-belief. It was built to impress, and to give a grand idea of Austria's power and consequence - exactly the sort of gesture one makes when one feels that one's power and consequence might be flagging. It certainly made a great impression on the young Adolf Hitler who, fuelled as he was by a gnawing inferiority complex, reacted to it in exactly the way he was expected to, writing in childishly overawed tones that "the entire Ringstrasse seemed to me like some enchantment from the Arabian Nights".

JUGENDSTIL

Established Vienna's insistence on clinging to an old order which had so clearly had its day profoundly exasperated the exponents of the new *avant garde*. To them the Ringstrasse represented all that was pompous and stuffy, revealed a complete absence of imagination and an apparent belief that nothing needed to change ever again. The need to break away - secede - from all that was what the Vienna Secession movement was predicated on. Gustav Klimt, as the Secession's guiding light (*see p. 62*), wanted to make a stand against what he saw as the fossilised tenets of art academe, as well as show Vienna what she was missing. Colour would replace black and white; sinuous curves would replace straight lines, and Vienna would catch up with Paris and

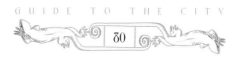
Berlin. In architecture a similar voice was provided by Otto Wagner (*see below*) and Josef Olbrich, the architect of the Secession building (*see below*).

Vienna Jugendstil - What to See Where

THE SECESSION BUILDING (Josef Olbrich, 1897-98) - A plot of land along the Ringstrasse had originally been earmarked as the site for this building. When the metropolitan authorities saw exactly what the young Olbrich proposed to build there, they blocked permission, and allocated another plot instead, in a less visible spot. Hailed as a cross between a mausoleum and a gasworks when it was first built, the Secession was almost totally destroyed by bombing in the Second World War - contemporary photographs show its golden laurel-leaf dome bobbing sadly above a sea of rubble - and for this reason the interior is undistinguished. Its exterior, however, is very interesting. Inspired by ancient Assyrian art and architecture, it was clearly meant to represent a sort of temple of art, with high priestesses and serpents around the doorway, and a central tenet of Secession philosophy emblazoned in gold above the lintel for all to see: "To every age its art, to art its freedom". The name of the Secession movement's periodical, *Ver Sacrum* (sacred spring), appears in classic Art Nouveau lettering on the front wall. Either consciously or unconsciously the architect borrowed a number of Vienna motifs from the past. The lizards around the doorway echo the lizards on the pulpit of the Stephansdom, while the tortoises that bear the huge laurel-tree pots at the entrance echo the tortoises of the

Detail of the gilded laurel-leaf dome on the Jugendstil Secession building.

Schönbrunn obelisk. Note how the laurel trees themselves are clipped to be living echoes of the golden laurel dome. The building (District 1, Friedrichstrasse 12) houses Klimt's Beethoven Frieze (*see p. 95*).

THE ANKER CLOCK (Franz Matsch, 1913) - This gold-and-green clock stands in Hoher Markt. It was created for the Anker Insurance Company, whose headquarters it adorns. The idea behind it - so they say - was to give a feeling of the passage of time, and thus inspire people to take out life insurance. It is topped by symbols of youth and age (a baby with a butterfly and a skeleton with an hour-glass). Below these is a golden sun, its rays shaped like little darts. At the bottom crouches a large lizard, the mythical basilisk of old Vienna (*see p. 177*). Figures from Vienna's history glide slowly across the clock face as the hours progress, with appropriately-chosen music heralding their arrival, and a muted chime on the hour. At twelve o'clock all the figures process by. On the clock face are the motifs of the old Vienna town flag (cross and double-headed eagle) and coats of arms representing professions and occupations. The historical figures appear as follows (the clock works on a twelve-hour system, so each figure appears

Detail of Franz Matsch's Anker Clock.

twice): I: Marcus Aurelius, the Roman Emperor who died at Vindobona (Roman Vienna); II: Charlemagne, founder of the Holy Roman Empire; III: Leopold VI, the Babenberg duke who first laid out a new town on the Hoher Markt site; IV: the minstrel Walther von der Vogelweide; V: Rudolf von Habsburg, founder of the dynasty, with his consort; VI: Hans Puchsbaum, master mason who worked on the Stephansdom; VII: the emperor Maximilian I; VIII: Andreas von Liebenberg, mayor of Vienna during the Ottoman siege of 1683; IX: Ernst Rüdiger von Starhemberg,

The Majolica House by Otto Wagner (1899).

commander of the city garrison during the siege; X: Eugene of Savoy; XI: Maria Theresa and her consort; XII: Joseph Haydn, composer of the hymn tune known as Austria (the former imperial national anthem).

THE KARLSPLATZ STADTBAHN PAVILIONS (Otto Wagner, 1899) - Intended as U-Bahn station entrances, one is decorated with stylised sunflowers and functions as a café in summer. The other is also decorated with sunflowers and an abstract design.

NOS. 38 AND 40 LINKE WIENZEILE - corner of Köstlergasse (Otto Wagner, 1899) - Two apartment houses, in all their dimensions like any other Historicist blocks, but with decoration on their façades that catapults them a million miles from Historicism. One is covered all over with pink creeping roses (made of majolica tiles), while the other is encrusted with gleaming gold leaves, and two bronze female heads call from the roof.

NB: More Jugendstil buildings are given in the section on Otto Wagner below. For information on Jugendstil painting, see pp. 62-3 and pp. 95-6.

MODERNISM & FUNCTIONALISM

A style as reliant on colour and ornament as Jugendstil was inevitably going to cloy sooner or later. The man who spoke out against it most vitriolically was Adolf Loos (*see below*), whose plain, deliberately unadorned counter-style gave Viennese tongues something to wag over and tut about for a good number of years. Modernism came to the fore during the Socialist Republic years of the 1920s and 1930s, with some monumental examples provided by the communal housing projects, the *Gemeindebauten*, financed by the city out of taxes levied on private property owners. A total of 200 architects, either working individually or in groups, designed the buildings, most of which are in outlying, traditionally working-class parts of town. Though the apartments themselves may not have been much bigger in surface area than the tenement flats that most workers were used to, they were all equipped with electricity, gas and running water. Not that they used it, mocked the *grandes dames* of the Ringstrasse. *Gemeindebauten* tenants had no idea what a bathtub was for - they used it for storing coal, to save themselves trips to the cellar. One of the best

The enormous, geometric Karl Marx-Hof, a workers' housing estate built in 1930.

and most famous of the *Gemeindebauten* is the Karl Marx-Hof at District 19, Heiligenstädterstrasse 82-92 (*see p. 200*). Built between 1927 and 1930, its 1,382 flats can accommodate up to 5,000 people, and its façade is so long that it takes three tram stops to get past it. Its even larger companion, the Friedrich Engels-Platz Hof (District 20, Friedrich Engels-Platz 1-10), was built by a pupil of Otto Wagner three years later. A year after its completion, in 1934, it was bombarded by government troops in their efforts to break the power of the *Schutzbund*, the socialist fighting force, for whom the "Engelshof" was a stronghold.

AN IMPORTANT
MODERN BUILDING - THE LOOS HAUS

Adolf Loos' best-known work is his "house without eyebrows" (the windows have no pediments) at Michaelerplatz 3, commissioned by the tailoring firm Goldman and Salatsch in 1910. Green-veined

marble clads the lower portion; the entrance is flanked by Tuscan columns in the same material. The green theme is taken up again in the plain lead roof. The upper storeys of the main façade are very plain. It is true that the windows have no sills or pediments, but some do have window boxes to articulate them. Loos' aim was to create something that was at once modern and timeless, a building that would encapsulate the curious paradox of permanence and change that characterised the Vienna he lived in. The building caused an immediate uproar. It is said to have upset Franz Joseph so much that he took to entering the Hofburg by a different gate so as not to have to look at it. And no wonder,

Green-veined Tuscan columns flank the entrance to the Loos Haus.

said some critics. So plain and dull a building could only have one aim: to make deliberate fun of the splendid Hofburg opposite. Modernisers were no more complimentary, sneering that it was not nearly daring or inventive enough. The building now houses the Raiffaisen Bank. The interior, also by Loos, is to some extent preserved, and it is worth going inside to see the original chunky stairway, the ceiling clock and old glass showcases.

A Handful of Architects And Their Buildings

Johann Bernhard Fischer von Erlach (1656-1723) - Born in Graz, the son of a stonemason, Johann Fischer trained under Bernini, and initially attempted to carve out a career for himself in Rome. Although unsuccessful, his studies of Rome's classical remains, as well as its Renaissance and Baroque buildings, stood him in good stead, and he went on to develop a style all his own, which fuses the Baroque with the Classical, and which found great favour with the Habsburg court. He was created Royal Court Architect and Court Engineer in 1694, and ennobled two years later, taking the title von Erlach. His works include the original design for Schönbrunn (1711), the National Library in the Hofburg (1722, *see p. 52*), the Winter Palace of Eugene of Savoy (Himmelpfortgasse 8, 1711), which mingles Baroque and Palladian elements and, definitely his most famous, the Karlskirche (1715-1737, *see p. 136*). Hijacked in a later century by pan-German nationalists

Interior of the Prunksaal of the National Library, with a statue of Karl VI in Roman guise. Karl commissioned the building from Fischer von Erlach.

as an architect of what they termed the "Reich style", Fischer von Erlach's reputation as the greatest architect of the Vienna Baroque nevertheless remains untarnished. His son, Fischer von Erlach the younger, was also an architect of note.

JOHANN LUKAS VON HILDEBRANDT (1668-1745) - The son of an army officer, Hildebrandt began his career as an army engineer, and was present at two of the campaigns led by Eugene of Savoy. He trained as an architect in Rome, and on coming to Vienna obtained a post as engineer to the court. It was Prince Eugene who helped him make his name: Hildebrandt built the Belvedere for him (*see p. 53*) between 1714 and 1723, and carried out enlargement work on his Winter Palace. When the supreme court architect Fischer von Erlach died in 1723, Hildebrandt was awarded a higher salary and commissioned to remodel the Reichskanzleitrakt section of the Hofburg (*see p. 44*). He never received the coveted title of Chief Court Engineer, however, which von Erlach had held. Apart from the

Belvedere, Hildebrandt's greatest achievements are his town palaces, such as the Palais Kinsky (Freyung 4, *see p. 154*), built in a style which spawned a whole school of imitators.

OTTO WAGNER (1841-1918) - The greatest exponent of Austrian Jugendstil, though he was influenced by Loos (*see below*) and turned more towards Functionalism later in life. A good juxtaposition of his two styles is provided by the eclectic, Historicist Grabenhof at Graben 14-15 (1876), and the mini skyscraper almost next door at Graben 10 (1894), which shows him moving slowly towards Modernism. His Postsparkasse (Georg Coch-Platz 2)

The Postsparkasse by Otto Wagner (1906). Wagner had already begun to move away from Art Nouveau towards Modernism.

Otto Wagner's Schützenhaus (1908) beside the Danube Canal, another building which fuses Jugendstil and Modernist elements.

was built between 1904 and 1906, interestingly seven years earlier than the massy, Historicist government buildings which stand facing it across the Ring - and in stark contrast. Whereas the architects of the Ringstrasse had been imitating earlier styles, and were content to create monoliths out of brick and moulded plaster pretending to look like hewn stone, Wagner had been infected by the teachings of Loos and wanted to conceal nothing, entirely happy that people should see that his Postsparkasse was clad in thin tiles fixed with aluminium nails. The same visibly tacked-on tiles technique was used for his Schützenhaus (1908) beside the Danube Canal in District 2 (Obere Donaustrasse 26), originally intended to serve the canal lock that was planned there.

ADOLF LOOS (1870-1933) - Above all Loos hated pretence. The Ringstrasse, with its brick and plaster masquerading as stone, had been bad enough. Jugendstil, however, was complete anathema to him. He detested its voluptuousness, declaring that ornamentation was a waste of labour, a waste of materials

A Vienna council house from the 1950s. The Socialist Realist decoration of the façade is a reminder that Vienna was partly under Soviet control until 1955.

refused to admit that the fault lay with the chair. The problem was with women's clothing, which was so constricting that the wearers were forced to perch, rigid and genteel, on the very edge of their seats, making a nonsense of a chair's centre of gravity. Of course it was going to fall over. Loos' bijou masterpiece is the American Bar (1908) in the Kärntner Durchgang, a tiny cocktail bar preserving its original fittings, and made to feel much more spacious than it is by the use of multiple mirrors.

FRIEDENSREICH HUNDERTWASSER (1928-2000) - The architectural ball is knocked into the other court once more by Hundertwasser, the prophet of "organic architecture" and mortal enemy of Functionalism. Profoundly eccentric as an artist and as an architect, half loony peace child and half impassioned spokesman for individualism, Hundertwasser was very involved with the green movement and conservationism, and a vociferous campaigner against Austrian accession to the EU. Born Friedrich Stowasser, he adopted the first name Friedensreich (which, appropriately

and a waste of money. As a member of turn-of-the-20th-century coffeehouse society, he expressed his distaste for the prevailing style of the times with his own anti-café, the Café Museum (1899, *see p. 110*), which aimed to banish clutter and twiddles and introduce functional purity. He boasted that his house on the Michaelerplatz (*see Loos Haus above*) used only "real materials". Loos also designed the interior of the clothes shop Knize (1909-13) at Graben 13 (*see pp. 144-5*). It is appropriate that Loos should have designed clothing stores considering his very decided views on fashion. When ladies persistently kept toppling off the chairs he designed, he to his philosophy, means "Empire of Peace") and translated the Slav "*sto*" in his name into the German "*hundert*". His aim was to devise a style of architecture that would bring man and nature closer together. He considered Functionalist architects such as Le Corbusier, Mies van der Rohe and Adolf Loos to be "irresponsible vandals", and advocated the demolition of every Bauhaus building, in an attempt to disentangle the "chaos of straight lines" to which we have doomed ourselves. His poster art includes *Save the Whales*, *Save the Seas*, and *Plant Trees Avoid Nuclear Peril*. His most famous

works in Vienna are the Hundertwasser House (District 3, Kegelgasse 36-38), a housing development opened in 1986, and the Spittelau municipal incinerator (District 9, Spittelauer Lände 45, guided tours available on 313 26 2705). Hundertwasser moved to New Zealand in 1999, and died a year later, aboard the QE2. He is buried in New Zealand, under a tulip tree as he requested. "There are no evils in Nature, only evils of Man" is one of the cornerstones of his philosophy, and where architecture is concerned, he believed that "the material uninhabitability of slums is prefer-

The Spittelau municipal incinerator by Friedensreich Hundertwasser.

The Hundertwasser House on the corner of Kegelgasse in District 3.

nence given to windows than to walls, in defiance of the "clichés" of academic architecture. Each apartment is different, making a stand against "imprisoned, enslaved, standardised man". In one of his architectural manifestos, Hundert-wasser writes that "Everyone should be able to - and be made to - build and thus be truly responsible for the four walls within which he lives. And he must also take the risk that any fantastical structure he erects may later collapse. If such a fantastical structure does collapse, however, it will usually develop cracks beforehand, so people will most likely be forewarned and able to escape". Hundertwasser's art is on display at the KunstHausWien, the former Thonet (*see p. 102*) furniture factory, which Hundertwasser adapted for his own purposes.

District 3, Untere Weissgerberstrasse 13. Open 10am-7pm every day.

able to the moral uninhabitability of utilitarian, functional architecture". The Hundertwasser House is built in accordance with this belief, with gardens on the roof, vegetation sprouting from the walls, and with uneven floors and with more promi-

ART GALLERIES
& MUSEUMS

THE KUNSTHISTORISCHES MUSEUM
District 1, Burgring 5
Open Tues-Sun 10am-6pm (Picture Gallery
and temporary exhibitions also open Thur 10am-9pm)

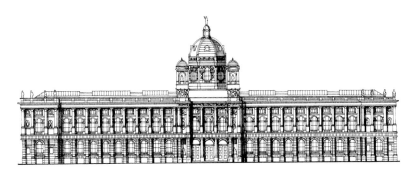

The art collection put together by the Holy Roman Emperors was - and is - one of the finest in the world. Titian painted a number of works for Karl V, as well as for Philip II of Spain, and it was Philip's nephew Rudolf II (1576-1608) who really began the work of putting Austria's magnificent collection together. Rudolf's collection, which he kept in Prague, included works by Arcimboldo (the famous images of human faces composed of fruit and vegetables) and Spranger, and it became so talked-about that 16th-century tourists flocked to see it. Other princes of the day soon began modelling their own collections on Rudolf's. Rudolf's brother Ernst, who was governor of the Habsburg Netherlands, purchased as many Brueghels as he could get his hands on, with the result that half of all the surviving works of Brueghel the Elder are now in Vienna. Ferdinand II's son Leopold Wilhelm bought up Charles I of England's collection when it was auctioned off after his execution in 1649. Other art-loving emperors were Ferdinand III (1637-1657), who owned a number of paintings by Velázquez; and Maria Theresa's father Karl VI (1711-1740), who had a weakness for Rubens and Rembrandt. Maria Theresa inherited her

The Kunsthistorisches Museum interior.

father's eye for art, and commissioned the now famous - and very lovely - series of Viennascapes from Canaletto's nephew Bernardo Bellotto. Maria Theresa's son, the *Volkskaiser* Joseph II, threw the imperial collection open to the public. That collection today forms the core of what can be seen in the Kunsthistorisches Museum.

THE BUILDING

Built in neo-Italian Renaissance style between 1871 and 1881 by Gottfried Semper and Karl von Hasenauer, the grandiose pile of the Kunsthistorisches Museum stands proudly opposite its twin, the Natural History Museum, with the statue of Maria Theresa, the matriarch of Austria, sturdily enthroned in between. The interior of the Kunsthistorisches is a real example of Historicist splendour, its walls, ceiling and stairway "almost too lavishly adorned with marble and stucco" - at least according to a 1920s edition of Baedeker. On the half-landing of the main stairway is the colossally violent statue of Theseus defeating the Minotaur, commissioned from Canova by Napoleon for a triumphal gateway he planned to erect in Milan, and intended to symbolise his subjugation of Europe by main force. Alas, poor Bonaparte, he never had the chance to enjoy the statue, for it was only completed in 1819, by which time Napoleon himself was history. The ceiling fresco above the landing is by the Hungarian artist Mihály Munkácsy and depicts the apotheosis of art. In the semi-circular lunettes beneath the fresco are paintings of the world's great artists by Hans Makart (*see p. 59*). In the spandrels under the cornice (on either side of the rounded archways) are paintings depicting art through the ages by Franz Matsch (*see p. 81*), Gustav Klimt (*see p. 62*) and his brother Ernst.

THE COLLECTION

Ground Floor: Home to three collections, the Collection of Classical Antiquities, the Egyptian and Oriental Collection, and the Kunstkammer collection of sculpture and decorative artifacts. Benvenuto Cellini's famous salt cellar is part of this collection.

First Floor: The Picture Gallery.

This is mainly what people come to the Kunsthistorisches to see - the collection includes some of the most famous images in the world. (*See plan overleaf for what to see where.*) An audio guide is included in the ticket price.

Second Floor: Collection of Coins and Medals.

NB: Vienna's foremost collection of Austrian art is held in the Upper and Lower Belvedere. For information about the works on display there, as well as about the artists, see Major Sights on p. 55.

The Herd Returning Home, one of the many works by Brueghel the Elder in the Kunsthistorisches Museum.

PLAN OF THE FIRST FLOOR OF THE KUNSTHISTORISCHES MUSEUM

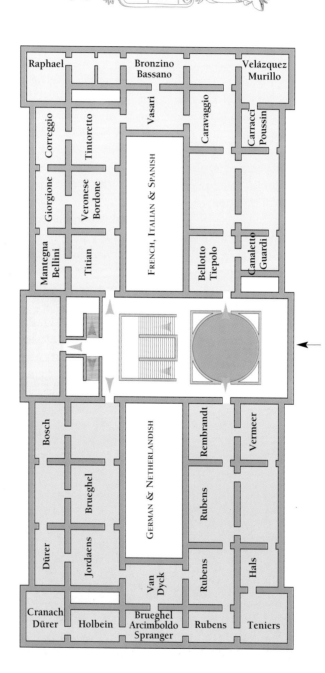

Raphael

Bronzino
Bassano

Velázquez
Murillo

Correggio

Tintoretto

Vasari

Caravaggio

Carracci
Poussin

Giorgione

Veronese
Bordone

Mantegna
Bellini

Titian

FRENCH, ITALIAN & SPANISH

Bellotto
Tiepolo

Canaletto
Guardi

Entrance

Bosch

Brueghel

GERMAN & NETHERLANDISH

Rembrandt

Vermeer

Dürer

Jordaens

Rubens

Van
Dyck

Rubens

Hals

Cranach
Dürer

Holbein

Brueghel
Arcimboldo
Spranger

Rubens

Teniers

JUGENDSTIL & THE SECESSION BUILDING
District 1, Friedrichstrasse 12. Open Tue-Sun 10am-6pm; Thur 10am-8pm.

The Vienna Secession, founded in 1897 by Gustav Klimt (*see p. 62*) and his followers, was an art movement that aimed to break away from Historicism, a style which had by then become intellectually and stylistically bankrupt. Klimt also wanted to introduce Vienna to new ideas from abroad, principally from France - which at the time meant Impressionism and Symbolism. Jugendstil came later, with the endeavours of the Secession members to create *Gesamtkunstwerke*, works which fused all disciplines of the arts together, and which would suffuse man's everyday life with art. Art was to be more than just decoration. Art, to put it boldly, was to be the new religion, the means by which man could get in touch with his finer feelings, find salvation, be redeemed. In 1898 the Secession artists built themselves an exhibition pavilion (*see p. 80*). Given that Klimt was the prime mover of the Vienna Secession, it is appropriate that the only permanent installation at the Secession building should be his *Beethoven Frieze*, which occupies one of the rooms in the basement.

The frieze was created for the Secession group's 1902 annual exhibition, and was intended as an adjunct to a statue of Beethoven by the "German Rodin", Max Klinger - it was never meant to be a lasting work of art. Klimt imagined that it would be destroyed when the exhibition was dismantled. Had it not been for the discerning eye of a collector, who bought the frieze in 1903, it would never have been saved for posterity.

INTERPRETING THE BEETHOVEN FRIEZE

Beethoven's idealistic streak, his ideas about a brotherhood of man, and his intensely emotional nature appealed to the Secession artists. His 9th Symphony was interpreted by Wagner as an expression of the human quest for happiness. In fact the text that Beethoven used in the symphony (Schiller's *Ode to Happiness*) expresses more than that; it also expresses the joy of being able to believe in a benign God, something that gets rather glossed over in Wagner's interpretation. Klimt ignores it too. His frieze identifies happiness as our supreme goal. To

"This kiss is for the whole world!"

dreams of sublime happiness. Then we see two wraith-like forms, a sort of banished Adam and Eve, kneeling in supplication before a knight in shining armour, with the incarnations of mercy (pardon for the suffering sinner) and ambition (the driving force which will lead us to our goals). Beyond these, in tortured, grisly file, come the personifications of gluttony, lasciviousness and grief, dominated by the shaggy, sub-human, gorilla-like monster Typhoeus, and the three gorgons with snakes in their hair. (The gorgons are complex symbols. In Greek mythology they are symbols of despair, though there is a parallel tradition which sees them as very beautiful. The personifications of the arts above the main entrance to the Secession building are, incidentally, represented as gorgons. What conclusion are we to draw? Typhoeus is more straightforward. A hideous monster and bane of mankind, his evil influence was brought to an end by Zeus, who laid him low with a thunderbolt.) In the third and final section of the frieze a golden harpist begins to play, and the ugly ape is banished - though surely his face re-emerges, metamorphosed into a golden, cheeky chimp-mask, in the final kiss scene? (*See picture*)

achieve it we have to battle with external evils and assailants - illness, insanity, misfortune - as well as with internal ones - lust, excess, greed. Bliss, when it does come, comes from the arts, in other words from creation rather than from the Creator. The famous lines of the fourth movement of the symphony are expressed pictorially in the final tableau of the frieze: joyful music, a bed of roses, and a universal love-in: *Seid umschlungen, Millionen! Diesen Kuss der ganzen Welt!* (Embrace each other now, you millions! This kiss is for the whole world!)

The frieze starts with a succession of floating female figures, dreaming

OTHER ART GALLERIES

MQ, THE MUSEUMSQUARTIER

District 7, Museums- platz 1 (formerly Messeplatz).

The main museums here are:

THE MUSEUM OF MODERN ART

(MUMOK, housed in the huge basalt bunker) - Contains a collection that runs from classic Modern Art to Contemporary, including Pop Art, Fluxus and Photo Realism along the way.

Open Tue-Sun 10am-6pm, Thur 10am-9pm.

THE LEOPOLD MUSEUM

(housed in the enormous white bunker) - Home to the private collection of Dr Rudolf Leopold. It is worth making time to see this museum. The exhibition space is light and airy, the rooms are comfortably large, and never over-stuffed with art. The major exhibits are as follows:

Ground Floor: A small collection of paintings by Klimt, Kolo Moser and Richard Gerstl. Gerstl (1883-1908) committed suicide after his affair with Schoenberg's wife Mathilde came to an end. There are also pieces

The former court stables, now converted into Vienna's Museumsquartier.

The black basalt bulk of the Museum of Modern Art (MUMOK) in the Museumsquartier.

of furniture by the Secession artists Kolo Moser and Josef Hoffmann, members of the Wiener Werkstätte (*see p. 103*), plus one or two by Loos (*see p. 87*), and a single Otto Wagner piece, a ceramic stove.

Third Floor: Egon Schiele. This is said to be the finest Schiele collection in the world. His own troubled relationship with his mother (*see p. 61*) is reflected in the number of works depicting mothers and children, always in an atmosphere suffused with suffering, death, dysfunction and disability.

Basement (U1): 19th-century works including Ferdinand Waldmüller (*see p. 58*) and Rudolf von Alt, as well as some lovely paintings by Emil Jakob Schindler (1824-1892), Austria's major 19th-century *plein-air* artist, exponent of a style known as Atmospheric Impressionism. More chairs by Loos, Hoffmann and Wagner, plus a few Thonet pieces as well.

Open Mon, Wed, Thur 11am-7pm, Fri 11am-9pm, Sat-Sun 10am-7pm.

ACADEMY OF FINE ART PICTURE GALLERY (*Akademie der bildenden Künste, Gemäldegalerie*) - Contains a collection of old masters including Bosch, Rubens, Rembrandt and Titian.

District 1, Schillerplatz 3, 1st floor. Open Tues-Sun 10am-4pm.

Major Temporary Exhibition Venues

Kunstforum
District 1, Freyung 8. Open 10am-7pm; Fri 10am-9pm.

KunstHausWien - Permanent Hundertwasser exhibition as well as temporary shows.
District 3, Untere Weissgerberstrasse 13. Open 10am-7pm every day.

Künstlerhaus
District 1, Karlsplatz 5. Open 10am-6pm; Thur 10am-9pm.

Palais Harrach - As much worth visiting for the art as for a glimpse of the interior of a former patrician palace.
District 1, Freyung 3. Open 10am-6pm every day.

Craft Movements

Biedermeier

Originally this was rather a sneering term, using the adjective *bieder*, which means naïve and clodding, and Meier, a common surname. Biedermeier, in other words, described the artistic horizons of Joe Ordinary. Now the term is used to refer to an entire age, the early 19th century "pre-March" decades of comfortable middle-class prosperity, when the loyal citizens of the emperor sat by their firesides reading homely literature, listening to the music

Portrait of Herbert Rainer by Egon Schiele. Both the Upper Belvedere and the Leopold Museum have collections of works by Schiele.

Village children frolicking in the sunshine on Corpus Christi morning. Examples of the Bieder-meier art of Ferdinand Waldmüller are on display in the Belvedere and Leopold Museum.

of Schubert, decorating Christmas trees, and not bothering their heads about politics. It describes the time before the revolutions that began in March 1848 swept like bush fires across Europe. Biedermeier art is thematically cosy and stylistically demure. Biedermeier furniture developed as a middle-class offshoot of the French Empire style, distinguished by solid craftsmanship, and making use of fruit woods, particularly cherry, which can be polished to a gleaming patina and which have a vivid, decorative grain.

WHERE TO SEE BIEDERMEIER

THE MUSEUM OF APPLIED ARTS (Biedermeier Room on the ground floor) *MAK, District 1, Stubenring 5. Open Weds-Sun 10am-6pm; Tues 10am-midnight* - Curated in an attempt not to be "dull" or "conven- tional", the display has no captions beside the exhibits, but rapidly-moving surtitles at ceiling-level instead, which make it almost impossible to digest the information in your own time. However, there

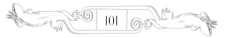
are detailed caption booklets on shelves beside the door, which will guide you round the display at leisure.

THE GEYMÜLLER SCHLÖSSL (MAK's Biedermeier Museum) - *District 18, Khevenhüllerstrasse 2. Open April-October during daylight hours.*

OTHER NOTED BIEDERMEIER NAMES
Some of the craftsmen who came to prominence in the Biedermeier period and who are still household names today

BÖSENDORFER - The original Bösendorfer piano manufactory was founded in 1828. Ludwig Bösendorfer, the founder's son, was something of a man about town, who used to strut the Ringstrasse in natty checked trousers and a top hat. One day, while watching the horses in Prince Liechtenstein's riding school on the Herrengasse, he noticed how good the building's acoustics were. He promptly rented a room and turned it into a concert hall. Music lovers found its atmosphere much more intimate than that of the Musikverein. When it was demolished in 1913, people even wept. Bösendorfer also teamed up with artists such as Hans Makart, who designed special pianos for the company. Today you can visit the Bösendorfer showroom at *District 1, Canovagasse 4. Open Mon-Fri 9am-6pm, Sat 9am-12 noon.*

LOBMEYR - Together with his Moravian wife, Josef Lobmeyr, a

glazier from Upper Austria, opened a shop in Vienna in 1822. The family worked hard to make ends meet, opening the shop at seven in the

Three of Hans Makart's Five Senses. Makart's taste for heavy drapery and palm fronds influenced late 19th-century interior design.

morning, and staying open until eight at night. By the time Herr Lobmeyr was succeeded by his sons, however, the shop had moved to smarter premises on the Kärntnerstrasse, and before long the firm was appointed official purveyor to the *k. und k.* court. The prototype of the decanter and wine glass set that has since become a top-selling classic was first made in 1856. Today the Lobmeyr shop & museum can be found at Kärntnerstrasse 26.

THONET - Michael Thonet (1796-1871) was a native of Germany who settled in Vienna at Metternich's suggestion, bringing with him his skill at making bentwood furniture. He exhibited his "Vienna bentwood chairs" to great acclaim at the Great Exhibition in London in 1851. His first commission in Vienna was from the Café Daum on the Kohlmarkt, where the Louis Vuitton shop now stands today. The Thonet shop is located at District 9, Berggasse 31 (closed weekends). There is also a very effective display of Thonet chairs in the Museum of Applied Arts (MAK). The chairs are placed in single file behind a semi-transparent screen, and illuminated from behind to produce a silhouette.

MAK, District 1, Stubenring 5. Open Weds-Sun 10am-6pm; Tues 10am-midnight.

Rocking lounger by Thonet.

THE WIENER WERKSTÄTTE

Inspired by the English Arts and Crafts Movement of William Morris, and more particularly by the work of the Scotsman Charles Rennie Mackintosh, the Wiener Werkstätte (Vienna Workshops) were founded in 1903 by Josef Hoffmann, a student of Otto Wagner, and Kolo Moser, one of the founding members of the Vienna Secession (*see p. 95*). Their aim was to raise craft to the same standing in people's minds as art, and to resist the commercial temptations of mass-production. In its heyday the Wiener Werkstätte had affiliated workshops in New York and Berlin, and its Vienna retail outlets were on the smartest streets in town, the Kärntnerstrasse and the Graben. Kokoschka, Schiele and Klimt were all at one time involved with the project. The danger of concentrating so much creative and artistic energy on every day objects was, inevitably, that applied artists would fall into the trap of over-design. In the Purkersdorf sanatorium on Vienna's western outskirts, for example, every detail, both interior and exterior, was designed by members of the workshop, even down to the last drainpipe and knife and fork. It is not recorded whether the inmates went mad or not. Reaction was bound to come, and come it did, with the furious polemics of Adolf Loos, the high priest of Functionalism (*see p. 87*). Loos loathed the idea of art for art's sake. For him, dignified restraint was what was truly refined, not showiness and gush. Besides, he argued, new solutions are never as good - never as intellectually rigorous - as the original ideas they seek to replace. Just as Esperanto - an invented construct - is inferior to Latin, the Wiener Werkstätte was a sham, and a feeble substitute for craftsmanship that is rooted in true culture. Economic difficulties in the decade following the First World War hit the Werkstätte hard. The co-operative went into liquidation in 1932, though WOKA, at Singerstrasse 16, still produces and sells reproduction Wiener Werkstätte lamps.

WHERE TO SEE WIENER WERKSTÄTTE WORKS

THE MUSEUM OF APPLIED ARTS - On the first floor.
MAK. District 1, Stubenring 5. Open Weds-Sun 10am-6pm; Tues 10am-midnight.

THE LEOPOLD MUSEUM - On the ground floor.
District 7, Musuemsquartier. Open Mon, Wed, Thur 11am-7pm, Fri 11am-9pm, Sat-Sun 10am-7pm.

OTHER MAJOR MUSEUMS

APPLIED ARTS MUSEUM (*Museum für angewandte Kunst, MAK*) - Covers applied arts of all periods from the Romanesque to the contemporary. Good shop with fun comtemporary-design artifacts and a good-looking restaurant (*see p. 210*).
District 1, Stubenring 5. Open Weds-Sun 10am-6pm; Tues 10am-midnight.

CLOCK MUSEUM (*Uhrenmuseum*) - Time-pieces stretching across almost 600 years.
District 1 Schulhof 2-Kurrentgasse 1. Open Tue-Sun 9am-4.30pm.

ETHNOGRAPHIC MUSEUM (*Museum für Völkerkunde*) - Important collection of classical antiquities, especially the Ephesus artifacts. Ephesus was excavated by an Austrian archaeological team.
District 1, Neue Burg, Heldenplatz. Open Wed-Mon 10am-6pm.

FOLKLORE MUSEUM (*Museum für Volkskunde*) - In the former summer palace of the Schönborn family. *District 8, Laudongasse 15. Open Tue-Sun 10am-5pm.*

NATURAL HISTORY MUSEUM (*Naturhistorisches Museum*) - Skeleton of a sabre-toothed tiger and other palaeontological exhibits, the prehistoric Willendorf Venus fertility statuette, and artifacts from the Hallstatt civilisation.
District 1, Maria-Theresien-Platz. Open Thur-Mon 9am-6.30pm; Wed 9am-9pm. Closed Tue.

THEATRE MUSEUM (Theater-museum). In the former town palace of the Lobkowitz family. District 1, Lobkowitz-Platz 2. Open Tue-Sun 10am-5pm; Wed 10am-8pm.

VIENNA HISTORY MUSEUM (*Historisches Museum der Stadt Wien*) - Exhibits on the city's history from ancient times to the present day.
District 1, Karlsplatz 8. Open Tue-Sun 9am-6pm.

COFFEE HOUSES

Vienna has been addicted to coffee since the late 17th century. For years stories circulated about a bag of coffee beans, discovered amongst possessions left behind by the routed Turkish troops in 1683, and about how the first coffee house opened shortly after. The stories have no truth to them. Vienna and London used to argue over which city had the first coffee house, but in fact it was neither of them. The very first coffee house in the world opened in Istanbul in 1554, followed about a quarter of a century later by an establishment in Turkish-controlled Buda. When in 1685 an Armenian trader by the name of Johannes Deodatus was granted a licence to sell coffee, tea and sherbet by the emperor Leopold I, his establishment came far behind coffee shops in London, Paris, Venice, Marseilles and even Oxford. The Viennese, however, more than the citizens of any of these other places (with the exception, perhaps, of Budapest), took coffee to their hearts. And there is reason to believe that coffee drunk with milk was truly a Viennese invention. The *Wiener Melange*, a mix of strong black coffee and warm frothy milk, is said to have been created as a way of making the taste of Herr Deodatus' beans less bitter.

From that followed a whole array of different ways to take one's coffee. The most commonly available today are listed below:

TYPES OF COFFEE

Fiaker Kaffee - coffee with whipped cream and a shot of cherry brandy to keep out the cold. The traditional favourite of Vienna coachmen.

Grosser (large) or Kleiner (small) Brauner - espresso coffee with a dash of milk or cream, often served in a separate jug so you can add as much or as little as you like.

Melange - coffee with frothed milk.

Verlängerter - American-style coffee. If you want cream with it, order it "*mit Obers*".

Einspänner - coffee with whipped cream, served in a glass.

A SELECTION OF VIENNA COFFEE HOUSES

CENTRAL

First opened in 1868 on the ground floor of the Austro-Hungarian Bank, the Café Central quickly became the favourite rendezvous for members of Vienna's intellectual circle (Adolf Loos, Arthur Schnitzler and Stefan Zweig were among its regular customers). Proud of its cosmopolitan - not to say worldly - atmosphere, the Central offered newspapers in 22 different languages. The eccentric writer Peter Altenberg (1859-1919) was a regular customer here - so regular that he gave "Wien 1, Café Central" as his correspondence address. The café now boasts a life-size statue of him, sitting moody and moustachioed beside the door. In the early years of the 20th century future Russian revolutionaries would meet here, no doubt plotting the overthrow of the Romanovs. Today the Central continues to offer newspapers, but most are in German. It is one of the pleasantest cafés in the city, with chairs and tables nestling amid a forest of pillars, and natural light streaming in from high windows on three sides. The *Centraltorte*, layers of walnut sponge and cream topped with chocolate, is delicious.

District 1, Herrengasse 14. Open Mon-Sat 8am-10pm; Sun 8am-6pm; Public Holidays 10am-10pm.

DEMEL

This café has been operating since 1786 and was one of the purveyors to the Imperial and Royal (*k. und k.*) household. It is without doubt the most beautiful in Vienna. Inevitably that makes it popular with visitors, but it doesn't matter: neither the quality of the cakes nor the quality of the atmosphere suffers. A covered inner courtyard stretches out towards the back, its walls mirror-clad, and with standard lamps constructed to remind you of palm trees. Adjacent to it there is a separate panelled cabinet for smokers. The best place to sit is definitely the front room, though. Its mirrored, jewel-chest interior makes it look exactly like one of those dainty children's

musical boxes where a ballerina twirls to a tinkly tune. Stucco-work ceilings are picked out in pastel colours; the floor is covered in 19th-century encaustic tiles. The cakes are

Refuge on a rainy day in the mirror-clad Demel on Kohlmarkt.

excellent, and the hand-made chocolates (exquisitely packaged) may be even better. Try a box of *"Auto-Chocolat"* for your glove compartment - even the most hardened motorist needs to stop from time to time for a mouth-watering, mint-flavoured morsel.

Vienna 1, Kohlmarkt 14. Open 10am-7pm every day.

Browsing through the morning papers at Café Diglas.

DIGLAS

With lots of tables and Thonet coat-stands packed into the L-shaped ground-floor of a solid old town house, Diglas first opened in the 1930s, when depressed Vienna was badly in need of a sustaining coffee or two (probably chicory in those days). Today it has a friendly, busy, bustly atmosphere, as well as an authentic Vienna café feel: plenty of traditional red plush banquettes and bentwood furniture. A good selection of Viennese breakfasts on offer, delicious soufflés and good cakes.
District 1, Wollzeile 10. Open from 7am; 9am on Sun.

GRIENSTEIDL

The old café Griensteidl, in the Palais Herberstein that used to stand on this site, was a "fairy temple" (or so contemporary newspaper articles described it) frequented by young Vienna literati and *belles esprits.* When the building was demolished in 1897, the coffee house closed and its clientèle moved *en masse* to the Central just up the road (*see entry on p. 106*). The present Griensteidl opened in 1990. Pleasant, well-lit and friendly, it would dearly like its walls to look less white and its upholstery less dazzling and to recover the dusty, dusky patina of yesteryear. Cigar-smokers are welcomed with open arms.

District 1, Herrengasse 1-3.

HAWELKA

Founded in 1939 (and still run) by the former manager of the Café Alt Wien (*see p. 176*). In the 50s it was a favourite meeting place for Viennese Bohemia, and Henry Miller came here whenever he visited Vienna. Today it has the aura of dogged refusal to change. But as the rock-candy stripes of the upholstery get steadily older and more worn, the clientèle remains young and fresh,

and the place looks very much like enduring for ever. Leopold Hawelka and his wife are still going strong, and their son and grandsons are fully part of the enterprise.

District 1, Dorotheergasse 6. Open Mon, Wed, Thur-Sat 8am-2am; Sun 4pm-2am. Closed Tues.

LANDTMANN

Founded in 1873 and still family-run today (though not by the Landtmanns), this large coffee house, a stone's throw from the Burgtheater and the Rathaus, makes a good refuge on a cold winter's day.

The smoky tenebrae of Hawelka, haunted by everyone from earnest poets to flighty socialites.

As you would expect from its location, it has been a traditional favourite with actors and politicians, and numbers Max Reinhardt, Gary Cooper, Clement Attlee and the Duke of Windsor among its former clientèle. The largest room, panelled in wood, perfectly recreates a late 19th-century atmosphere, even down to the upholstery, which is curiously reminiscent of the brown, leaf-patterned suites in Franz Joseph's Schönbrunn apartments. A popular Sunday-morning breakfast spot.
District 1, Dr Karl Lueger-Ring 4. Open 8am-midnight every day.

MUSEUM

Opened in 1899, this was Adolf Loos's (*see p. 87*) first great work, and was greeted enthusiastically, described as "the springboard for all interior design". The light fittings were originally naked bulbs (which is maybe taking Functionalism a teeny bit too far), though gas lamps were also allowed, in case the electricity should fail. Wittgenstein came here frequently, as did Klimt, Schiele and Kokoschka. Though little is left of the original fixtures and fittings, the place remains a draw. Neither the coffee nor the cakes are the best in town, but Café Museum still

Café Museum, down at heel but still stylish, and much loved.

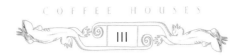

SACHERTORTE & IMPERIALTORTE

The original *Sachertorte* - chocolate sponge smothered in apricot jam and encased in chocolate icing - is said to have been invented in 1832 by Franz Sacher, a 16 year-old kitchen boy in the employ of Prince Metternich. Sacher passed the recipe on to his son, Eduard, who, with his wife Anna, founded the hotel. A legal battle with the Demel coffee house over who had the right to label their cake "*original Sachertorte*" dragged on for many years, and was finally settled in 1955: Demel lost. Today the Sacher recommends that its *Torte* be eaten with cream. Originally it was served with a little glass of cognac, which on raw winter days seems more comforting, and on hot summer days less likely to stick in your throat. The permitted ingredients of true *Sachertorte* are officially set down in the Austrian Alimentary Codex. Not to be outdone, the Hotel Imperial also created its own cake, the *Imperialtorte*. Layers of wafer and marzipan are coated in thick chocolate, and the whole thing comes in an elegant box. Because it uses no cream, it keeps a relatively long time, and makes the perfect extravagant gift.

exudes the unmistakable tobacco-breath aura of urban bohemian life. One of the chairs that Loos designed for the Museum is now on display in the basement of the Leopold Museum (*see p. 98*).
District 1, Friedrichstrasse 6. Open 8am-midnight every day.

SACHER

Attached to the hotel of the same name, the Sacher is one of Vienna's most famous institutions. Founded in the latter half of the 19th century, the hotel and its coffee house gained their full renown after 1892, when the management was taken over by the founder's widow, Anna Sacher. A woman of forceful personality, the cigar-toting, lapdog-loving Anna turned the hotel into a meeting-place for Vienna high society. Courtiers, politicians and artists all flocked to her door, and the hotel's 13 *chambres séparées* became famous for the deals concluded, liaisons begun, backs stabbed and ententes broken within their walls. The Sacher's most famous offering today is its *Sachertorte* (*see above*), and people are still flocking to the hotel's coffee house to sample it. In fact, because *Sachertorte* is what almost everyone asks for, the selection of other pastries is limited. Try to time your visit not to coincide with a tourist coachload, or you might find yourself joining a queue that snakes halfway up the street. Is it worth it? Anna Sacher was a shrewd business-woman, but even she might have found it rather too much.
District 1, Philharmonikerstrasse 4. Tel: 514 56 0.

LITERARY VIENNA -
A SELECTION OF THE CITY'S WRITERS

FRANZ GRILLPARZER (1791-1872)

Austria's greatest playwright. Grillparzer first embarked on a career as a civil servant. He detested it, and never rose above a very middling rank, perhaps because of a poem he wrote following his mother's suicide, which offended both the Catholic Church and the emperor. His personal life was equally slow-moving. Though engaged for many years, he could never persuade his fiancée to tie the knot. His early plays drew loud boos and hoots of derision from Viennese theatregoers, which drove him to a life of utter seclusion. When recognition finally did come to him, he was too old and embittered to care.

Favourite coffee house: An inn on the Spiegelgasse, now a bank.

ARTHUR SCHNITZLER (1862-1931)

Schnitzler's doctor father disapproved of his son's ambition to write. He also despaired of his ardent nature. Finding that the 16 year-old Arthur had slept with a prostitute, he presented him with an illustrated tract on venereal disease. Dutifully Schnitzler took a degree in medicine, but he was never able to take the profession seriously. He frequented the Café Griensteidl, and was a great friend of Sigmund Freud, who considered Schnitzler his "double", doing for literature what Freud was doing for psychoanalysis. Considering that both men seem to have seen sex as the basis of everything we think, feel and do, this was possibly quite near the mark. Schnitzler's best-known work is *La Ronde*. Turning as it does on his favourite topic, it provoked a week-long obscenity trial.

Favourite coffee house: Griensteidl.

HUGO VON HOFMANNSTHAL (1874-1929)

The son of a Sephardic Jewish bank manager, Hofmannsthal married a bank manager's daughter, though his own interests were a long way away from the world of finance. His career took off when he met the composer Richard Strauss. He provided the libretto for Strauss' *Elektra*, and - much more famously - for *Der Rosenkavalier* (*see p. 116*).

Favourite coffee house: Central.

ROBERT MUSIL (1880-1942)

Born in Klagenfurt, Musil moved to Vienna at the age of two. His finances were always precarious, but Part One of his *Man Without Qualities* inspired well-wishers to set up a Musil Society, with the aim of financing him through Part Two. Musil was embarrassed to discover that Thomas Mann, whom he had always despised as the voice of the bigoted liberal elite, was one of the founders of the society. *The Man Without Qualities* (which Musil never completed) combines the overarching with the minute - the author's own Vienna milieu and the collapse of a world empire.

Favourite coffee house: Museum.

STEFAN ZWEIG (1881-1942)

Biographer, poet, essayist and short story writer, Zweig was a friend of Rodin, Rilke and Toscanini. He was greatly interested in Freud, and made use of the teachings of psychoanalysis in his historical biographies. Nazi persecution of Jews drove him to England. Later he moved to Brazil, where he became fatally depressed, and eventually committed suicide. His posthumous novella, *The Royal Game*, uses chess as a symbol not only for Nazism, but also as an extended metaphor for human existence, where men are mere pawns in the control of superior forces.

Favourite coffee house: Beethoven (District 9, Universitätsstrasse 11).

MUSIC

Vienna has long been famous as a musical city. Ever since the emperor Maximilian I founded a court orchestra in 1498 (as well as the ancestor of the Vienna Boys' Choir), the ruling Habsburg dynasty has shown a marked fondness for music, turning out not only aficionados but gifted performers and composers as well. Court music performances were private affairs at first, with friends and family members doing the singing and playing. Later professional musicians began to be invited to provide entertainments. In the mid 17th century Leopold I - himself a keen musician - built the first opera house, the Hofoper, whose performances were free for all. In 1778 Joseph II founded a new opera house with the aim of developing native opera (as opposed to the French or Italian styles). Since then the city has been associated with some of the best and most famous composers the western world has produced. Schubert and Strauss were native Viennese; Haydn, Bruckner and Mozart were native Austrians; Mahler, born in Bohemia, was a son of the empire; Brahms

The golden Grosser Saal of the Musikverein.

and Beethoven became Viennese by choice, producing some of their finest work here. Schoenberg and his disciples treated the public's ears to something entirely new, with their atonal system.

Inevitably Vienna has sought to cash in on her musical traditions, with period-costume performances of Mozart advertised in every hotel lobby. But a music-loving city Vienna nevertheless remains. The zealous mayor Karl Seitz, addressing the crowd outside a new housing project in the late 1920s, declared that "Vienna was once a city of song. We shall make her a city of work!" He did not succeed. Long lunch hours, plenty of coffee breaks, and a good concert in the evening is still the Viennese ideal. It is a measure of how seriously the Viennese take their music that during a wartime performance of Brahms' *Requiem* the audience remained staunchly in their seats even after an air raid began.

MAJOR MUSICAL VENUES

There are many places to hear music in Vienna. The Kursalon in the Stadtpark regularly puts on concerts of Vienna evergreens by Mozart and the two Strausses. The Konzerthaus (District 3, Lothringerstrasse 20) is another major venue, while former palaces turn over their gilded salons and churches give over their chancels to music ensembles all year round. The two most important and most beautiful places to hear music in Vienna are the two given below.

THE OPERA HOUSE (*Staatsoper*) - The first of the grand new Ringstrasse buildings to be completed, the opera opened in 1869 with a performance of Mozart's *Don Giovanni*. The building's romantically eclectic style is intended to be reminiscent of the Venetian Renaissance, a deliberate tribute to the origins of opera. The Viennese public did not take to the opera house at first, and neither did Franz Joseph. Allegedly driven to despair by the lack of imper-ial enthusiasm, one of the architects, Eduard van der Nüll, committed suicide before the official opening. A few months later the other architect, August Sicard von Sicardsburg, died of a heart attack. Dismayed by these twin calamities, Franz Joseph in future limited his public pronouncements to the stock phrase "It's very nice. It gave me great pleasure". The interior is dec-orated with frescoes by the leading artists of the day, notably Moritz von

Impostor? Wherever you go in Vienna there's a man - or a woman - pretending to be Mozart.

Schwind's (*see p. 58*) *Magic Flute* sequence in the loggia above the main entrance. There is also a bust of Mahler by Rodin in the foyer. During the Second World War the opera house was hit by a bomb, and the resulting fire completely gutted the auditorium. It reopened in 1955 with a performance of *Fidelio*, a work which had premiered in Vienna in 1805, conducted by Beethoven himself.

District 1, Opernring 2. Information and tickets Tel: 514 44/2250. Box office at District 1, Hanuschgasse 3. www.wiener-staatsoper.at

Guided tours of the opera house are available in English at the times posted beside the Kärntnerstrasse-facing entrance. NB: The opera house is closed in July and August, though guided tours are still given during these months.

THE MUSIKVEREIN - Completed in 1869 under the auspices of the *Gesellschaft der Musikfreunde* (the Society of Music Lovers), the Musikverein was designed by the Danish architect Theophil Hansen (*see p. 69*). Half Greek temple half Renaissance villa, the use of contrasting light and dark colour on the façade is a conscious imitation of Brunelleschi. The main auditorium, the *Grosser Saal*, is a great gilded box. The conductor Bruno Walter used to swear by its acoustics. The small concert hall is named after Brahms, who worked as musical director here. The Musikverein is now home to the Vienna Philharmonic, which in its time has been conducted by the famously strict Mahler, as well as by Toscanini, Furtwängler, Hindemith, Klemperer and von Karajan, to name only a handful.

District 1, Karlsplatz 6. Box office open Mon-Fri 9am-7.30pm; Sat 9am-5pm. Tel: 505 81 90. www.musikverein.at

For a multi-sensory tour through the world of music, there is the **Haus der Musik Wien**. Housed in the building where the Vienna Philharmonic was founded in the mid 19th century, this modern museum aims to make music "not just audible, but also visual and palpable". A hands, ears and eyes-on approach to the world of sound, covering Vienna's rich musical heritage and the men that made its name, as well as the whole human aural experience.
District 1, Seilerstätte 30. Open 10am-10pm every day.

CLASSIC VIENNA MUSIC

OPERA: DER ROSENKAVALIER - When the young Viennese poet Hugo von Hofmannsthal met the German composer Richard Strauss, he probably didn't realise that the hand of fate was steering him towards fame. *Der Rosenkavalier* - for which von Hofmannsthal produced the libretto - is still one of the world's best-loved operas. The soppy-but-feel-good tale of the older woman who nobly gives up her young lover to a girl his own age, in

Fountain outside the romantic Historicist opera house, a building which the Viennese public did not like at first. Both architects died of despair before the official opening in 1869.

the process saving said young girl from marriage to a drunken sot, is set in 1740s Vienna, the age of Maria Theresa. In fact the Marschallin herself (the older woman of the story) is named Marie Therese. The role of the Rosenkavalier himself is always played by a woman, which makes the pantomime mood of the whole thing all the more marked, especially when the drunken Baron Ochs (pun intended) falls in love with him/her and predictable high jinks ensue.

WALTZ MUSIC - or anything by either of the Johann Strausses. Strauss the Elder (a German who settled in Vienna) wrote the *Radetzky March*, celebrating the victory of Field Marshal Radetzky over the revolutionaries in Italy in 1848 (*see p. 21*). It was the younger Strauss who was the "Waltz King". His *Blue Danube* originally had words as well as music. It received its first public performance in 1867, sung by the Vienna Male Voice Choir, but the words were so inane that the production was a flop. Today, the words abandoned, the *Blue Danube* has become an indispensable ingredient of any *Viennese Soirée*-type compilation album. And the tune is so infectiously upbeat that it is difficult not to be swept along by it - or to wish that you were being swept around a glistening chandelier-lit ballroom by a beautiful beau in evening tails.

Schrammel musicians with accordion and the traditional double-necked guitar.

URBAN FOLK: SCHRAMMEL - If Vienna has a folk music as such, it is definitely Schrammel, the cheerful *Weinkeller* stuff you hear in the *Heurigen* (*see p. 199*). It takes its name from the brothers Johann and Josef Schrammel, musicians whose traditions were grounded in salon music and military oom-pah tunes, and who turned to folk as a way of making a living. In 1877, fusing elements of all three styles, they founded a popular quartet of two violins, guitar and clarinet, playing the compositions of Alois Strohmayer, the father of one of the quartet's members. Today the clarinet has been replaced by an accordion, but Schrammel music lives on, and CDs of it are plentifully available - try EMI Austria at Kärntnerstrasse 30.

THE WALTZ

The word *Walzer* comes from the German verb meaning to whirl or turn, movements which for a long time were explicitly frowned on in the dance hall. A late 16th-century public notice warned that "Ladies must comport themselves with modesty and male persons are to refrain from whirling. Whosoever will turn immodestly in defiance of this order will be brought to jail". The waltz as a dance has its origins in the round dances of mediaeval times, the German *ländler*, and the *langhaus* of the *Linzer Geiger*, a group of strolling players who travelled up and down the Danube. The waltz as such first appears in around 1750 in the Tyrol and Styria, as a peasant dance danced by couples, who turned in each other's arms in 3/4 time. Before long this dance of

Johann Strauss the younger, king of the Vienna Waltz, apotheosised into the golden boy of glorious kitsch.

the working man became popular with the aristocracy as well, although it still lacked the sanction of official approval. Waltzing orgies at the Mondschein dance hall near the Karlskirche were routinely raided by the police. And then, in 1775, Maria Theresa caused a stir at Schönbrunn, when she requested her orchestra to strike up a *ländler*. The noble families soon followed her lead, and before long they were sneaking off to their servants' dance parties to grope and be groped - the sedate minuets of their ballrooms never gave much opportunity for the "lewd grasp and lawless contact" that Byron wrote of in his apostrophe to the waltz. By the early 19th century all disapproving tongues had been stilled, and the Viennese were waltzing till dawn - so tirelessly in fact, that many foreign visitors found it all a little too much. When Napoleon agreed to marry the emperor's daughter Marie Louise, he also decided to take waltzing lessons. *Tanzpaläste* - glittering palatial dance halls - began to spring up like mushrooms. One, the Sperl in Leopoldstadt, was used for lavish evening entertainments during the Congress of Vienna. Annagasse 3, where the Tenne night club stands now, is the site of the Neues Elysium, a subterranean *Tanzpalast* and pleasure grotto, which in its 19th-century heyday contained several stages, restaurants, a mini train and a pasha's harem.

A Handful of Composers & Their Connections with Vienna

Classics & Romantics

Every single one of these composers is a household name, and their music is familiar across the globe. Yet all had their origins in Vienna, either because they were born in the city, because they studied and trained here, because their patrons had connections to the city, or because it was the Viennese public who first applauded their efforts.

Franz Joseph Haydn (1732-1809) - Born in Rohrau, the son of a wheelwright, Haydn lived in Vienna as a boy, receiving lodging and a stipend as a chorister in the Stephansdom. Forced to leave the choir when his voice broke, he spent the next eight years in a dingy garret on the Kohlmarkt, scraping together a living giving music lessons and playing the organ in a monastery church in Leopoldstadt. His career took off after 1761 when he entered the service of the Hungarian prince Miklós Esterházy "the Ostentatious" at his palaces in Fertőd (Hungary) and Eisenstadt (Austria). Under the terms of his contract, he was a sort of "composer laureate", required to compose works when his patron desired them, and allowed to compose independently only with permission. He composed many of his finest symphonies during this period, and as his fame grew, the rules of his contract were relaxed. When Miklós Esterházy died, the family continued to retain him, but he was free to travel. He visited London, where two of his most famous works, the *Surprise Symphony* and the *Clock Symphony* were composed. On his return to Austria, he worked for Esterházy's grandson, another Miklós, known as "Il Magnifico". Under his aegis Haydn produced two of his best oratorios, *The Creation* and *The Seasons*. In 1800 Princess Esterházy arranged for him to give a concert to entertain Nelson and Lady Hamilton, who were passing through Austria at the time. Lady Hamilton raised offended eyebrows by paying no attention to the music, talking noisily all the way through it, and refusing to leave the card table, where she won a considerable amount. In his latter years Haydn lived in Vienna, in the house that is now the Haydn Museum (*see*

Wolfgang Amadeus Mozart, perhaps the most "Viennese" of all composers, although his home town was Salzburg.

below). When he occupied the city in 1809, Napoleon, not normally famous for his kindness and consideration, gave orders that no harm was to come to the aged composer. "Don't be afraid," Haydn reportedly comforted his servants during the French offensive on the city, "As long as I am here, no harm will come to you." He was right. Napoleon sent a posse of soldiers to guard his house. Haydn died in his sleep later the same year.

Haydn Museum, District 6, Haydngasse 19. Open Tue-Sun 9am-12.15 & 1pm-4.30pm.

WOLFGANG AMADEUS MOZART (1756-1791) - A native of Salzburg, Mozart began his career in the service of its Archbishop. Wearying

of drudge-work, and the restrictions which were placed on him in the post, he came to Vienna in 1781, hoping to make his own way on his own two feet. He was by no means a stranger to the city. As a tiny boy his father had paraded him in the imperial and noble salons on one of his promotional tours, and at Schönbrunn his curly locks and astonishing keyboard skills had famously charmed the empress Maria Theresa. Her son Joseph II, though an accomplished cellist with a fine singing voice, found Mozart hard to appreciate. He commissioned an opera from him for his new opera house, but when confronted with the result, *The Abduction from the Seraglio*, he famously remarked "Good Lord, my dear Mozart, what an awful lot of notes!" Joseph's Spanish sister-in-law Ludovica was blunter. "German bilge" was her reaction to *La Clemenza di Tito*. Mozart knew that his public was hard to please. In a letter to his father he complained that he had to cater either to dunces or to pseuds. "If you want to be appreciated you must either compose stuff so facile that any coachman could pick up the tune, or so obscure that people will go wild for it precisely because no sensible person could like it." The house where he wrote *The Marriage of Figaro* is now the Mozart Museum. He lived here from 1784 to 1787 with his wife and son, a housemaid and a cook, and wrote of it fondly as the "nicest house I ever lived in". He was forced to move to smaller quarters when he could no longer afford the rent. A great genius doomed to an early grave, Mozart's music is inevitably a blend of brilliance and immaturity. The brilliant passages are so very brilliant, though, that you forgive the slightly corny movements that intersperse them.

Figarohaus, District 1, Schulerstrasse 8 (entrance from Domgasse). Open Tue-Sun 9am-6pm.

LUDWIG VAN BEETHOVEN (1770-1827) - Born in Bonn, Beethoven first came to Vienna at the age of 17 to meet Mozart and show him his music. Five years later he moved to the city permanently, provided with a stipend by Maria Theresa's youngest son Max Franz (see p. 189).

Beethoven, fiery composer with a gaze like the Ancient Mariner. He provided much of the live entertainment at the Congress of Vienna in 1814.

He lived at over sixty addresses in Vienna, and composed many of his masterpieces here. An intensely moody, emotional man, Beethoven had revolutionary, panglossian ideals and believed in the establishment of a peaceful and united human brotherhood. His *Eroica* symphony was originally dedicated to Napoleon, but when Napoleon declared himself Emperor of France, Beethoven angrily scrubbed the dedication out, remarking bitterly that Napoleon had turned out to be no more than an ambitious little tinpot posturer. During the Congress of Vienna, convened after Napoleon's exile to Elba, Beethoven provided much of the entertainment, conducting a gala performance of his works in the Hofburg. His only opera,

Fidelio, has come to be seen as a symbol of escape and freedom, and was the first piece to be performed at the re-opened Opera House after the Second World War. The house where Beethoven lived longest - and which was famously a horrifying spectacle of dirt and disorder when he inhabited it - has now been turned into a museum.
Beethovens Wohnung, District 1, Mölker Bastei 8. Open Tue-Sun 9am-12.15 & 1pm-4.30pm.

FRANZ SCHUBERT (1797-1828) - A private man and a private composer, Schubert totally lacked the ability to cultivate the kind of aristocratic patrons who could have helped him. Always poor, very shy, and without even a piano of his own, he composed largely for his circle of friends, setting their poems to music, writing waltzes and *ländler* for them to dance to, and *lieder* for them to sing at the now legendary *Schubertiade* get-togethers. His symphonies were never performed in public in the way we understand it today, but in private houses where small, amateur music societies congregated. His music is a perfect mirror of the Biedermeier era: light and tinkly, pretty and carefree, neat and well-crafted on the surface, but with a dark harmonic world underneath,

full of discordant undertones and repressed passions. Schubert died of typhus, the great Vienna disease, at the age of 31. Both the house where he was born and the one where he died have been turned into museums.
Schubert-Geburtshaus, District 9, Nussdorferstrasse 54. Open Tue-Sun 9am-12.15 & 1pm- 4.30pm; Schubert-Sterbewohnung, District 4, Kettenbrückenstrasse 6. Open Tue-Sun 1pm-4.30pm.

ANTON BRUCKNER (1824-1896) - Born into a peasant family in Upper Austria, Bruckner made no effort to turn himself into an intellectual, reading almost nothing at all except the Bible. Almost totally uninterested in politics or ideas of any kind, he nevertheless loved nature, something that comes across very powerfully in his works. Never able to rid himself of his strong provincial accent, he was rather sneered at by the liberal Viennese arts establishment, who execrated his music as "noise", and regarded him as a foolish old bumpkin, rendered even more foolish by his incurable attraction to very young girls, all of whom rejected his proposals of marriage. Bruckner didn't taste success until the age of 60, with his 7th Symphony, which remains one of the most instantly appealing. His music is eclectic but never too daring, sometimes blowsy and sentimental, with passages of great grandeur and great beauty, and others of strange, unresolved restlessness. Always a diffident man, he submitted himself and his works to the opinions of interfering friends who suggested ways to "improve" them. Bruckner's modest, unposturing genius was just the sort of thing to appeal to the conservative-minded Franz Joseph, who was kind to him in his last years, giving him free lodging in the former porter's lodge of the Upper Belvedere.

JOHANNES BRAHMS (1833-1897) - Born in Hamburg, the son of a double-bass player, Brahms chose to live and work in Vienna, which despite being the capital of an enormous empire, had an ineradicably provincial feel to it, which he liked. He called it "the village" and meant it as a compli-

ment, saying it was the only place he could work satisfactorily. He had lodgings on the Karlsplatz, and was for a time musical director at the Musikverein. Adored and lionised by Ringstrasse society, his music - a sort of classical chassis padded with soft, romantic upholstery - is accessible without being facile; sophisticated without being pretentious. In a strange way it manages to appeal both to the tone-deaf and to listeners with true musical understanding.

Tombstone of Johannes Brahms, the son of a German double bass-player, who made his fame and his fortune in Vienna.

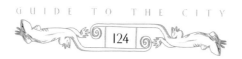

THE MODERNS

GUSTAV MAHLER (1860-1911) - The son of Bohemian immigrants to Vienna, Mahler famously said of himself that he was "thrice homeless: a native of Bohemia in Austria, as an Austrian among Germans, and as a Jew throughout the world". As a Jew he was not eligible to be director of the Vienna Opera, so he converted to Christianity. Damned if he did and damned if he didn't, when Hitler came to power, his music was banned because he was Jewish. Although many now hail Mahler as the greatest composer of his generation (there is even a virtual shrine to his memory on the Internet), during his lifetime he was recognised mainly as a great conductor. His reign at the Vienna Opera (1897-1907) was notoriously strict, as he strove to root out everything that was sloppy and slapdash. When people complained that he was trampling on tradition, he replied that "tradition is laziness". He spent his last years in America, as conductor of the Metropolitan Opera.

ARNOLD SCHOENBERG (1874-1951) - A convert to Lutheranism at the age of 24, Schoenberg is famous for inventing atonal composition, a system whereby the music has no set key signature, and which attracted a whole host of imitators. Like so many true innovators, however, he was not nearly as zealous as his converts, and the greatest atonal composer of them all returned to tonal composition in later life, just as he also returned to the Jewish faith he had abandoned as a young man.

ANTON VON WEBERN (1883-1945) - A pupil of Schoenberg, Webern's early enthusiasms were mediaeval polyphonic masters, particularly Heinrich Isaac. Webern's atonal composition gives way later on to a twelve-note method which takes him back to controlled polyphonic harmony. His orchestral arrangements of Bach and Schubert are highly accessible, and a good introduction to his style. To an untrained ear he sounds better with the bourgeois discipline of a theme and a melody behind him. Much of what he wrote has a furtive brittleness to it, and an astonishing delicacy. The sound of the silences is as important as that of the notes.

METTERNICH AND THE CONGRESS OF VIENNA

Count Klemens Wenzel Lothar Metternich (1773-1859) arrived on the scene at Austria's hour of greatest need. Napoleon was tearing Europe to pieces, and Europe, in those days, largely meant Austria. Metternich was not able to save the Holy Roman Empire, but there was plenty that he did salvage. His great skill was to appear to be appeasing Napoleon while in reality allying himself with Russia and Prussia against him. It was his idea to blunt Bonaparte's claws by marrying him to Archduchess Marie Louise, daughter of Franz I, in 1810. Then he sharpened his own claws, reformed the Austrian army, and resoundingly defeated Napoleon at the Battle of Leipzig in 1813. In gratitude Emperor Franz raised his "beloved Metternich" to the rank of Prince, and in this guise Metternich presided over the lavish Congress of Vienna, which convened after Napoleon's exile to Elba to redraw the map of Europe, making sure that as much of it as possible fell to Austria's share. The Congress was one of the most extravagant political summit meetings in history. Tradesmen all over Vienna had a field day, making small fortunes from the crowned heads and other dignitaries present. Metternich organised grand balls and *soirées*, had Beethoven conducting gala performances of his own music, took his guests hunting in the Vienna Woods and dancing into the small hours at the Sperl in Leopoldstadt, the grandest and most glittering *Tanzpalast* of them all. In 1821 he was made State Chancellor, an office which had been vacant since the days of Kaunitz (*see p. 166*), and instituted a repressive regime which relied on a secret police force and ruthless press censorship to maintain law and order. In self-defence Metternich argued that freedom obtained through revolution would not be freedom but anarchy, and that the press, far from being an expression of public opinion, was no more than the opinions of individual journalists. While he may have been right in theory, his methods made him deeply unpopular, and the revolution he so dreaded inevitably broke out, in March 1848. He was told that he must go or else the mob could not be calmed. He resigned immediately, fled to England in disguise, and found sanctuary in Brighton.

RELIGIOUS MONUMENTS

Vienna today is, to all intents and purposes, a Catholic city. But it was not always so. It was re-converted during the long Counter Reformation, which spanned most of the 16th and 17th centuries. While Spain visited the Inquisition on her heretics and England punished hers by burning them at the stake, Vienna - along with Poland and Hungary - was surprisingly tolerant, or tolerant to a degree. Most of the Habsburg rulers preferred to use persuasion rather than violent coercion to bring erring sheep back into the fold. Protestantism had a long tradition in the region, stretching back to the days of Jan Hus (1370-1415) in Bohemia. For much of the Middle Ages the reigning Catholic Habsburgs did not use Vienna as a permanent capital and the city's inhabitants were left alone to practise their own religion. A sizeable section of the German population had embraced the ideas of Martin Luther, and Vienna had come to be regarded as a Protestant city. Alongside the Protestants, many of the merchant classes were Jews, and there were sizeable pockets of Orthodox Greek and Armenian traders as well.

In 1519, Karl V came to the throne. Karl was the grandson of Ferdinand of Aragon, who, together with his wife Isabella, had expelled the Jews from Spain and sent the inquisitors to spread the fear of God among heretical Protestants. Karl admired his grandfather, and expressly wrote to the Electors of Europe to let them know that "we wish to follow in his footsteps". One of Karl's great pre-occupations was getting Luther excommunicated. In 1521 he split his Habsburg dominions in two, keeping Spain and the New World for himself and transferring Austria and her dependencies to his brother Ferdinand. Ferdinand was a pious Catholic, but he was not a fanatic. He believed that the best way to combat the infidel (Jews and Protestants) was not by torturing and murdering them but by forcing them to convert, simply by making life diffi-cult for them. He passed a law forbidding them to set up in business, and in 1551 he called in the Jesuits, who set up teaching colleges to woo the popula-tion back to the Mother Church. His aim was to enforce the principle of *cuius*

The interior of the Jesuit Church, the most triumphant expression of sacred Baroque archi-tecture in Vienna.

regio eius religio, which had been established at the Peace of Augsburg in 1555, and which required all subject peoples to practise the religion of their rulers.

As the century wore on, the Counter Reformation question became largely a matter of imperial whim. Ferdinand's successor Maximilian II had strong pluralist sympathies. He described himself simply as a Christian, refusing to qualify the description by specifying a particular denomination. Protestants were given the right to worship in private, and in 1574 in public as well. Triumphant, the Lutherans went too far. When some members of the Protestant nobility insulted the Catholic Church by riding into the Stephansdom on horseback, Maximilian's successor, Rudolf II, attempted to contain the situation by passing a law decreeing that no non-Catholic could hold Viennese citizenship. Rudolf's heart was not really on the Catholic cause, though. He was far more interested in his studies in astronomy amidst the Protestant nobles of Prague. It took the famous defenestration of 1618, when Bohemia responded to a visit from imperial Catholic envoys by simply bundling them out of a Prague castle window, to get the Counter Reformation going in any meaningful sense. The envoys were unharmed. They fell onto a refuse tip in the castle moat - but even so, the emperor Ferdinand II - who came to the throne in 1619 - was not amused. He responded by launching the Battle of the White Mountain, which all but wiped out the Bohemian aristocracy. His successor Ferdinand III continued his aggressive pro-Catholic policies, as did Leopold I (1657-1705). After 1683, when the Ottoman menace was laid to rest once and for all, Leopold turned his attention to wresting Vienna back from the clutches of Lutheranism and Jewry. Knowing

The initials of the Three Kings, sandwiched between the date of the new year to come, are chalked on doors all over Vienna during Advent.

The high altar of the Karlskirche, execut-
ed to designs by Johann Bernhard Fischer
von Erlach.

that his realm was made up of a complex mix of peoples and cultures, he looked to religion as a unifying force. He was also a man of his time. He firmly believed that non-Catholics would burn in eternal hell fire unless he intervened to save their souls.

THE JEWS IN VIENNA

Jews first settled in Vienna in the 12th century, and in 1238 were granted extensive privileges by the last of the Babenbergs, Friedrich the Quarrelsome, whose quarrels were with Mongols and Magyars, not with his own subjects. In the late 13th and early 14th centuries, Vienna's Jews were regarded as the leading community of German Jewry, and the city even served as a refuge for Jews fleeing from persecution elsewhere. It was not until the 15th century that persecution came to Vienna, under Albrecht V, "scourge of the unbeliever". In 1421 he accused the entire community of being in league with the Protestant Hussites of Bohemia against the Catholic Habsburgs of Austria, and demanded that every Jew in the city should be baptised forthwith. Two fates were in store for those who refused. The wealthy ones were flung into jail; the poor ones were set afloat on the Danube in a rudderless boat, and left to the mercy of the currents. Many did convert. Many did not - and various other methods of coercion were tried on them: bribery, starvation, burning at the stake… Eventually all Jews who declined to be baptised were banished beyond the city walls, and their property was confiscated.

Over the next two hundred years, given the more or less tolerant climate in Vienna, things went quiet again, and the Jews trickled back, taking advantage of the fact that the Holy Roman Emperors were more bent on keeping the

Ottomans out of their realm than on persecuting hard working tailors, merchants and goldsmiths. Then came the reign of Ferdinand II. In 1621, having dealt with the Protestants (*see above*), he turned his attention to the Jews, expelling them once again from the inner city, and forcing them to settle outside the walls. The new Jewish area became what is now District 2, on the further side of the Danube Canal. They were only left in peace there for half a century. In 1670 Leopold I banished them again, named their area Leopoldstadt after himself, and converted their temple on the Grosse Pfarrgasse into a Catholic church, to which he gave the inspired name Leopoldskirche. Not that Leopold was an unmitigated monster. Politically and militarily his reign was a success. He was a talented musician, a gifted linguist and a good family man, being steadfastly faithful to each of his three wives (one after the other, of course). But he had been educated by Jesuits and originally intended for the Church. As a zealous and militant Catholic, he saw Protestants and Jews as sinners who could not hope to enjoy clemency. Most Austrian rulers for the next century felt the same way.

After Joseph II's Edict of Tolerance (*see p. 132*), things changed. The Jews ceased to be harried, and were allowed to return to their homes, By the late 19th century Leopoldstadt was largely Jewish. Vienna's anti-Semites of the 20s and 30s used to remark sneeringly that the reason the statue of Admiral Tegetthoff, which stands at the edge of the Prater, was equipped with a telescope, was because he was vainly scanning the horizon for a Christian face. When the Nazis seized power and annexed Austria, they drew up plans to raze much of Leopoldstadt to the ground and construct an enormous mock-Roman forum for speeches and rallies. Thankfully the plans never left the drawing board.

THE HOLOCAUST MEMORIAL AND THE JUDENPLATZ MUSEUM

In 1997 Vienna erected a memorial on the Judenplatz, the centre of mediaeval Jewish life in the city, to commemorate Austrian victims of the Holocaust. The plinth of the memorial is engraved with the names of the places and camps where Austrian Jews were murdered. The nearby museum (Judenplatz 8) gives full documentation on the 65,000 Austrian Holocaust victims, with information on where and how they were killed. Exhibition rooms in the museum

basement cover Jewish life in Vienna until 1421, the date of their expulsion from the Judenplatz enclave. An underground passage leads to the remains of the mediaeval prayer house and school, destroyed in a pogrom at that time. *The museum is open Sun-Thur 10am-6pm; Fri 10am-2pm.*

THE STADTTEMPEL

This Classicist synagogue, built by Josef Kornhäusel (*see p. 163*) in 1824-6, stands on the site of a much older mediaeval prayer house, built by the Jewish traders who had colonised this part of Vienna in the early middle ages. When the Jews returned to the inner city after the declaration of the Edict of Tolerance (*see p. 132*), they chose to build a new synagogue on the site of the old, though it still took the community decades to secure planning permission. They had to endure numerous delegations from the emperor Franz I, visiting the site to assess whether the building was really necessary. A quirk of Joseph

The postman on his morning rounds in the Judenplatz. On the left you can see the stark grey bulk of the Holocaust memorial.

II's tolerance laws forbade synagogues and Protestant churches to betray their function, which explains why outside of the Stadttempel does not resemble a place of worship at all. It was the only one of 24 synagogues in Vienna that was not completely destroyed by the Nazis in 1938.
District 1, Seitenstettengasse 4.

Vienna has another Jewish museum, the Jüdisches Museum Wien, at District 1, Dorotheergasse 11. You can also visit their website at www.jmw.at

THE EDICT OF TOLERANCE

Joseph II (1780-1790) was consumed by reforming zeal. While his mother, Maria Theresa, was alive, the imperial household was riven with quarrels about it. As soon as she died, Joseph felt free to act. One of the first things he deemed necessary was better education for the common people, as well as better social provision: schools, hospitals, orphanages. During his reign people of all faiths were given new freedoms, including the right to wander in the Prater along with every other Vienna citizen. A noble lady is said to have acidly remarked that by flinging so many things open to the public the emperor was ensuring that nowhere in the city was safe for people of gentle blood. Why did Joseph want to spend so much time with the lower orders? Joseph responded with the much-quoted

The Stadttempel, Vienna's inner-city synagogue. The strict rules that governed non-Catholic places of worship mean that it was not allowed to look like a synagogue from the outside.

The façade of the Toleranzhaus on Fleischmarkt, on the site where the Edict of Tolerance was proclaimed in 1782. The gilded cameo relief is of Joseph II, author of the Edict.

put-down that if he wanted to spend all his time with his equals, he would have to go and cool his heels in the *Kaisergruft*.

One of Joseph's central concerns was religious reform, and this was one of the few things on which he and his Chancellor, Maria Theresa's trusted Kaunitz (*see p. 166*), agreed. Church was to be subservient to State, and the state itself was to be better centralised. Joseph was watching events in revolutionary France with interest. He even warned his sister, Marie Antoinette, that if she and Louis did not manage to contain the revolution, the results would be "atrocious". Joseph believed in reform, but he did not believe in ceding power to the people. His Catholic reforms included the closure of 18 monasteries and convents in Vienna, on the grounds that they performed no useful function. Monks and nuns who ran schools and seminaries and tended the sick were a desirable thing and on the whole were reprieved. Those who did nothing all day but count rosary beads and meditate on scripture found their orders suddenly dissolved. "We want educated brethren who can teach philanthropic values," he said, "not *fainéants* mooching about in rags."

The Edict of Tolerance, passed in 1782, was one of the cornerstones of Joseph's ecclesiastical reforms, and it made the lives of all Vienna's non-Catholics considerably easier. Jews were not to be persecuted, Protestants were to be allowed to worship freely, and both were once again allowed to build places of worship - but with the curious proviso that they must not carry any outward symbol of their function. The Lutheran church now has a tower, but it was not built until 1887. The Greek Orthodox church gained its bell tower in the same year. The *Stadttempel* synagogue (*see above*) remains plain and unadorned, with only the Hebrew lettering over the entrance to give its secret away.

CHURCHES

Inevitably - given the historical conditions outlined above - the places of worship of greatest architectural and artistic interest in Vienna are the Catholic churches. Four of the best appear below.

NB: *The Stephansdom is covered in Major Sights on pp. 37-41.*

THE AUGUSTINERKIRCHE - Originally this was the church that served the adjoining Augustinian monastery, which was founded in Vienna in the early 14th century. The original Gothic entrance façade, facing the Josefsplatz, was swamped in Baroque cladding by Maria Theresa's court architect Nikolaus Pacassi, so that now it is entirely flush with the square. The interior was re-Gothicised by Joseph II's court architect von Hohenberg who, in the course of his anti-Baroque campaign, dumped an altar painting by Maulbertsch (*see p. 55*) onto the rubbish tip. Hohenberg's work was successful, though. The interior of the church today is cool, lofty and serenely peaceful - unless the organist is practising, in which case the whole building becomes a sound-box. Badly damaged by fire in the 1848 revolution, and again during the Second World War, the church nevertheless preserves the magnificent marble tomb of Marie Christine, Maria Theresa's favourite daughter, with its carving of mourners entering a pyramid-sepul-chre. Above the tomb entrance is carved the Latin panegyric "best of wives". Above that is a cameo portrait of the deceased. The tomb (in the south aisle) was made by Canova in 1805 and is considered one of his masterworks. (Marie Christine is not resting in peace inside it; her body is in the *Kaisergruft, see p. 146.*) It was in this church, on April 24th 1854, that Franz Joseph - much against his domineering mother's wishes - married the romantic, beautiful and wayward Elisabeth of Bavaria, niece of the mad Ludwig, who built a personal theatre for himself in Munich (he was to be the sole member of the audience), and tried to persuade Wagner to take up residence with him, and compose operas for his solitary delight. Some tongues whispered that Elisabeth had inherited the family dottiness. She certainly had a solitary streak; but Franz Joseph was blinded by love, and married her despite all warnings. The marriage (*see p. 25*) was a disaster. These walls were also witness to the proxy marriage of Napoleon to Marie

Allegory of the Jesuit Order by Franz Anton Maulbertsch.

Louise of Austria (*see p. 20*). In the Loreto Chapel, (entrance beyond Marie Christine's tomb), there are rows of little silver urns concealed behind the altar. Each one contains the embalmed heart of a Habsburg. The church's high altar, though mediaeval in style, dates from 1874. On the north side, note the amusing Holy Dove in the pulpit canopy, hovering with very red, sharp claws, threatening to land on the preacher's head.

District 1, Augustinerstrasse 3.

THE JESUIT CHURCH - The Church of the Ascension of the Virgin, dedicated to St Ignatius Loyola, founder of the Jesuits, and St Francis Xavier, evangeliser of Goa, was built between 1627 and 1631 under the auspices of the ferociously Catholic emperor Ferdinand II. It is without any doubt at all the most triumphant - and triumphalist - expression of the Counter Reformation in Vienna. The interior (1703-1707) is by the Jesuit father Andrea Pozzo, master of the *trompe l'oeil*, whose other works include the Jesuit churches in Rome and Dubrovnik. The result of his labours in Vienna is overwhelming, and the pillars that run the length of the nave are probably the fattest marble pillars anywhere in the world. Great twisted

Solomonic columns in red and green marble flank the nearest and furthest side-altars on both sides of the church. No expense was spared on this interior; everything is gilded, and the pews and confessionals have elaborate marquetry work. The whole effect is of magnificent excess, and is curiously pleasing in its opulence. Pozzo's *trompe l'oeil* gives a soaring, uplifting feel to the building, which saves it from ponderousness. A white stone in the central aisle marks the spot from which the *trompe l'oeil* dome is best appreciated. Fans of Pozzo should also visit the Franciscan Church (Franziskanerplatz 4) to see his enormous *trompe l'oeil* high altar. *District 1, Dr Ignaz Seipel-Platz 1.*

THE KARLSKIRCHE - The swansong of Vienna's greatest Baroque architect Johann Bernhard Fischer von Erlach (*see p. 85*. He died before it was completed and the project was taken over by his son), the Karlskirche was commissioned by the emperor Karl VI in 1713 (completed 1737), as a votive church to give thanks for the passing of the plague. Architecturally it is a perfect encapsulation of Baroque principles: a basic square box disguised by the wealth of architectural detail and flummery tacked onto it. When it was first built, it stood in solitary splendour among the watermeadows of the

Wiental, the valley of the River Wien. It must have looked rather fine then, much finer than it does now, stranded on the over-paved, over-expansive Karlsplatz. The church is surmounted by a great dome. Viewed from a distance, in fact, it is remarkable just how much of the building *is* dome. The two towers on either side are modelled on Trajan's column in Rome (though Trajan's column lacks an elongated Baroque pill-box on top), and as such are symbolic of the Holy Roman Empire itself: Christianity and the conquering might of Rome grafted together. The towers are decorated with carved scenes from the life of St Carlo Borromeo (1538-1584), a tireless church reformer and outspoken critic - despite his speech impediment - of lazy and immoral clergy. He later became Archbishop of Milan, and is patron saint of plague survivors, which is why the church is dedicated to him. The tympanum across the entrance portico has a bas-relief depicting Vienna and the death of the plague. Inside the church you get a full appreciation of how enormous the dome really is (78 metres high) - you need to crane your head back as far as it will possibly go to see Rottmayr's fresco of St Carlo Borromeo praying for an end to the plague and of his apotheosis. The baptismal chapel (on your immediate left as you stand at the back of the

Fischer von Erlach's monumental Karlskirche, reflected in the Karlsplatz fountain.

church facing the high altar) has an altarpiece of Christ and the centurion by Daniel Gran (*see p. 52*). Walking clockwise round the church from here, you come to the Chapel of the Assumption, with an altarpiece by the Venetian artist Sebastiano Ricci, who also worked in London, and who had been a contender for the dome of St Paul's Cathedral. This *Assumption of the Virgin* was painted in 1733-34, and is supposed to be his last great work, though some think that it was painted largely by his assistants - hence the rather inelegant Mary ascending to heaven on a doughy-looking cloud. Ricci's health was very poor when he worked on this piece. He suffered terribly from gall stones, and died on the operating table in the year the altarpiece was completed. The high altar was executed to Fischer von Erlach's designs. Immediately opposite the Chapel of the Assumption is a chapel with another altarpiece by Daniel Gran, showing St Elizabeth of Hungary dispensing alms. Devoted to her husband Louis, Margrave of Thuringia, Elizabeth was devastated when he died of plague in 1227 (the plague connection is presumably the reason for her inclusion here). Instead of marrying again, she chose a life of austere piety under the direction of her confessor, the sadistic Conrad, who beat her frequently until finally she died, worn out, at the age of 24. She was known for her generosity to the poor, particularly to children.

District 1, Karlsplatz. Open Mon-Sat 9am-12.30pm & 1pm-6pm; Sun 1pm-6pm.

THE MINORITENKIRCHE - The Church of the Friars Minor (Franciscans), and one of the most interesting in Vienna. From the outside you can clearly see what a jumble of buildings and rebuildings took place to create what stands today. Between 1569 and 1620 the church was used by Vienna's Protestants. After the accession of the fiercely Catholic emperor Ferdinand II the Franciscans returned, only to be dispossessed by Joseph II, who gave the church to Vienna's Italian community, who still use it today. The stumpy tower was once a steeple: its flèche was knocked off by a Turkish cannon ball in 1683. The main west doorway preserves some original 14th century carving: St Francis (headless now) receiving the stigmata, with a hedgehog and a rabbit in the undergrowth beside him. The tympanum of the Crucifixion over the main door was executed to the design of one of the monks, Jacobus Parisiensis (c. 1350).

The interior of the church is unusual for its extraordinary width, the two aisles being almost as wide as the nave. The pillars and vaulting of the main nave are original, the rest is much later: the re-Gothicising work of Joseph II's court architect von Hohenberg is clearly visible in the rather Strawberry Hill style of the walls and tracery, especially to the south of the main altar. The mosaic copy of Leonardo da Vinci's *Last Supper* was created at the request of Napoleon between 1806 and 1814. Napoleon, it is said, had seen the original in Milan, looked on it with covetous eyes, and ordered that it be transported to Paris. When this proved technically impossible, he ordered a copy instead.

District 1, Minoritenplatz.

The Minoritenkirche.

A Handful of Doctors & Philosophers

The 19th and 20th-century Viennese schools of science, philosophy and medicine produced discoveries, theories, systems and analyses which have had a profound influence on the whole course of modern life and thought. Here are four of the best-known of Vienna's many prodigies.

SIGMUND FREUD (1856-1939) - Born in a part of the empire that is now the Czech Republic, Freud moved to Vienna at the age of three. During his military service in the Austrian Army, he would act as impromptu doctor when the need arose. Later he went on to become Professor of Neurology at Vienna University. His work in the field of psychoanalysis received almost no official recognition, and was mainly conducted in his own time. Every Wednesday evening he would invite a group of like-minded people - the Freud Circle - to a gathering at his rooms in the Berggasse. When he published his *Interpretation of Dreams* in 1899, it went almost unnoticed. In 1938 Nazi persecution induced Freud to move to England, where he imagined himself landing at Pevensey to vanquish the Anglo Saxons, just as William the Conqueror had done in 1066. Freud's former practice rooms are now open to the public. *Vienna 9, Berggasse 19. Open 9am-5pm every day. www.freudmuseum.at*

ALFRED ADLER (1870-1937) - When dangerously ill with pneumonia as a small boy, Adler overheard his father predicting that he was almost certain to die. Then and there Adler vowed that if he survived, he would become a doctor and fight fatal disease. He qualified in 1895. Adler was one of the first people to appreciate the greatness of Freud: in gratitude, Freud invited him to join his circle. Unable to accept the ultimate Freudian view that everything is traceable to sex, Adler went on to set up a circle of his own. The main tenet of his system of "individual psychology" was that ailments and neuroses stem from the whole person and their environment, and should be diagnosed and treated accordingly - an idea which was to revolutionise child psychology. Adler's most famous coinage is the term "inferiority complex".

LUDWIG WITTGENSTEIN (1889-1951) - After studying at Cambridge under Bertrand Russell, Wittgenstein went to Norway where he lived alone in a log cabin, working on the philosophical ideas which were to become his famous *Tractatus*. He then abandoned philosophy, only to return to it - and to Cambridge - in 1929. Wittgenstein never really enjoyed university life, and would advise his students against going into academia, saying that it was enough to stifle anyone - except him, because he could "generate my own oxygen". After a failed madcap jaunt to Soviet Russia, where he had decided he wanted to work in a factory (no factory would have him, and the only job offer he received was from Moscow University, as Professor of Philosophy), he returned to Cambridge where he died, having lived, in his own words, "a wonderful life".

SIR KARL POPPER (1902-1994) - Born in Vienna, Popper emigrated to England to escape Nazi persecution, and spent over 30 years at the London School of Economics, where he dominated western debate on the Philosophy of Science. His *The Open Society and its Enemies* attacks Plato and Marx, whom he saw as providing spurious intellectual support for Fascists and Communists. The term most associated with his name is "falsifiability": if a theory is falsifiable, Popper believed, it is good science. Systems of belief based on non-falsifiable premises he termed pseudo-science.

PART III

GUIDED WALKS

Each of these walks is designed to take between 45 minutes to an hour. By visiting museums, churches or cafés along the way, you can make them last a whole morning or afternoon.

Key streets and sights are marked in bold throughout.

p. 141   WALK ONE -
South from the Graben

p. 149   WALK TWO -
In and Around the Freyung

p. 157   WALK THREE -
From Am Hof to the Bermuda Triangle

p. 167   WALK FOUR -
East of the Stephansdom

p. 173   WALK FIVE -
Between Wollzeile and Fleischmarkt

Each walk is preceded by a detailed map showing the route. A map of all five walks in their city-centre context can be found on p. 234.

Spire of the Stephansdom reflected in the Haas Haus.

WALK ONE

Arn
Hof

P

Kirche
am Hof

Nagler
Haarf. Irisg.
Bognerg.
Seitzerg.
Tuch-
lauben
hof
Steindlg.
Tuch-
Peters
pl.
Jung-
fernsg.
St. Peter

Paris erg.
Kurreng.
Kleeblattg.
Jordan-
pl.
Schul-
terg.

Landskron g.
Wildpret-
mkt.
Milch
Kühfussg.
Freisinger g.
Goldschmiedg.
Brandstätte
Bauern
Jasomirgott
str.

Hoher
Markt

Judeng.
Fisch-
hof
markt
Ertl
g.

D.
Friedmann-
Pl.
Rot
Lichten-
steg
Guter

U3

Kohlmarkt
str.
Graben
str.

Kramer
Totenturm
Wollzeile
Archbish.
Palace

Merpl.
Habsburger
Stallburgg.
Bräuner
Dorotheer
Dorotheum

STEPHANSPL.
Jewish
Museum
Planking.
Seilerg.
Spiegelg.
Glücksg.
Göttweiher g.
Kärntner
Durchgang
Neuer
Donner
Markt g.
Marco-
d'Aviano-
g.
Maltheser
Kirche
g.

Stephans-
pl.
Stephansdom
P
Schu

U1,3
Kärntner
Str.

Nikolai
g.
Blut
Singer
Weihburg
Blumen-
stockg.
Bali-
Rauhensteing.
Lilieng.
Franziskaner-
pl.

Himmelpfort
Johannes

1.

sefs-
platz
Augustinerkirche
Augustinerstr.
Augustiner-
bastei
Hanusch.
Lobko-
witz-
pl.
Führich
Kaisergruft
Tegetthoffstr.
Albertina
pl.
Mayse derg.
Philharmo-
nikerstr.
Opera
Opern
P
Kruger
Walfisch
Mahler
Anna
St. Anna
St. Ursula
Seil
stätte
Seiler
Fichte
Schwarze
Schelling

SOUTH FROM THE GRABEN

The Graben, once a muddy ditch, is now Vienna's smartest shopping street. This itinerary includes two interiors by Adolf Loos, the scene of a mediaeval execution, plus a famous café and snack bar.

This walk begins in the **Petersplatz**, a wide square of old Vienna town houses, with the Baroque *Peterskirche* squeezed into the middle, occupying almost all the available space. The house on the north-east corner of the square, at **Milchgasse 1**, is where Mozart lodged when he first came to Vienna in 1781, having escaped the claustrophobic atmosphere of Salzburg. It was here that he wrote *The Abduction from the Seraglio*, commissioned by Joseph II, and it is also where he met his wife, Constanze Weber, the daughter of his landlord.

Interior of the clothing shop Knize, created by Adolf Loos (1909-1913).

Leopold I kneels in prayer on Fischer von Erlach's plague monument. The plague, personified as an ugly old crone, falls to her death beneath him.

Leaving the main entrance of the Peterskirche behind you, go out into the Graben along a short, stubby street, the Jungferngasse. In the middle ages the street was spanned by a covered bridge, from which a young man fell to his death trying to creep from his own house on one side to the bedroom window of his lover on the other. News of the illicit affair spread all over town, and the girl was punished by being made to walk barefoot to the church where she was stuck in the pillory.

On reaching the wide, pedestrian **Graben**, turn left. This street, the name of which means ditch, was once exactly that, a deep, muddy moat running outside the walls of the Roman garrison town. It was only in the late 12th century that it was filled in and turned into a city street, the work being financed with ransom money obtained for the release of the crusader king Richard the Lionheart, who had been kidnapped by the Duke of Austria and locked up in Dürnstein castle. Today the Graben is lined with expensive shops and filled with pavement cafés in the spring and summer. In the centre of it is the

plague monument (*Pestsäule*), put up to give thanks for the passing of a plague outbreak which hit Vienna in 1679, leaving around 10,000 dead in its wake. Built to the design of Vienna's greatest Baroque architect, Johann Bernhard Fischer von Erlach (*see p. 85*), it shows the emperor Leopold I, represented true to life with his colossal Habsburg jaw, kneeling in prayers of thanksgiving while a cherub obligingly holds his crown for him. Below him the plague, personified as a hideous old crone with withered breasts, is struck down by a firebrand.

On the right hand side of the street, at No. 13, is the gentlemen's outfitters **Knize**, with an interior and shopfront designed by Adolf Loos (*see p. 87*) between 1909 and 1913. In its clean-lined simplicity it forms a marked contrast to the lace doily-style decoration of the late 19th-century main façade. Knize, which has been in business since the 1850s, was formerly purveyor of dress uniforms to the Turkish Sultan and the Shah of Persia, hence the coats of arms above the shop door. Loos himself had very particular ideas about fashion, and though a Functionalist to the bottom of his heart, he certainly didn't believe in dressing down. "I am a Communist," he once declared, "The only difference between me and the Bolsheviks is that they want to turn everyone into proletarians. I want to turn everyone into aristocrats".

Further along the street on the same side, at No. 10, is the **Ankerhaus**, a building by an architect who fell deeply under Loos' spell. Otto Wagner (*see p. 86*), once the High Priest of Jugendstil, became more and more Modernist in his approach. His Ankerhaus (1895), a sort of squat skyscraper, fuses elements of the two styles. The studio on the top floor, which Wagner designed for his own use, was used in more recent years by Friedensreich Hundertwasser (*see p. 88*).

At the end of the Graben there is an open square (Stock-im-Eisen

Platz) giving on to the Stephansdom, with the modern **Haas Haus** (1990) on your left. The building caused an uproar when it was first built, but now most Viennese seem to have got used to it. At No. 3 stands the old **Equitable Palais**, a monumental 19th-century office block (1890-1) with elaborate bronze doors - note the white bell-push at about waist-height on your left, inserted into the mouth of a grotesque. The hallway of the building is well worth a look, with its Escher-esque stairway, opulent marble walls and covered atrium, clad top to bottom in majolica. Above the topmost arch of the covered court-yard the word "Equitable" is picked out in swags of majolica foliage and crayfish.

Stock-im-Eisen Platz is named after an old tree trunk (the **Stock im Eisen**, "stick in iron") now preserved behind glass on the outside corner of the Equitable Palais. The trunk is the middle section of a 15th-century fig tree, enclasped in an iron band, and filled with iron nails, hammered into it by itinerant locksmiths, one by one, for good luck, a practice which began when the tree was still alive. By the early 19th century the tree had acquired mystic status, and when Hans Christian Andersen wrote about it in 1842, he had fully swallowed the story that it was the only remnant of the prehistoric, dinosaur-filled swampy forest that had once covered the Danube floodplain.

Turn right into Kärntnerstrasse now, and first right again at the folk-dress shop Lanz Trachtenmoden, into the Kärntner Durchgang. Here, on your left, you will find the tiny **American Bar**, another work by Adolf Loos (*see p. 88*). At the end of the street turn left down Seilergasse and into **Neuer Markt**, formerly the flour market, where milled grain from the Hungarian Great Plain was sold to the bakers of Vienna. At No. 15 on your right, you will find the jeweller Köchert, who made the little jewelled stars that Empress Elisabeth wore in her hair (*see picture on p. 45*). The **fountain** in the centre of the square is an allegory of Providence, with statues symbolising four of Austria's rivers and the role they played in the country's prosperity. It was the first ever non-religious piece of sculpture commissioned for a public place in Vienna. What you see now is a copy. The original statues were made of lead, and were the work of Georg Raphael Donner (1739). The face of the central figure, Providence herself, was whispered to have been modelled on the face of Donner's mistress, the wife of his landlord. Whatever the truth, the whole ensemble was too much for the family values of Maria

Theresa (perhaps it was the youth with the trident that did it, bent half double with his bottom in the air). In 1773 the statues were removed and sent away to be smelted down. Fortunately for posterity, the man charged with this job spotted their artistic value and kept them. Donner died in poverty and is buried in a pauper's grave. The original statues are now on display in the Lower Belvedere (*see p. 55*).

At the far end of Neuer Markt, on the right, stands the **Capuchin church**, whose vaults (the *Kaisergruft*) are the last resting place of the Habsburg rulers and their consorts (minus their hearts, which are buried in Augustinerkirche, and their entrails, which are buried in the Stephansdom). They are entombed in a long and lugubrious file of metal sarcophagi. Though a painted admonition above the entrance to the crypt calls for "*Silentium!*", the insistent voices of tour guides fills the air, along with the exhaled breath of all the visitors, which is causing the coffins to corrode. It is hard to imagine those bones can be resting in peace. (*The Kaisergruft is open from 9.30am to 4pm every day.*)

Turn right now down Gluckgasse, past a shop offering wine and underwear (*Wein und Wäsche*), and into **Lobkowitz Platz**. It was here, in

1408, that the mayor of Vienna, Konrad Vorlauf, was beheaded by Duke Leopold Habsburg. The charge against Vorlauf was that his taxes were exorbitant. Although the craftsmen and artisans who had to pay the taxes supported Duke Leopold, Vorlauf's friends among the nobility rose up against him, setting up the 11 year-old Duke Albrecht as ruler in his stead. Leopold died of an apoplexy, and Albrecht went on to become the persecutor of Vienna's Jewish community (*see Walk Three*).

Lobkowitz Platz is dominated by the Palais Lobkowitz at No. 2. The Lobkowitzes were a noble family from Bohemia, the most famous of whom is Prince Joseph (1772-1816). Left partially crippled by a childhood accident, and unable to serve his country on the battlefield, he turned his attention to the arts instead, funding his own private orchestra, turning the ceremonial hall of the family palace into a concert hall, and extending financial support to Joseph Haydn. Beethoven's *Eroica* premiered here privately in 1804. It was originally dedicated to Napoleon, but when he declared himself Emperor of France later the same year, the disillusioned Beethoven scrubbed out Napoleon's

The Capuchin church on Neuer Markt, whose vaults contain the mortal remains of 139 Habsburgs.

The open-sandwich buffet Trześniewski, a popular snack bar in Dorotheergasse.

name and dedicated the piece to Lobkowitz instead.

Turn right now down Spiegelgasse, where you will soon pass, on your left, the back of the **Dorotheum**, formerly a convent, now Vienna's premier antiques auction house. Turn left up Plankengasse to the **Lutheran church**. Originally attached to a convent dissolved by Joseph II as part of his Edict of Tolerance in 1782 (*see p. 133*), the church was snapped up by the Lutherans, and became Vienna's first legitimate Protestant church. Turn right down Dorotheergasse and walk along it, past the Casanova Revue Theatre (of *Third Man* fame). In this out-of-the-way sidestreet the Casanova has been bold enough to put up a neon sign of a naked dancing girl. In the family-filled Graben there is a similar sign, but the girl is clad in a blue evening dress. If Casanova knew what tawdry thrills were being advertised in his name he would appreciate the irony of it. The Vienna that he knew offered a much more barren experience. "In Vienna," he lamented in his memoirs, "the severity of the empress made the worship of Venus difficult. A legion of vile spies,

who were decorated with the fine title of Commissaries of Chastity, were the merciless tormentors of all the girls. The empress did not practise the sublime virtue of tolerance for what is called illegitimate love." The Graben, once famous for its strolling prostitutes, the *Grabennymphen*, was cleaned up by Maria Theresa, and Casanova had a bleak time of it.

Dorotheergasse offers two places to end this walk. **Café Hawelka** at No. 6 (*see p. 109*), or **Trześniewski** further down on the other side, where people stand at tables outside, drinking tiny *Pfiffs* of beer and tucking into the buffet's famous open sandwiches.

WALK TWO

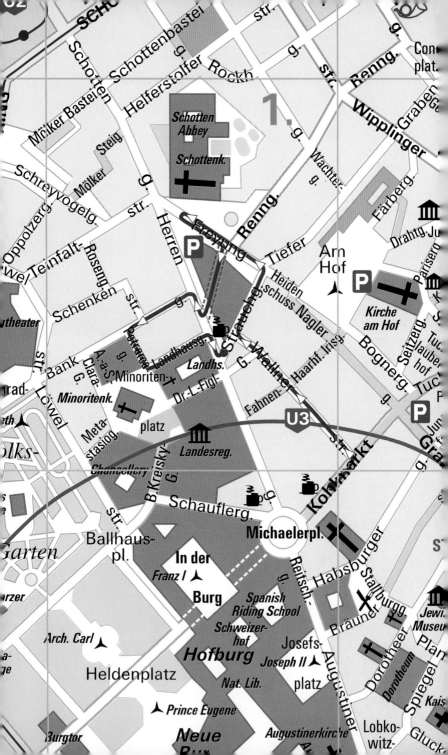

IN AND AROUND THE FREYUNG

The old town palaces of the nobility crowd the streets to the west of the Hofburg and down towards the Freyung. Two famous coffee houses, a statue stuffed with cigars, and the hero of the siege of Vienna are all part of this itinerary.

This walk begins in the **Kohlmarkt**, once, as its name suggests, a charcoal market, and now a pedestrian shopping street where you will find one of Vienna's oldest and most illustrious confectioners (Demel, *see p. 107*), as well as the House of England, Scotland and Wales and the House of Gentlemen, "specialist outlet for British menswear". The Viennese taste for *le style anglais* is said to have germinated at the Congress of Vienna in 1814 (*see p. 125*), when the sartorial dash cut by Wellington and Castlereagh

The Freyung Passage. Previous page: View of the Freyung.

The Order of the Golden fleece hanging above the main entrance to the Palais Batthyány.

caused a major stir, and inspired a whole generation of Viennese dandies to nag their tailors for something along the same lines. Sadly the British ladies were not so admired: they were generally agreed to be the dowdiest women in Europe.

Turn out of Kohlmarkt into **Wallnerstrasse**, a street full of former patrician palaces. The plain building on the left with the modern upper storeys (No. 3) is the Palais Lamberg, formerly home to the ill-fated Count Franz Philipp, who was sent to Budapest in 1848 to dissolve the newly declared independent Hungarian parliament. His reception committee was a revolutionary mob with murder in their hearts; Lamberg was stabbed to death on the pontoon bridge as he tried to cross the Danube. On the other side of the road, at No. 4, is the **Palais Esterházy**, built in the late 17th century by Paul Esterházy, Palatine of Hungary, and a talented amateur composer (his religious song-cycle, *Harmonia Caelestis*, is available on CD). When Napoleon's troops occupied Vienna in 1809, the French marshal Bessières quartered himself here - perhaps hoping for a return of the favour France had conferred on the Esterházy family: Napoleon had offered the crown of Hungary to Miklós Esterházy "Il Magnifico". Further down on the same side, at **No. 8**, is a house that was once the French embassy, from where the *Tricolore* was flown in 1798, causing the blood of loyal Austrians to boil. The *Tricolore* was the symbol of the French republic, and one of the ways France had obtained its republican status was by guillotining Marie Antoinette, the daughter of Austria's much-loved matriarch Maria Theresa. A raging mob stormed the palace and tore the flag to shreds, and later the same year the building was sold to a banker, Johann Geymüller, who held literary and musical *soirées* here, at one of which Grillparzer (*see p. 112*) met Kathi Fröhlich, the woman he loved for almost half a century but never got round to marrying. Nearby Fahnengasse, "Flag Street", takes its name from the ignominious *Tricolore* incident. Geymüller's summer villa is now a museum of Biedermeier furniture (*see p. 101*).

At the end of Wallnergasse turn right down Strauchgasse, a narrow street that was leads into the **Freyung**. The Freyung is a broad, irregularly-shaped square, once the site of a huge outdoor market and fair, which not only had stalls full of produce, but puppeteers and tightrope walkers to entertain the crowds, and colossal ox roasts to feed them. Today it hosts an organic farmers' market. The name Freyung, meaning liberation, comes from the fact that three days' amnesty was granted to runaway serfs, outlaws and political black sheep who managed to reach the square and the protection of its monastery. Walking anti-clockwise round the square you come first to the **Kunstforum** at No. 8-9, a gallery that hosts excellent temporary exhibitions. Beyond that, at No. 7, is the *Schubladkastenhaus* ("chest-of-drawers house") so-called because that is what it reminded the Viennese of. The drab grey colour of its façade is the legacy of Joseph II: a keen reformer and, in his paternalistic way, keen to improve the lives of his subjects, he was sometimes too joylessly utilitarian in his approach. The **Freyung fountain** consists of an allegorical figure of Austria surrounded by the rivers Danube, Elbe, Po and Vistula, symbolising the extent of the empire's dominions. Hollow inside, the cast iron figures are said to be stuffed full of cigars, smuggled into Austria by the sculptor, who had had the statue made in Munich. By the time the statue arrived in Vienna, in 1846, the sculptor had fallen ill, and by the time word got around that the figures were full of cigars it was too late - the statue had been erected.

Next door to the *Schubladkasten-haus* are the **Schotten Abbey** and its church, saved from dissolution by Joseph II (*see p. 133*) because of its famous grammar school (Johann Strauss was a pupil here). The Schottenkirche contains the tomb of Ernst Rüdiger von Starhemberg, Vienna's hero in her hour of need in 1683, but more of him later. The abbey building itself is by the early 19th-century architect Josef Kornhäusel, and is interesting for the way it plays with Classicism, stretching the pediment out to enormous lengths, and barely articulating the windows and the bays (there are no pilasters on the courtyard side, and only the merest hint of pediments). The "*Schotten*" who founded this abbey were not Scots at all, but Irish Benedictines who had settled in Regensburg, from where they came to Vienna with the Babenberg duke Heinrich II, when he transferred his court to the city in the 12th century. There is a memorial to Heinrich fixed to the abbey wall, commemorating him under his nickname *Jasomirgott*, a soubriquet said to have come about because of his fondness for the oath "So help me God" - "*ja so mir Gott helfe*".

Beyond the Schotten Abbey, at No. 4, stands an icing-sugar dream, von Hildebrandt's **Palais Kinsky** (1716). Today it is owned by a bar pianist-turned-businessman, who has built his own mausoleum at the back of the courtyard, ready to receive his body when the day comes. There are auction rooms on the first floor, and it is worth going up the grand, Atlas-borne stairway to see them. Note the series of chubby *putti* wrestling their way along the top balustrade. The early 19th-century Count Kinsky who lived here was a keen music patron who did much to assist Beethoven, including giving him a stipend if he would agree to stay in Vienna and not move back to Germany. Beethoven dedicated a number of works to Countess Kinsky, whom he described as "the most beautiful woman in Vienna - and the fattest".

Going back down the other side of the Freyung now, turn right into the **Freyung Passage**, an exuberant mid 19th-century arcade of shops, with painted vaults and a gurgling fountain beneath the high central dome. The arcade brings you out into Herrengasse. Turn right and then immediately left into Bankgasse, a narrow street once again home to an enfilade of aristocratic piles. The **Palais Batthyány** at No. 2 has the Order of the Golden Fleece hanging over the door, an order of chivalry - Austria's equivalent of the Order of the Garter - founded in 1429 in Bruges by Philip the Good of Burgundy. With the marriage of Maximilian I to Mary of Burgundy the head of the House of Austria also became head of the order, though when the Habsburg house split into an Austrian and a Spanish line, the order split as well. The Batthyánys were members of the Hungarian aristocracy, and not always loyal to the Habsburgs. By the early 19th century they were beginning to show radical tendencies. One freed all the serfs on his southern Hungarian estates; another, much more famously, became the first Prime Minister of Hungary, after the country rose up and formed its own government in 1848, declaring itself independent of Austria. Chaos ensued. The ineffectual emperor Ferdinand abdicated in favour of the very young, very conscientious but very inexperienced Franz Joseph. After securing military aid from Russia, Franz Joseph defeated the Hungarians, dissolved their parliament, and put Batthány in front of the firing squad. Hungary never forgave him.

Turn left down Petrarca-Gasse and into the **Minoriten-Platz**, a pretty cobbled square dominated by the former Minorite church (*see p. 138*).

The Habsburg eagle breaks its chains and takes control of the tools of production. Doorway of the Ministry of Science and Education, formerly the Palais Starhemberg, on Minoriten-Platz.

A statue of the artist Rudolf von Alt (*see picture on p. 38*) sits outside with his sketchbook and pencil.

On your right at No. 5 the Ministry of Education, Science and Culture occupies the former **Palais Starhemberg**, built for Ernst Rüdiger von Starhemberg, who commanded the hard-pressed city garrison in their victorious stand against the Turks in 1683 (*see p. 15*), and who died in this house in 1701. Think of him at twelve noon, when all the church bells in Vienna begin to peal. After his victory it was decreed that at midday every day the church bells should ring out all over Christendom. In the former Austria-Hungary they still do.

With your back to the Starhemberg palace, turn left down Landhausgasse and right into **Herrengasse**. The elegant Classicist building on the corner (Herrengasse 13) is the former *Landhaus*, the County Hall of Lower Austria. When the capital of the province moved from Vienna to St Pölten in 1986, the building lost its function, though its role in history is assured. The popular revolution of 1848 was sparked off here when, on March 13th, the Hungarian lawyer-turned-freedom-fighter Lajos Kossuth, known for his inflammatory oratory, gave a speech in the *Landhaus* courtyard that sent his audience on an anti-Habsburg rampage.

Opposite the *Landhaus*, on the other side of the street, is the **Café Central** (*see p. 106*). An instant success when it opened in 1876, the nicotine-stained literati who had formerly haunted the Griensteidl on the Michaelerplatz moved *en bloc* to the Central when the Griensteidl closed down. Next door to the Central, at No. 12, is a house with two proto-Socialist bas-reliefs (1915). One, with the Latin legend "Machinery moves the world", shows bald men with beards hauling at an enormous cogwheel against a background of smoky factory chimneys. The other shows burly men hauling flour sacks off ships, with the motto "Healthy trade is the basis of happiness". They don't look conspicuously happy, it has to be said, perhaps because this building, formerly a bank and then the Chamber of Commerce, is not as Socialist Realist as it looks, being built in an age when the focus was still more on employers' profits than on employees' benefits.

You can either end the walk in the Central, or continue up the street to the reincarnated Griensteidl (*see p. 108*).

Small galleries and clock shops cluster around the old Gothic walls of the Kirche am Hof.

WALK THREE

Essling

Werdertor

Concordia-
platz

Renng.

Wipplinger

Graben

Rudolfs-
platz

Heinrichs-

Salz

Gölsdorf

Gon-
zagag.

Salzto

gries

Morzin-
platz

P

Franz-Josefs

Str.

Salzto

Rupr.
stiege

Maria am
Gestade

Passauer Pl.

Am
Gestade

Ma.
stiege

Schw.

Sterh.
erstiege

Vorlauf

str.

Stern

Marc-Aurel-

Str.

Rupr.
g. g.

Salz

Ruprechts-
kirche

Seitenst.

D.

g.

Raben str.

Färberg.

Gloss.

terg.

Himme

Altes
Rathaus

St. Salvator

Salvator g.

Jordan

Drahta
Juden-
pl.

Parisserg.

Schul-
terg.

lauben

Landskron g.

g.

Hoher
Markt

Judeng.

Fisch
hof

Friedmann-
Pl.

P

P

Kurrentg.

Kirche
am Hof

Steindlg.

Seitzerg.

Tuch-
lauben-
hof

Tuch-

Milch

Kühl-
fussg.

Kleeblattg.

Wildpret-
mkt.

Brandstätte

Bauern

markt

Kramer

Fisch-
hof

Lichten-
steg

Ertl

Rot

g.

Gutenberg

Bäck

Bognerg.

g.

P

Peters
pl.

Jung-
ferng.

St.
Peter

Freisingerg.

Goldschmiedg.

Jasomirgott
str.

Rotenturm

Wollzeile

Archbish.
Palace

Stroher

Graben

str.

Stephans-
pl.

Stephansdom

P

Schuler-

STEPHANSPL.

U1,3

Kärntner

Str.

Nikolai

Blut

Domg.

Dom

Singer

Grünangerg.

Stallburgg.

räuner

Jewish
Museum

Göttweiher
g.

Kärntner
Durch-
gang

Weihb

Lilieng.

Salzto

Salz

FROM AM HOF TO THE BERMUDA TRIANGLE

Am Hof lies adjacent to the Judenplatz, once the heart of the mediaeval Jewish quarter. The oldest church in Vienna, the Jugendstil Anker Clock, a relic of the Ottoman siege, and a house without a ground floor are all part of this walk.

This walk begins in **Am Hof**, site of the first royal residence in Vienna. You are standing on very old stones here. The wall around the Roman garrison town stretched along the axis formed by Naglergasse today, and Am Hof was the site - more or less - of the Roman *praetorium*. Today it is a wide cobbled square with some pretty façades and steep tiled roofs, dominated in its centre by a **statue of the Virgin Mary**, erected to give thanks for a lucky escape in 1644, during the Thirty Years War. The Swedish army had massed

The broad square of Am Hof, flanked by steep-roofed houses and a fire station.

Franz Matsch's Jugendstil Anker Clock (see p. 162). The figure on the left is Andreas von Liebenberg, mayor of Vienna during the siege of 1683, who lived in a house on Am Hof.

outside Vienna preparing to attack. Instead of responding with an army to repel them, the emperor fell to his knees in the Burgkapelle and prayed for deliverance. Not the most heroic of tactics, but it appears to have worked, as the Swedes did not attack the city after all. The statue faces the church of the Nine Choirs of Angels, or **Kirche am Hof**, from whose balcony Pope Pius VI dispensed blessings to the crowd in 1782, when he came to Vienna to remonstrate with Joseph II and his proposed measures to subordinate church to state (*see p. 133*).

On the opposite side of the square stand the buildings of the **Central Fire Department**, the most interesting of which is the ornate No. 10, the former city arsenal (hence the decorative weaponry all over the façade), with its huge golden-tongued double-headed eagle. It was Fischer von Erlach (*see p. 85*) who first suggested setting up a fire department, to combat the outbreaks of fire which continually threatened his creations. Nothing was done until 1848, however, when the revolutionary mob stormed the arsenal building, looking for weapons with which to equip themselves for street battle. In response the emperor moved the arsenal to the outskirts of the city, and set up a fire department here instead. Another building in the present Fire Department complex, No. 7, stands on the site of the house of Andreas von Liebenberg, Vienna's mayor at another crisis point in her history, 1683, the year of the Ottoman siege (see p. 15). Having done his utmost to boost his citizens' morale, Liebenberg died before he heard the news that the Turks had been defeated and his city was free.

With the fire station on your left, head diagonally to your right up Drahtgasse. You now enter a world of narrow, zig-zagging cobbled streets with names like Ledererhof (Leatherman's Court) and Färbergasse (Dyers' Street), named after the craftsmen who once colonised them. Drahtgasse brings you into the **Judenplatz**, once the heart of the Jewish quarter of Vienna, until the Jews were expelled in 1421. Their expulsion was the work of Duke Albrecht V, who demanded that every Jew convert to Christianity or face banishment. Those who refused baptism were expelled from the city and their property was seized. The house at **No. 2**, confiscated in 1421, came into the possession of a man called Johann Jordan, who put up the

relief of Christ's baptism in the River Jordan, partly as a play on his own name, and partly to rub in the point that the Christians had taken over. The Latin inscription below the baptism scene speaks disparagingly of the Jews as "heathen dogs".

The Judenplatz today is one of Vienna's most unspoilt enclaves, a delightful square of pavement cafés and handsome façades. A grimmer note is struck by the concrete bunker in the centre, the **Holocaust memorial** commemorating the murder of over 65,000 Austrian Jews in the death camps of Auschwitz, Belsen and Buchenwald between 1938 and 1945 (see p. 130).

Turn up Parisergasse now. At the bottom you will see the back of the Kirche am Hof, in its original Gothic form (the Baroque façade was added much later), with tiny little art galleries and watchmakers' shops built up against the walls. Turn left, crossing Schulhof, and loop left again into the picturesque **Kurrentgasse**, a street whose name has got nothing to do with water: it is named after the tax collectors who once lived in the area. Kurrentgasse brings you back into the Judenplatz, with Fischer von Erlach's former Bohemian Court Chancellery (1714) straight in front of you. Go towards it, and then turn right into Jordangasse, with the

Bieradies bar and restaurant on the corner. Narrow cobbled streets like Jordangasse, lined on both sides with buildings so tall that the sun only penetrates late in the day if at all, are typical of old Vienna. Today they are purely picturesque. In former centuries they were notoriously smelly and dirty, and ideal breeding grounds for typhus, the "Viennese disease", which claimed so many lives, including that of Franz Schubert. Nevertheless, the fine exterior appearance of the houses impressed foreign visitors, even though Lady Mary Wortley Montagu deplored the fact that the buildings contained such a hotch-potch of social classes that "the apartments of the greatest ladies, and even of the ministers of state, are divided but by a partition from that of a tailor or shoemaker".

Jordangasse takes you out into Wipplingerstrasse, with a grand but grimy building, the **former Town Hall** (*Altes Rathaus*), straight ahead of you. In its courtyard stands a fine fountain by Georg Raphael Donner (*see p. 146*) representing Andromeda chained to her rock, while a gallant Perseus gallops to the rescue.

Turn right up Wipplingerstrasse until you come to **Hoher Markt**. Built alongside the old Roman Via Principalis, this is the oldest square in Vienna - though sadly it does not look like it now. It was reduced to little more than a bomb site in the war. Nevertheless it has a claim on history as the possible place where Marcus Aurelius died in the year 180. In later centuries Vienna's main market took place here, and it was also, until the beginning of the 18th century, a place of public execution. Until 1848 the public pillory also stood here. Removing it was one of the 1848 revolutionaries' symbolic acts, signalling that the populace was no longer prepared to be ritually cowed. On the left of the square are two solid-looking buildings belonging to the Anker Insurance Company, linked one to the other by a second-floor bridge decorated on its underside by a globe with signs of the zodiac borne by four sphinxes. The clock which decorates the bridge, the famous **Anker Clock** (*see also p. 81*), was made in 1913 to designs by the Jugendstil painter and sculptor Franz Matsch, a friend and contemporary of Klimt. Every hour, when the clock strikes, a figure from Viennese history moves across its face. Many of them - as one would expect - are Habsburgs, but not all. Also included are Hans Puchsbaum (*see p. 37*), the mayor Andreas von Liebenberg, Joseph Haydn, and the minstrel Walther von der Vogelweide.

Georg Raphael Donner's
Andromeda Fountain,
in the courtyard of the
old Town Hall (Altes Rathaus)
on Wipplingerstrasse.

Do not go under the Anker bridge, but turn up Judengasse, which after a while opens out into a broadish square of old town houses. This area, known as the **Bermuda Triangle**, was once a throbbing hive of all-night bars, until local residents protested at the constant din. Now they are mostly closed down. Turn right down Seitenstettengasse, where you will find the **Stadttempel** synagogue at No. 4 (*see p. 131*). It was built by Josef Kornhäusel (1782-1860), a Classico-Biedermeier architect who built himself a tower-house with no street-level entrance, only an iron drawbridge, so that he could use it as a refuge from the suspicious nagging of his jealous wife (you can see it at Judengasse 14 - *Kornhäuselturm*). Once in Seitenstettengasse, go immediately left through an archway which takes you out directly in front of the oldest church in Vienna. The stumpy-towered **Ruprechtskirche**, dedicated to the early 8th-century saint St Rupert, is built on a sort of high platform, from where you can look down onto the Danube Canal. The houses along the canal quayside were destroyed in 1945, as the Nazis put up one last desperate effort against the advancing Allies. Before the river was regulated, navigable arms of it lapped around the foot of the plateau we are standing on. Street names like Salzgasse (Salt

St Rupert carrying a barrel of salt - his emblem - tucked into a forgotten nook at the back of the ancient Ruprechtskirche.

Street) commemorate the boats that came by and docked their cargoes to the waiting dealers and customs officials who occupied this part of town. St Rupert has a salty connection himself. Having successfully evangelised Regensburg, the Bavarian seat of the Babenberg dukes who ruled Austria in the early Middle Ages, he went on to develop the salt mines of Salzburg, where he also founded a monastery. His emblem is a barrel of salt - and perhaps the Danube salt dealers of the Salzgasse chose to dedicate their church to him because he was patron of their trade. In a forgotten corner at the back of the church stands a one-armed statue of St Rupert clutching his salt barrel.

Retrace your steps now and turn right down Sterngasse. The house at No. 3, formerly a Roman military bath house, has a **stone cannonball** suspended in a niche in its façade, with a plaque telling you that it was shot from a Turkish cannon stationed across the Danube in Leopoldstadt, in July 1683. Straight ahead is a vista of not particularly picturesque busy streets, with the delicate lacework spire of the church of **Maria am Gestade** (*see p. 74*) rising above them. Go down the steps, across Marc Aurel-Strasse into the continuation of Sterngasse, and then left into Fischerstiege, a street which takes its name from the fishermen who worked the waterways here, and built their church, Maria am Gestade, on a piece of elevated ground safe from the river floodwaters. Go up the steps and into Salvatorgasse. The **Salvatorkapelle** at No. 5 has a lovely Renaissance doorway, one of the few remaining examples of Renaissance architecture in Vienna. Originally the chapel was a private chapel in the home of the wealthy citizen and magistrate Otto

Haimo. When he took part in an anti-Habsburg uprising in 1308, however, his house and chapel were seized, by Friedrich the Handsome, and given to the city. The citizens of Vienna, instinctively anti-Habsburg as they were, never forgot Otto Haimo and his gallant stand. He even became something of a cult figure: under the corrupted name of Ottenhaim, he became a saint, and people would come to the chapel to worship him. Eventually things got so bad that in 1515 Pope Leo X sent a special Papal Bull banning the cult as a heresy and having the chapel remodelled and dedicated to the Holy Saviour. The present doorway dates from around 1520.

Turn right at the chapel and right again down Stoss im Himmel to come out in Wipplingerstrasse, with the back of the Bohemian Court Chancellery ahead of you, a mixture of Baroque and Classicist elements in true Fischer von Erlach style. To end the walk go straight on down Fütterergasse and back into the Judenplatz, where there are plenty of places to sit and relax or get a bite to eat (the Bieradies serves slices of bread with various toppings, which you eat off a wooden board with a knife and fork).

Overleaf: Early afternoon in Weihburggasse.

An Officer & A Gentleman

Prince Eugene of Savoy
(1663-1736)

Born in Paris, the son of the Count of Savoy and his Italian wife. When Eugene's father died, his mother embroiled herself in undignified squabbling for a place in Louis XIV's bed, until implicated in a poisoning scandal, whereupon she fled the country. Eugene, a pallid, sickly boy, was brought up by a sour-tempered aunt. He had always dreamed of joining the army, and when his application was rejected he left France to seek his fortune in Austria, despite the fact that Louis XIV had expressly banned Frenchmen from serving in the Imperial Army (see p. 16). Though Eugene was present at the siege of Vienna in 1683, his role in defeating the Turks was minimal. Three years later, though, together with Charles of Lorraine, he was ejecting them from Buda, after which he went from victory to victory, eventually winning back all of Hungary, plus Transylvania, Croatia and Slavonia. Eugene also fought alongside Marlborough at the Battle of Blenheim - against his native France - and in his later years turned his attention to statecraft, with a style of diplomacy that relied heavily on the use of bribes. In his last years Prince Eugene lost his touch, and found himself passed over in favour of other counsellors. As Frederick the Great of Prussia said, "he outlived his own glory". Maria Theresa was kinder. "When he died," she is reported to have said, "fortune stopped smiling on Austria".

Count Wenzel Anton Kaunitz
(1711-1794)

As State Chancellor, Kaunitz served first under Maria Theresa, then under her son, Joseph II, and finally under his brother, Leopold II. All three rulers were of a reforming turn of mind, and all three realised how precarious the vast Austrian empire was becoming. Kaunitz helped to reform the tax system, set up a rudimentary civil service, an imperial chancellery and something resembling a modern ministry of foreign affairs. Maria Theresa totally trusted Kaunitz, and largely let him have his own way. Joseph II kept him on a tighter rein, and Kaunitz found little outlet for his vanity - for vain he certainly was. He would spend hours at his dressing table, administered to by a whole retinue of servants, each of whom had a different function to perform: combing, powdering, perfuming, manicuring... Though he supported many of Jospeh's reforms, especially his desire to subordinate Church to State (Kaunitz was notably rude to Pope Pius VI when he visited Vienna to argue against the reform programme), he eventually grew out of patience with the emperor and came to view him as "the wrecker of the empire". Leopold II, Joseph's successor, was, if anything, even more radical. "The most important thing for princes to realise," he wrote to his sister Marie Christine, "is that all men are equal". Kaunitz, sensing that his day was well and truly over, resigned in 1792 and devoted the last two years of his life to his art collection.

Walk Four

Jordan- Schul- Lauben Landskron g. Hoher Markt Judeng. Friedmann- Pl. Griechen Hafersteig K.

Schulterg. Kammer-spiele Griechen k.

Seeblattg. Wildpret- mkt. Kramer Fisch hof markt Rot Lichten- steg Fleisch Köllnerhofg. Gras- hofg. Wolfeng. Dracheng. Kan. ope.

Kühfussg. Brandstätte Bauern Freisinger g. Jasomirgott str. Goldschmiedg. Ertl g. Gutenberg Sonnenfels Bäcker Heiligen- kreuzer- Hof Schönlatern Jesu. g. U. K.

Roterturm Wollzeile Archbish. Palace Strobel Windhaagg. Essigg. Dr.-Ig.-Seipel- Pl.

Stephans- pl. Stephansdom P Schuler- Woll str. Zedlitz

HANSPL. U1,3 Nikolai g. Blut Dorotg. Grünangerg. str.

Göttweiher g. Kärntner Durchgang Singer Kumpf g. Riemer Jakoberg. An der Hülben Stube

Weihburg Lilieng. Franziskaner- pl. Francisc. Church stätte Liebenberg g.

Neuer Kärntner Str. Blumen- stockg. Ball. Rauhensteing. P Coburgbastei Gartenbau- promenade

Donner Markt g. Himmelpfort P Seiler Weihburg

Marco- d'Aviano- g. Johannes 1. stätte

Maltheser Kirche St. Anna Anna St. Ursula

Berg. Kruger Seiler Fichte Schelling RING PARK Kursalo.

Walfisch str. Schwarzen Johannesg.

Mahler

EAST OF THE STEPHANSDOM

The winding alleys to the east of the Stephansdom include the streets where Mozart lived and died, where Schubert had his favourite tavern, and where Prince Eugene of Savoy built his magnificent Winter Palace.

This walk begins in the Stephansplatz, outside No. 5a. Go through the courtyard, which takes you out into the cobbled **Domgasse**. Here you will find the entrance to the **Figarohaus**, where Mozart lived (*see p. 121*) and, at No. 6, the **Haus zum Roten Kreuz** where, according to the legend, Vienna's first ever coffee house opened after a Polish trader called Kolschitzky found a bag of coffee beans left behind by the routed Ottoman army. Kolschitzky definitely did have a license to sell coffee, and

The Kleines Café on Franziskaner-Platz, with the Franciscan Monastery in the background.

Café Frauenhuber, one of several establishments in this part of town with a strong musical connection (see p. 172).

he did open a coffee house on this site, but it was not Vienna's first. That accolade goes to the patriarch of Vienna's Armenian community, who opened for business in 1685.

Retrace your steps a little way now, and turn left into **Blutgasse**, (Blood Alley), another cobbled street of tall house-fronts and hidden courtyards that gets its name - so the legend goes - from the blood of the Teutonic Knights, massacred here in the middle ages. At the end of the street, turn left into Singerstrasse (the pretty **church of the Teutonic Knights** is to your right at No. 7, and worth a detour) a

street originally colonised by dyers from Sünching in Bavaria (the name is a corruption - it has nothing to do with singers). Immediately opposite is the fine façade of the early 18th-century **Palais Neupauer-Brauner**, built for a newly-rich merchant family in the style of von Hildebrandt. The statues around the portal are a direct copy of the group on the Bohemian Court Chancellery in the Judenplatz (*see Walk 3*). Further along on the same side, at **No. 18**, is the house where the Fröhlich sisters gave their famous soirées, with Franz Schubert on the piano, and Franz Grillparzer pining for the love of Kathi Fröhlich, the girl he never got round to marrying (see p. 112). Walk on until you get to the corner of Grünangergasse on your left, erstwhile home of the Green Anchor tavern (No. 10), a favourite haunt of Schubert and his circle. One New Year's Eve after a long drinking session, Schubert and his friends emerged into the street to find it covered in snow. At the corner of Singerstrasse they started a snowball fight, though Schubert declined to join in.

Cross Singerstrasse now, and go into the **Franziskaner-Platz**, a pretty square of tall old houses, many with windows flush with the wall, generally a sign that they are 18th rather than 19th century. It is also home to one of Vienna's cosiest bars, the snug, stylishly old-fashioned **Kleines Café**. The grey and white building on your left, with its extraordinary "decoration" of sunken discs, is the **Franciscan Monastery** (1621), reprieved by Joseph II during his frenzy of convent closures in the late 18th century (see p. 133). Most of the other monasteries in this area - where they used to stand almost shoulder to shoulder - were not so fortunate. The Franciscan church adjoining the monastery has a *trompe l'oeil* high altar (1707) by Andrea Pozzo (see p. 135). The pillars are real, but the rest

is an illusion. Were you fooled?

At the end of the square, turn left into Weihburggasse to peep into the courtyard of No. 16 on the right, an excellent example of an early 18th century Baroque burgher's house. Leave Weihburggasse now, and turn through an archway into **Ballgasse**, a narrow, cobbled alley filled with restaurants and antique shops. At No. 8 you will find a furniture restorer, operating out of premises acquired in 1722 by the Vienna guild of carpenters, and which in turn occupied the premises of the former Ballhaus, a kind of early theatre where Italian and German troupes performed for the public, and which gave the alleyway its name.

At the Alte Blumenstock café (another former beer tavern beloved by Schubert) the alleyway forks. Take the right fork, with the Stadheuriger Gigerl on your left. This brings you out into **Rauhensteingasse** (Rough Stone Street), which boasts a rough stone cube hanging from a pair of iron pincers over the doorway on your left. The building at **No. 8** on the right stands on the site of the house where Count Walsegg came to see Mozart, to commission a Requiem Mass from him, in memory of his dead wife. Mozart wrote the *Requiem* in a semi-delirium, and died shortly before he finished it.

Rauhensteingasse brings you out into **Himmelpfortgasse**. The name means Gate of Heaven Street, and comes from a 14th century legend concerning a runaway nun from a convent that once stood here. At the time she made her escape she had been on gate duty, and had simply laid the key down beside a statue of the Virgin that stood guard beside the convent entrance, and walked away into the street. Seven years later, disillusioned with what she had found in the big bad world outside, she returned. And - miracle of miracles - no one had noticed her absence. Every time her name had come up on the gate duty rota, the statue had come down from its plinth and done it for her. The nunnery became known as the Convent of the Heavenly Gate Keeper, and the street eventually took on a corrupted form of that name.

Looking left down the street you will see, on your right, the long façade of Prince Eugene of Savoy's former **Winter Palace** (No. 8), with the gilded crowns and escutcheons above its three great entranceways glinting as they catch the light. Begun in 1696 by Fischer von Erlach (*see p. 85*), enlargements were carried out later on by von Hildebrandt, who completed the building in 1724. Prince Eugene died here in 1736. Each of the doorways is flanked with bas-reliefs showing heroic deeds and strongman acts aplenty, along with scenes from classical mythology. Today the palace is home to the Finance Ministry, and sadly its grand rooms (hidden from view from the street by *frou-frou* curtains) cannot be visited. If you talk nicely to the porter, he might let you in to see a glimpse of the grand stairway, borne by Atlas figures in the style that von Hildebrandt so loved.

Opposite the Winter Palace is the *"kaiserlich und königlich"* bric à brac shop, selling broken radios, old teddy bears, souvenir mugs, plaster busts of Wagner and signed photographs of Romy Schneider in her film role as Empress Elisabeth. If you haven't the strength for a browse, collapse into one of the red plush seats of the **Café-Restaurant Frauenhuber**, founded in 1788 by Maria Theresa's personal chef, and where Mozart and Beethoven once gave concerts to the public.

Facing page: The picturesque Griechengasse, which leads from Fleischmarkt down towards the Danube Canal.

WALK FIVE

Salztorbr.

Gölsdorf g.

platz

Gon-
zagag-

Salztor

Lilien-
brunn-

Gredlerstr.

STR.

Lilien-
g.

N.21

Sch-
hof

Morzin-
platz

gries

Str.

Marienbr.

SCHWEDENPL.

TABOR

Vorlauf
str.

Franz-Josefs-

Rupr.
stege

Schwe

Stern

Marc-Aurel-

Salzg.

Ruprechts-
kirche

U1,4

P

Rupr.
g.pl.

Seitenst.

N,1,2

21

Franz-Jose

Hoher

Judeng.

D.

g.

Griechen

Hafnersteig

Kai

Laurenzerberg

Au-

Raben str.

str.

Kammer-
spiele

g.

Fleisch

Griechen k.

markt

winkel

bastei

Markt

Fisch-
hof

Rot

Friedmann-
Pl.

Lichten-

markt

steg

Köllnerhofg.

Gras

hofg.

Wolfeng.

Hauptpost
amt

Kramer

Ertl

g.

Gutenberg

Sonnenfels

Heiligen-
kreuzer
Hof

Dracheng.

P

Kammer-
oper

Rotenturm

Wollzeile

Bäcker

Wind-

Schönlatern

Univers.
K.

Barbara
g.

Archbish.
Palace

Essigg.

Strobe

Riemerg.

Jesu

g.

Dr.-Ig.-Seipel-
Pl.

Predigerg.

Dominikaner

hans-

P

Schuler-

Domg.

str.

Dominican
Church

Stephansdom

Nikolai
g.

Blut

Wollzeile

Dr.-Karl-
Lueger-P

Singer

Grünangerg.

str.

Zedlitz

bastei

RING

Lilieng.

Weihburg

Kumpf

Riemer

Jakoberg.

Stubenbastei

g.

Schube

Rauhensteing.

Blumen-
stockg.

Franziskaner-
pl.

str.

An der
Hülben

Liebenberg-

Cobdeng.

g.

Am

Bait

Francisc.
Church

g.

Coburgbastei

g.

Gartenbast

melpfort

Seiler

Weit

stätte

BETWEEN WOLLZEILE AND FLEISCHMARKT

This part of town contains some of Vienna's most picturesque streets, full of places to eat and drink, and as bustling with life now as when they were home to a prosperous community of merchants and traders.

This walk begins in the **Diglas café** on Wollzeile. Coming out into the street, turn left, and walk up Wollzeile, past the proud shop sign of the *k. u. k. Hofzuckerbäcker L. Heiner*

on your right. Even though designating oneself purveyor to the *k. und k.* (imperial and royal) court is meaningless today, plenty of old businesses still make much of the old distinction in their shopfronts.

When you reach the old-fashioned A. Katzer stationer's, turn right into a **narrow parade of shops** that links Wollzeile with Bäckerstrasse. Just inside, on the right, is the

View of Fleischmarkt, looking towards the neo-Byzantine Greek Orthodox church.

Late mediaeval wall painting in Bäckerstrasse showing a cow playing backgammon with a wolf, and said to be an allegory of the tussle between Catholics and Protestants.

popular Figlmüller, where office workers and businessmen recharge their batteries at lunchtime with enormous *Wiener Schnitzels* and glasses of dry white wine.

Walk through the passage, which brings you out into Lugeck, a small square dominated to your right by the enormous 19th-century Wüstenrot building, with its twin turrets and statue of Friedrich III over the immense doorway. Friedrich III was never a popular ruler (*see p. 40*), but it was he who gave Vienna the right to use the double-headed eagle as its badge. Turn right up **Bäckerstrasse**. This ancient street was once the Roman highway to Carnuntum, capital of the province, the ruins of which lie halfway between Vienna and the Hungarian border. In the middle ages the street was tramped by itinerant craftsmen, and many of its houses are of mediaeval origin. At **No. 7** on the left hand side is a house with pretty painted glass signboards advertising Franz Nemetschke's piano shop. Go through the gateway and you find yourself in a **Renaissance courtyard**. The arcades are now walled in, but the balustrades and rounded arches are still clearly visible. In the left-hand corner at the back, there are two stone drinking troughs fixed to the wall, in the part of the courtyard where horses were once stabled. Now pushchairs are stabled here instead. The artist Friedrich von Amerling (*see p. 58*) once lived in this building, and stored his wrought iron collection here. The wrought iron is still there, rusting gently on the first floor exterior wall.

Continuing up Bäckerstrasse, pass the **Café Alt Wien** on your left, a fiercely old-fashioned haunt that rarely sees the sunlight and has barely seen the 21st century. But for the contemporary fly posters all over the walls, one might be forgiven for thinking that the world had ended in 1965. Across the street at **No. 12** you will see a fragment of 17th-century wall painting. A bespectacled cow is playing backgammon with a wolf, neatly manoeuvring a counter with its hoof. The image has been interpreted as a satire on Protestantism: the wily, lupine Lutherans trying to outwit the plodding (but learned) Catholic Church.

Go down the alleyway immediately opposite the cow, cross the next street, and go ahead, slightly to the right, into **Schönlaterngasse**. This is rightly famed as one of Vienna's prettiest streets. It takes its name from an ornamental lamp, the Schöne Laterne, a copy of which you will see fixed to the wall of No. 6. The original is preserved in the Vienna History Museum. Today the street offers a selection of restaurants and good-looking bars, and makes an excellent place to come for a pre-dinner drink or an after-dinner nightcap and stroll. At No. 7 on the left, just where the road curves, is the so-called **Basiliskenhaus**. It gets its name from the legend of a monstrous basilisk, half lizard and half bird, which took up residence in the well and poisoned the water supply of the whole area, and whose hideous visage turned anyone who beheld it to stone. A baker's apprentice who lived in the

house then hit upon the idea of holding up a mirror to the basilisk's face. Sure enough, the creature fell down in a deadly swoon, and then spontaneously combusted. The name of the baker's apprentice was Georg - clearly this is a homespun Vienna version of the legend of St George and the dragon. Just inside the doorway, behind a grille on the right, is the shaft of the old well.

With the Basiliskenhaus in front of you, turn left into **Heiligenkreuzerhof**, a broad cobbled yard, home to the University of Applied Arts and a couple of violin makers' workshops. Though the architecture is largely 18th century, the Hof is built up on a very old, early mediaeval nucleus of buildings, belonging originally to the Cistercian monastery at Heiligenkreuz, east of Vienna. That monastery is most famous today as being the burial place of Mary Vetsera (*see p. 26*). When her body and Prince Rudolf's were discovered, in an attempt to avoid a scandal, Mary's father and uncle wedged her corpse in a sitting position between them in their carriage, and galloped post haste to Heiligenkreuz, where she was buried without a whisper.

The most famous of the Cistercians is St Bernard (d. 1153), Abbot of Clairvaux, and it is to him that the chapel on the immediate left as you enter the Hof is dedicated. St Bernard brought austerity to a fine art. He should not be confused with the other St Bernard, patron saint of mountaineers and dispenser of drams of brandy. At the beginning of his tenure as abbot, Bernard of Clairvaux had his monks eating boiled beech leaves. Halfway along the right-hand wall there is a small statue of him, holding cross and nails.

A wooden postern gate at the far end of Heiligenkreuzerhof takes you out into Grashofgasse. At the end of it turn right and then right again into **Fleischmarkt**. This ancient market-place, former site of the butchers' guildhall, was colonised in the 18th century by Greeks, who controlled Vienna's trade with the Balkans and the Levant. Immediately in front of you is the red brick and gold Greek Orthodox church, with the Issakides carpet shop attached to it, proof that Levantine traders are still active in the area today. Walk towards the church, noting the decorated upper-floor façade of **No. 7** on your left (1899), originally a building belonging to the Julius Meinl coffee company, and sporting reliefs showing coffee being grown and harvested and then shipped to the dainty tables of genteel Vienna. The three coats of arms are those of the three major trading ports of Hamburg, Trieste and the City of

London. A plaque in the building's entranceway tells you that Billy Wilder (Hollywood director of *Some Like it Hot, see p. 181*) lived here as a schoolboy, between 1914 and 1924.

Immediately before the church, also on the left, is the picturesque, ivy-hung **Griechenbeisl** restaurant (*see p. 207*), from which the equally picturesque Griechengasse leads downhill towards the Danube Canal. In the courtyard of No. 7 you will see a Gothic residential "tower block", the only surviving **mediaeval skyscraper** of several which once stood in the area.

The Griechenbeisl was formerly a favourite haunt of Greek merchants and local mercers. The famous song *Ach du Lieber Augustin* was said to have been composed here (around 1678), by the minstrel and piper Augustin N, whose relief now adorns the restaurant façade. His song laments the sorry state of Vienna, which was suffering an outbreak of plague: "There was partying every day. Now all we've got is plague: just a corpse jamboree. Oh, Augustin, you might as well just go and lie down in your grave!" Augustin's own life was saved, so they say, by his inordinate fondness for wine. Once, after a night of particularly reckless carousing, he fell into a drunken sleep in the street. Mistaken for a plague victim and taken for dead, his supine body was

The house with the Renaissance courtyard on Bäckerstrasse, once home to the artist Friedrich Amerling, still contains his collection of wrought iron.

hauled away and flung into a mass grave. He woke the next morning feeling fit as a flea, and climbed out of the pit, miraculously uninfected. His survival was popularly attributed to the huge amount he had drunk - which is perhaps not as mad an idea as all that. Wine is known to possess anti-bacterial qualities; in fact people routinely used to add it to their drinking water to reduce the risk of cholera.

Opposite the church, at No. 18, is the so-called **Toleranzhaus**. It was from the house that formerly stood on this site - where the Greek and Jewish districts of Vienna meet - that Joseph II's Edict of Tolerance was proclaimed in 1782 (*see p. 132*). Later the same year work began on constructing the **Greek Orthodox church**. The 18th-century original had neither bell tower nor street-facing portal, because these were proscribed for non-Catholic places of worship. Today's Byzantinesque building is the work of Theophil Hansen (*see p. 69*), and was done at a time (1887) when Austria's rulers were much more *laissez faire* about such things. The Greek community gave Hansen the commission because before coming to Vienna he had worked for many years in Athens. The church is usually kept locked, but an elderly lady emerges at intervals to give little rote-learned tours. The late 18th-century iconostasis is worth seeing. After the tour the lady likes her palm to be crossed with silver. There is a donation box for the purpose as well, but she prefers to take a few euro cents direct.

Across the third floor of the Toleranzhaus is an inscription that reads: "This house is transient; Joseph's fame everlasting. He gave us tolerance. His tolerance gave him immortality". The building at **No. 19** (now home to the central Post Office and the Castelnuovo Pizzeria) is the remodelled former Dominican convent of St Lawrence, dissolved as part of Joseph's implacable anti-

monastic reform programme. One man's tolerance is another man's bane. The pluralist tradition of this area is still alive and well, though. Diagonally opposite the Griechenbeisl is a courtyard which is home to Vienna's Buddhist Society, as well as to a New Age bookshop and vegan restaurant. Take your pick to end the walk. In summer the Griechenbeisl has a terrace on the street, protected from cars by thick shrubs. Otherwise, retrace your steps to the Schönlaterngasse, where the Lukas bar at No. 2 solves the religious debates by using an old altarpiece as a shelving system for bottles of liqueurs and spirits.

Crowds gather in Schönlaterngasse to hear the story of the loathsome Basilisk.

SILVERSCREEN WIEN - A SELECTION

BILLY WILDER

The man who rose to be one of the Hollywood's greatest ever directors was born Samuel Wilder in a little Austro-Hungarian town (Sucha, now in Poland) in 1906. His father ran a chain of railway cafeterias. His mother had visited America and developed a fixation with Buffalo Bill: she nicknamed her son Billy. Wilder moved to Vienna as a boy. After leaving university he went to Berlin where he got a job as a paid dancer, entertaining lonely ladies at *thés dansants*, from where he moved on to a career as a journalist. When the tide of Nazism began to rise, he went to seek his fortune in the US, where he had numerous successes as a director and screenplay writer. *Ninotchka, Sunset Boulevard, The Seven Year Itch, Double Indemnity, Some Like it Hot* and *Irma La Douce* are just a handful of Wilder's many classics. He died in Beverly Hills in 2002.

HEDY LAMARR

"The most beautiful woman in the world" was born Hedwig Kiesler in Vienna in 1914, the daughter of a bank manager and a pianist. Her acting ability was discovered by Max Reinhardt, who gave her work in Berlin: but it was never for her ability that she became best known. The 1933 film *Ecstasy*, in which she skinny dips in a lake and runs naked through a forest, rocketed her to instant fame. Her breasts were the first ever bared on screen, and the film was banned in the US. In 1937 she escaped her arms-manufacturer husband and went to Hollywood, reinvented as Hedy Lamarr. Her dark beauty formed a stark and fascinating contrast to the traditional platinum peaches of the day. Her greatest box-office hit was *Samson and Delilah* (1949). Lamarr died in 2000, having lived in almost total seclusion for many years.

THE THIRD MAN

Based on a novel by Graham Greene, this classic film of post-war Vienna shows a city divided into four zones, occupied by the allied powers, and poverty-stricken. Old ladies wrap themselves in eiderdowns to keep warm, down-and-outs haunt the dustbins, and racketeers are rife. Most unscrupulous of these is Harry Lime (Orson Welles), who finally meets his end in the municipal sewers, in what must be one of the most famous scenes in European cinema. The Josefsplatz, the Hotel Sacher, the Casanova Revue Theatre and the ferris wheel in the Prater are the film's other famous backdrops. Today you can follow in the footsteps of Lime on a Third Man Tour (see p. 221).

PART IV

PLACES TO GO

This section offers two trips outside the centre of town, one to the summer palace of Schönbrunn, east of the city centre, and the other to the suburb of Grinzing, famous for its vineyards and *Heurigen* (wine taverns).

Details of how to get to each are included in the text.

p. 183 Schönbrunn

p. 198 Grinzing

p. 200 A Good Day Trip

183

SCHÖNBRUNN

District 13, Schönbrunner Schlossstrasse.
Underground line 4 from Karlsplatz to Schloss Schönbrunn (direction Hütteldorf)

The summer palace of Schönbrunn, with its vast ornamental park, was Maria Theresa's favourite residence, and it is mainly to her that it owes its present character. After her death (1780) it was little used, until Napoleon installed himself here in 1809 when he invaded Vienna. The emperor Franz Joseph was born here, and he died here too, in 1916. On November 11th 1918, in the Chinese Room, the last Emperor of Austria, Karl I, signed a letter renouncing all involvement in Austrian state affairs. The palace and its park are now open to the public, and are a favourite weekend destination for Viennese families.

Until the mid 16th century there was a mill on the site, which made use of the waters of the river Wien. On one of his hunting forays to the area, the emperor Maximilian II was so impressed by the delicious spring water that he bought the mill and converted it into a hunting lodge. In 1683 the successor to that building was hit by Turkish artillery and burst into flames. Ten years later Johann Bernhard Fischer von Erlach (*see p. 85*) was commissioned to produce designs for an imperial summer residence. He came up with a plan for a truly enormous palace, situated on top of the Schönbrunner Berg, where the Gloriette (*see p. 195*) stands now, a design that was intended to put Versailles well and truly in the shade. Tempting as it no doubt would have been to trounce *le roi soleil*, the proposal was deemed far too expensive, and von Erlach was asked to submit another, which he did and which was accepted. Construction work on the main building was completed in 1713. The palace that stands today is not nearly as Baroque as von Erlach's original, because it was altered and modified under Maria Theresa after 1743. The largely Rococo interiors are the work of her court architect Nikolaus Pacassi.

NB: Winter and early spring are the best times to visit Schönbrunn: in high summer its grand dimensions are dwarfed and dominated by the sheer number of visitors and tour-bus stampedes. Opening times are given on p. 193.

The main gate to the palace is flanked by slender obelisks still topped by the golden eagles which Napoleon put there to imprint his stamp on the place. The main gate takes you into the *cour d'honneur*, the *Ehrenhof*, with its two small ornamental fountains. It was in this courtyard that a 17-year-old tradesman's apprentice, Friedrich Staps, ran at Napoleon with a kitchen knife as he was presiding over the changing of the guard in 1809. Immediately to the right of the gate (behind the souvenir shop and café) is the *Schlosstheater*. Life in such a huge palace would be intolerable without a theatre, Maria Theresa maintained, and so she built one, initially to provide a bit of family fun for herself and her children, who enjoyed amateur theatricals, though later it became the venue for premieres of operas by Gluck and Mozart, and professional actors were invited to give performances to a select audience. Napoleon requested a performance of Racine's *Phèdre* here. The request was granted, but the language of the production was German. Napoleon had to follow the performance from a French text in his lap.

THE PALACE

There are three main things to see inside Schönbrunn. The apartments used by Franz Joseph and Elisabeth; those used by Maria Theresa and her family; and the decorative, bijou cabinets of lacquer and *chinoiserie*.

NB: Because the rooms and exhibits themselves are mostly uncaptioned, in order to know what you are looking it you need to join a guided tour or use an audio guide (included in the ticket price). This means that you will either be confined to your own little sonic world, or be part of a large group, unable to tour the rooms at your own pace. The descriptions that follow of the major apartments of Schönbrunn aim to solve that problem. The rooms are numbered on the plan below in the order that you will visit them. Only rooms of particular interest are described.

SCHÖNBRUNN - FIRST FLOOR PLAN

Garden Side

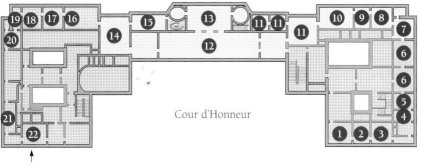

Cour d'Honneur

Tickets

  Franz Joseph & Elisabeth's apartments

  Maria Theresa's apartments

  Decorative apartments

❶ FRANZ JOSEPH'S AUDIENCE CHAMBER: The first emperor to use this room for audiences was Joseph II (1780-1790), who began the tradition in the first place. Any subject who wished to bring a request or a grievance before the emperor was theoretically allowed to do so - it would be interesting to know how many plucked up the courage. Franz Joseph took the obligation seriously and granted over a quarter of a million audiences during the course of his reign, though most were not to humble peasants from far-flung corners of his realm. The room is furnished with handsome walnut panelling and a beautiful gilt-wood chandelier.

❷ FRANZ JOSEPH'S STUDY: Franz Joseph's predilection for the colour brown is seen here in the wall hangings and the upholstery. His choice of the spartan over the luxurious is reflected in the simple bentwood chair at his desk. His obsession with his wife, whose *farouche* emotional nature he never understood, is betrayed by the multiple portraits of her that hang here. Even the portrait of Franz Joseph himself has a bust of Elisabeth lurking in the background.

❸ FRANZ JOSEPH'S BEDROOM: Once again, the colour scheme is brown, and the autumnal leaf-pattern upholstery is the same as in the study. As in his bedroom in the Hofburg, Franz Joseph has a plain, narrow iron bed. This particular bed is the one in which the aged emperor died, in November 1916. Alarmed by the disastrous turn the First World War was taking, he had asked to be woken at three the following morning, as there was "so much to be done", and died in his sleep. Hearing the news Katharina Schratt, his estranged mistress, came to say her goodbyes, laying two white roses on his breast. He lay in state for five days as the people of Vienna, probably knowing that they were on the losing end of the war, filed past to pay their last respects - not only to a dead man, but to the end of an era.

On your way out of the room, look left to see Franz Joseph's water closet, complete with padded seat and ventilation shafts in the ceiling. Left to his own devices, the emperor would probably not have bothered to have it put in. Sisi, however, was keen on running water and electricity. Thanks to her, Schönbrunn's lighting was fully electric by 1891, and it was Edison himself who helped install it.

❹ ELISABETH'S DRESSING ROOM: Note the scales, included in the furnishings so that Sisi could keep an eagle eye on her weight to make sure that it never went above her ideal 50 kg - not much for a woman who stood 172 cm in her bedroom slippers. All the bottles and brushes and mirrors are the originals, including a travelling vanity chest. Photographs of the empress adorn the walls, some of them quite obviously touched up to remove any signs of advancing age.

❺ ELISABETH'S BEDROOM: Here Sisi replaced the 18th-century red brocade wall hangings with blue silk, giving for a somewhat lighter, more feminine atmosphere. In theory this was the imperial couple's marital bedroom, though after the first few years of their life together, Franz Joseph probably spent relatively little time here, apart from the brief reconciliation period that came in 1866-67, when he was licking his wounds after his defeat at Königgrätz (see p. 22) and the execution of his brother Maximilian (see p. 46). Elisabeth was a woman to whom extreme emotion came easily, but Franz Joseph was not the man to inspire it. It is doubtful whether any real, living, flesh-and-blood man could have satisfied her thirst for romance. A strange mixture of burning passion and icy *froideur*, Elisabeth's name was never convincingly linked with any lover's, though perhaps there may have been something between her and the dashing English captain Bay Middleton, with whom she went fox-hunting in Ireland. Poor Franz Joseph was out of his depth: he longed for tranquil domestic contentment.

❻ ELISABETH'S SALON & RECEPTION ROOM: Elisabeth had the walls of the first room, her small private salon, re-hung in light-coloured silk. It was here that she would retreat into her own world, read the romantic poetry of Heine, compose gushing verse of her own, and study Hungarian with her trusted Magyar ladies-in-waiting or modern Greek with her funny little tutor Christomanos, whom she took everywhere with her, and who hung about her, half in love with her, like a devoted spaniel. When duty called for a formal reception, she would use the room next door, with its classic Schönbrunn white-and-gilt *boiserie*. It is dominated by a portrait of the 20 year-old Franz Joseph in Field Marshal's uniform. Before Elisabeth, another unhappy empress haunted these apartments: Maria Josepha of Bavaria, second wife of Joseph II. Chancellor Kaunitz (*see p. 166*) forced the marriage on Joseph, but it was a dismal failure. Joseph found poor Josepha physically repulsive,

describing her has having "a spotty face and appalling teeth". It would be interesting to know whether the beautiful Sisi - whose own teeth were also famously appalling, and who was a direct descendant of the lonely, unloved Josepha - ever thought about her.

7 THE NURSERY: This room forms part of the suite used by Maria Theresa's children. The empress (she was never empress in her own right, only as the wife of the Holy Roman Emperor; her title as ruler of Austria was Archduchess) had 16 children, of whom three died as babies and three in their teens. This room contains portraits by an unknown artist of the six surviving daughters:

Maria Anna, 1738-1789 (*immediately in front of you as you enter*): Her father's favourite, strong-willed and tomboyish, interested in

The formal gardens of Schönbrunn by Bernardo Bellotto, nephew of Canaletto.

botany and numismatics. She never married, and became an abbess in Klagenfurt.

Maria Elisabeth, 1743-1808 (*next to Maria Anna*): The most beautiful of the daughters, Maria Elisabeth was lined up to make a dazzling marriage, until smallpox took away her looks and suddenly no one would have her. She also became an abbess.

Marie Christine, 1742-1798 (*left of the entrance*): Maria Theresa's favourite, a great lover of art and a keen amateur painter (*see Room 19 below*). She was the only daughter to make a love-match: to Prince Albert of Saxe-Teschen (*see p. 52*).

Maria Amalia, 1746-1804 (*next to the bathroom door*): Of all the daughters the least close to her mother. She married the Duke of Parma.

Maria Karoline, 1752-1814 (*holding a paper with portrait*): When her elder sister Maria Josepha died aged 16 in 1767, Maria Karoline was packed off to take her place as wife to the bluff, uncouth King of Naples, famous for his misshapen nose and his habit of eating pasta with his fingers. Maria Karoline was energetic and intelligent where her husband was idle and dissipated. She took over the business of ruling Naples and preserving it (with the help of Nelson and Sir William Hamilton) from the French threat.

Marie Antoinette, 1755-1793 (*next to Maria Karoline*). The ill-fated queen of France, who met her death on the guillotine.

Leading off the nursery is a little cabinet where the unloved empress Maria Josepha is thought to have taken her solitary breakfasts.

The embroidered nosegays on the walls are the work of Maria Theresa and her daughters.

8 THE YELLOW SALON: Used variously as a bedroom by Maria Theresa and her sister-in-law, as well as as a study by Franz I. It is hung with paintings by the Swiss artist Jean Etienne Liotard, probably from Maria Theresa's own collection.

9 THE BALCONY ROOM: This room was used latterly as the bedroom of Archduchess Maria Valerie, youngest daughter of Franz Joseph and Elisabeth, born in 1867, at a time when the couple had briefly patched up their differences. Elisabeth lavished a stifling affection on Valerie, calling her the great love of her life. The walls are hung with more portraits of Maria Theresa's children. Four of her sons survived to adulthood:

Joseph, 1741-1790 (*central figure in the central portrait*): Became Holy Roman Emperor after his father's death in 1765, at which date Maria Theresa also elevated him to the position of co-regent. His brief reign as Archduke of Austria (1780-1790) was a time of great reform (*see p. 132*).

Leopold, 1747-1792 (*left-hand figure in the same portrait*): A gifted administrator and a sensitive reformer (*see also p. 166*), Leopold was Grand Duke of Tuscany until his brother Joseph's death. His reign in Austria was all too brief - a mere two years.

Ferdinand, 1754-1806 (*top left-hand portrait on the right wall*): Became Duke of Modena,

Portrait of Maria Theresa's son Joseph II with his brother Leopold. Both men were keen reformers who worried that Austria could easily go the same way as revolutionary France, where their sister, Marie Antoinette, was queen.

Theresa's Rococo palace, was used by Maria Theresa for *soirées* and evening entertainments. It was here that the six year-old Mozart charmed her with his skills on the harpsichord in 1762. A shallow, built-in cupboard houses a little altar where newly-appointed ministers of state were traditionally sworn in.

11 THE ROSA ROOMS: The name of these three rooms comes from the artist of the wall paintings, Joseph Rosa, whom Joseph II appointed as keeper of the Imperial Picture Gallery. The painting immediately on your left as you enter the first room shows a romantic view of Schloss Habsburg, the dynasty's original seat in Switzerland. The painting was commissioned by Maria Theresa.

12 THE GREAT GALLERY: The grandest room that Pacassi created for Maria Theresa, this great banqueting hall and ballroom is decorated with gilt-capitalled Corinthian pilasters running the length of the walls, and gilded groupings of martial implements (breastplates, swords, banners, *fasces* and halberds) at intervals above the cornice. The three ceiling frescoes were painted by an Italian

and led the Austrian army to defeat against Napoleon in 1805, just days before the Battle of Trafalgar. His ruthless regime in Italy contributed to growing Italian resentment of Austrian rule.

Max Franz, 1756-1801 (*top left-hand portrait on left wall*): Became Elector and Archbishop of Cologne. A man of great humanity. As he said himself, "I have no wife and family, no mistresses or bastard children to provide for," so he spent his life trying to help the poor and needy. He gave a stipend to the struggling young Beethoven when he came to Vienna to study under Haydn.

10 THE MIRROR ROOM: This room, which perfectly preserves the style of Maria

P L A C E S   T O   G O

190

artist in 1762. The one above your head as you enter depicts the fruits of peace: agriculture, trade, art and science. The farther one depicts the art of war. The central fresco shows the crown lands of the empire paying homage to Maria Theresa and Franz Stephan.

13 **THE SMALL GALLERY & CHINESE CABINETS:** The smaller, garden-facing gallery was used by Maria Theresa for family events and evening gatherings of family and close friends. On each side of the gallery is a small *chinoiserie* cabinet where gilded Rococo frames enclose lacquerwork panels, round the edges of which the golden swirls are twisted outwards to form brackets supporting blue and white porcelain vases. Both cabinets have secret stairways leading to them, and Maria Theresa used to summon Kaunitz (*see p. 166*) here for secret confabulations

Marie Antoinette, Maria Theresa's fun-loving, irresponsible daughter who ended her life on the guillotine in 1793.

during the summer. In fact Kaunitz was in demand so frequently that he even had his own summer residence just outside the Schönbrunn park gates.

14 **THE CEREMONIAL HALL:** The star exhibit of this room is an amazingly detailed scene by the Swedish artist Martin van Meytens (Maria Theresa's court painter) and his studio. It shows the Bourbon princess Isabella of Parma's ceremonial entry into Vienna as the bride of Archduke Joseph, later Joseph II. Isabella sits stiffly upright, fluttering with nerves in her carriage of blue and white froth, being subjected to last-minute advice from an eager-faced attendant. The procession is seen approaching the Hofburg, about to pass through an elaborate triumphal arch. The building of the National Library with its two golden globes can clearly be seen in the background. Thanks to the diplomatic efforts of Chancellor Kaunitz, Austria and France were - temporarily at least - on friendly terms. To seal this friendship it was decided that Joseph should take a Bourbon bride. The two teenagers were married in 1760, and were blissfully happy for three years. Isabella died together with her infant daughter in 1763, plunging both Joseph and Maria Theresa into profound gloom.

Further paintings by Meytens in this room include the wedding ceremony itself (in the Augustinerkirche, *see p. 134*), the wedding banquet in the Hofburg (something of a scrum, by the looks of it, with more people spectating than sitting down to eat), and a portrait of Maria Theresa, the ultimate matriarch, in a huge hooped skirt covered with lace.

15 THE EQUESTRIAN ROOM: Noted for a series of horse portraits executed for Maria Theresa's father, Karl VI, whose great legacy to Vienna is the Spanish Riding School (*see pp. 43-4*). The artist, Johann Georg Hamilton, was the son of a Scots still-life painter who had emigrated to the continent.

16 THE BLUE CHINESE SALON: The *chinoiserie* wallpaper dates from the 18th century. It was here, on 11th November 1918, that the emperor Karl I - whose bust is placed in front of the window - signed a paper renouncing all involvement in Austrian state affairs. He refused to abdicate entirely, and was sent into exile (*see p. 26*). The pair of tables with gilt legs and *pietra dura* tops decorated with fruit, flowers and birds, are of Florentine make.

17 THE LACQUER ROOM: Glossy walnut panelling is almost entirely covered in elaborately carved gilt frames containing genuine oriental panels, purchased for an enormous sum by Maria Theresa, who had thrown herself into the task of creating jewel-box apartments to console herself for the death of her husband, Franz Stephan, in 1765. His

posthumous portrait hangs on the main wall in a frame surmounted by the crown of the Holy Roman Empire. It was commissioned by his widow, as was the double portrait of the two sons who were later to become emperors, Joseph and Leopold. The portrait of Leopold's wife, Maria Ludovica of Spain, hangs opposite. Mozart composed the opera *La Clemenza di Tito* to celebrate Leopold's coronation as King of Bohemia. Maria Ludovica dismissed the piece as "German rubbish". Whether she held the same opinion of her husband the gossip-mongers don't say. The rather heavy, crude-looking floor is not contemporary with the room, but was laid in the 19th century.

18 THE NAPOLEON ROOM: Napoleon occupied Vienna twice, in 1805 and 1809. The second time round he installed himself in Schönbrunn, and it was thought that he used this room as his bedroom. Later in the same year the Austrian army defeated him at Aspern, just east of Vienna, and peace terms were drawn up in the Treaty of Schönbrunn, signed in this palace, with the Austrian archduchess Marie Louise (*see picture on p. 10*) as the sacrificial offering: she was to marry Napoleon. The son of that marriage, Napoleon Franz, was given the title King of Rome, and held it until Napoleon finally fell in 1815, whereupon he became the Duke of Reichstadt. It was a piece of terrible bad luck for the poor boy to be fathered by Napoleon. Deeming him potentially dangerous, Metternich refused to let him leave

The Schöner Brunnen (beautiful spring), which gives Schönbrunn its name. It once supplied the drinking water for the imperial family.

Schönbrunn, where he lived for almost all of his lonely life. He died of consumption in this room in 1832, at the age of 21. The room's furnishings include his emaciated death mask and a crested lark in a cage. He is purported to have claimed the bird as his only true friend in the world.

19 THE PORCELAIN ROOM: The elaborately carved swags of fruit and foliage and the crossed parasols that adorn this room are painted blue and white in imitation of Chinese porcelain, hence the room's name. The "Chinese" drawings in pale blue ink are the work of Maria Theresa's consort, Franz Stephan, and their daughter Marie Christine. Franz Stephan and Marie Christine, together with Marie Christine's husband Albert, founder of the Albertina graphics collection, are the subjects of three of the four cameo heads. The design for the room, which makes heavy use of vertical axes and has nothing whatever of the Rococo about it, was the work of Joseph II's wife Isabella of Parma, the fourth head.

20 THE MOGHUL OR "MILLIONS" ROOM: The rosewood panelling and golden *rocaille* frames that fill this room seem almost crude and unsubtle when contrasted with the exquisite Indian miniatures inserted into

them. Each represents a scene from 16th and 17th-century Moghul court life - elephants and horses carrying warriors into battle, a prince out hunting, a princess at her toilet, meals being prepared and eaten - and each is a little gem for the delicacy of its artistry and the wealth of its detail. The room also contains a little portrait of Maria Theresa in widow's weeds. The amount of money she spent on these rooms drove her son Joseph to distraction.

21 THE RED SALON: Formerly a library, now interesting for its portraits. Three emperors are shown in the robes of the Order of the Golden Fleece. From the left as you enter they are Leopold II, Franz I by the Biedermeier portrait painter Friedrich von Amerling (*see p. 58*), and Ferdinand I. Franz I looks very stern indeed - and he had every right to be. He was the emperor whom Napoleon effectively deposed (*see p. 34*). Franz's two daughters were both forced into political marriages. Marie Louise married Napoleon, and Marie Leopoldine, whose portrait stands in the corner, married the Emperor of Brazil, whose rough treatment caused the miscarriage which killed her at the age of 29.

22 THE STATE BEDCHAMBER: The early 18th-century canopied bed with its sculpture-in-textile hangings belonged to Maria Theresa, although she used it in the Hofburg, not here - and even then she did not use it for sleeping in, but to give ceremonial audiences in her bedjacket or to show off her latest newborn. This is the room (though not the bed) in which Franz Joseph was born, in August 1830. He died 86 years later, in the corresponding room of the palace's opposite wing.

The palace is open every day 8.30am-5pm (April-June & Sept-Oct); 8.30am-7pm (July-August) and 8.30am-4.30pm (Nov-March).

THE GROUNDS

Schönbrunn's ornamental park that was built by Maria Theresa, following the French fashion of the time - ruthlessly making nature obey the rules of geometry - remains largely intact or has been reconstructed. Though the style was very out of date by the latter decades of her reign, the empress clung to it tenaciously, her only concession to newer, more romantic concepts of the picturesque being the fake Roman ruins. Succeeding emperors who preferred a wilder, more Capability Brown style of garden did not choose Schönbrunn as the place to construct their bowers and grottoes. Schönbrunn was left as a monument to the *grande dame.*

The main features of the park are listed below. All are also clearly marked on the plan overleaf.

THE SCHÖNER BRUNNEN: In the eastern (left-hand) half of the ornamental garden is a stone kiosk built over the *Schöner Brunnen.* The "beautiful spring" that gives Schönbrunn its name and that so charmed the emperor

Maximilian II, was "rediscovered" by the emperor Matthias, whose monogram is carved on a stone set into the kiosk's right-hand wall. The spring is now guarded by a nymph, from whose pitcher it flows. Franz

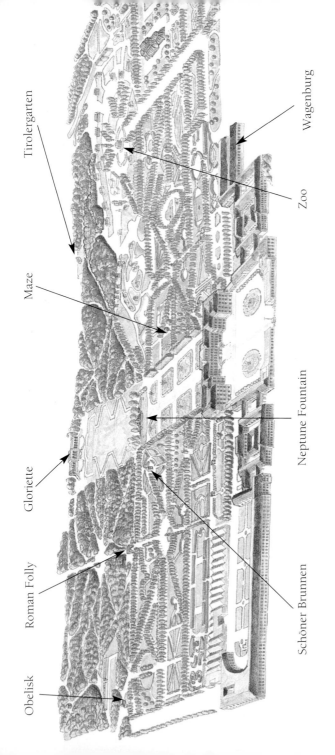

Tirolergarten

Wagenburg

Zoo

Maze

Neptune Fountain

Gloriette

Roman Folly

Schöner Brunnen

Obelisk

THE PALACE AND GARDENS OF SCHÖNBRUNN

Joseph and Elisabeth used this as their drinking water. Every day a fresh supply would be taken to the Hofburg on a draycart, and when the imperial pair travelled they would take flasks of it with them. Beyond the spring, at the very edge of the park, is the **OBELISK** on which Maria Theresa had the story of the Habsburg dynasty carved in mock hieroglyphics. The tortoises on whose backs the obelisk stands were originally gilded.

THE ROMAN FOLLY (1778): The work of Johann Ferdinand von Hohenberg, who became court architect to Joseph II, and who was a leading exponent of the new style, leading away from the Baroque and towards Classicism.

THE NEPTUNE FOUNTAIN: What the Habsburgs may have lacked in taste they certainly made up for in dimension. This huge writhing group of human and animal flesh rendered in stone, at the end of the central avenue of the ornamental garden, took the sculptor Franz Anton Zauner ten years to complete (1770-1780). It shows Thetis, the mother of Achilles, begging Poseidon to let her son come home safely from the Trojan War. He didn't.

THE GLORIETTE: Situated on top of the Schönbrunner Berg, Fischer von Erlach's original projected site for the palace itself, the Gloriette is a triumphal classico-Renaissance colonnade built to celebrate Austria's victory over Frederick the Great of Prussia at the Battle of Kolin in 1757. Despite Frederick's impassioned urging of his men to hurl themselves pell-mell into the jaws of death ("You dogs! Are you hoping to live forever?"), he was massively outnumbered, and the defeat forced him to withdraw once and for all from Bohemia. Less than six months later, Frederick inflicted a crushing defeat on Austria at the Battle of Leuthen, but construction of the Gloriette went ahead anyway. It was completed in 1775, and the architect was Ferdinand von Hohenberg. The view from the Gloriette over Vienna to the hills beyond is magnificent. The central section has been glassed in and is now a café. If you feel like more sustenance than coffee and a cake, however, walk a little further through the woods to the **GASTHAUS TIROLERGARTEN**, which will give you a good Austrian lunch of *Tiroler Knödel* (a bacon and herb dumpling) with sauerkraut and a mug of white wine *g'spritzt* (with soda water).

THE MAZE: By the end of the 18th century mazes were disappearing from courtly pleasure gardens. The vogue had turned, and everyone was mad about the nature-run-wild look, not about razor-sharp topiary and parallel lines. Maria Theresa ignored fashion. A maze she wanted and a maze she got.

THE ZOO: Famous as the oldest zoo in the world, it was founded by Maria Theresa's husband, Franz Stephan, in the middle of the 18th century. The octagonal pavilion in the centre, where Maria Theresa liked to take her breakfast in the summer months, also dates from that time. Franz Stephan began the process of stocking the zoo with exotic animals. Before that the only animals to roam Schönbrunn had been pheasants and minor game. He and his successors sent teams of scientists to the West Indies, Brazil and the Cape of Good Hope to collect specimens.

THE WAGENBURG: The old stable block, which now contains a museum of coaches and carriages. Some of the best displays are those where the actual carriage itself is

accompanied by a contemporary painting which features it. The 18th-century coronation coach, for example, is featured in a painting of Joseph II's coronation in Frankfurt. The magnificently hideous Rococo sleigh that once whisked the ample matriarch Maria Theresa across the snow can be seen in a painting of imperial personages whirling about the icy Hofburg on horse-drawn sledges - perhaps on ice that had been specially imported from the countryside by retinues of put-upon servants. Sympathisers with France's revolutionary mobs used to mutter furiously about the needless toil

Snowy scene outside Schönbrunn, with Maria Theresa's gilt Rococo sleigh in the foreground. When snowfall in town was not heavy enough to allow sledging and tobogganning, the empress would have cartfuls of snow specially imported from the suburbs so that she and her family could enjoy winter sports in the courtyard of the Hofburg.

created by the imperial family's self-indulgent frolics.

The most memorable exhibit in the Wagenburg is the huge, sombre funerary coach with its black velvet and moiré taffeta drape that was used for the funeral cortèges of Crown Prince Rudolf, Empress Elisabeth, Franz Joseph, and most recently, of Karl I's widow the Empress Zita, who returned to Vienna to be buried in 1989. There is also a child's carriage built for the Duke of Reichstadt (*see p. 191 above*), which was pulled by two specially trained merino sheep. The final exhibit is a sleek green limousine, which at the same time as bringing the Habsburg vehicle fleet into the modern age is also ironically the car in which Karl I and his family were driven into exile in Switzerland. Switzerland agreed to take Karl on condition that he forbore from dabbling in politics. It proved too tall an order. When Hungary's short-lived Soviet-style commune fell in 1919, the country did not declare itself a republic as Austria had done. Hoping that there might be a role for him there, Karl applied (he had already been crowned King of Hungary in any case). He was cruelly snubbed by Admiral Miklós Horthy, who had set himself up as Hungary's regent. Poor Karl was left cap in hand, begging to be allowed somewhere to live. Eventually he went to the only country who would take him, Portugal, who granted him and his family asylum on Madeira.

The Wagenburg is open March-Oct 9am-6pm every day; Nov-March 9am-4pm Tue-Sun.

Entry to the Schönbrunn park and grounds is free, though individual entry fees are charged for the zoo, Wagenburg, maze and palm house.

GRINZING

"Ich möcht' wieder einmal in Grinzing sein," as the old song goes, *"Beim Wein, beim Wein, beim Wein!"* I'd love to be in Grinzing again, with wine, wine and more wine! If you want to taste Austrian wine in the raw, Grinzing is the place to go. Now a suburb of Vienna, lying on the city's north-eastern fringe, Grinzing was once a separate village, and still retains a lot of its old rustic charm.

Right up until the end of the 17th century, vineyards covered much of what is now central Vienna. All that is left of them today is a tiny cluster in a corner of the Schwarzenbergplatz, still tended and maintained by the Mayer am Pfarrplatz winery (*see p. 202*), but for sentimental rather than commercial reasons. After 1683, when the Ottoman menace was quelled for good and construction in the inner city began to take off, the wine growers moved out to the hillsides of Grinzing, Nussdorf and the Kahlenberg. That wine tradition is still going strong in the form of the *Heurigen*, country-style taverns where you can sit out in the courtyards under

Whiling away a sunny afternoon in one of the famous Grinzing Heurigen. The musicians sitting at the table are playing traditional Viennese Schrammel music.

The Reinprecht Heuriger in Cobenzlgasse, with its traditional pine branch over the door signalling wine to sell.

the vine-shade and drink to your heart's content and your head's mortification. In the old days a *Heuriger* would sell wine only, and people would bring along their own picnic food to eat. Nowadays the *Heurigen* offer buffet food: hearty cuts of ham and cheese, pickles, salads and breaded meats. The Grinzing wine-tavern tradition as it exists now is principally a 19th-century phenomenon, though the *Heurigen* are far older than that. The first opened for business in the 15th century, and in the late 18th century more and more began to spring up, after Joseph II lifted the tax on new wine and granted winemakers permission to sell their own wine on their own premises, the *Heurigen* have been popular, with winemakers scrambling to sell all their wine before the next grape harvest came in. The word *Heuriger* comes from the German for "this year's", referring to the new vintage. As soon as the wine was ready to drink, the *Heuriger*-keeper would traditionally put a spring of pine on a pole outside his tavern as a sign that he had wine to sell. Today you still see wine cellars with pine branches *ausg'steckt* - but whether they are ever taken down is open to question. Still, there is a definite *Heuriger* season, from March/April to early November. Opening hours are usually from 3pm. The wine is traditionally served in mini glass tankards, by the quarter (*viertel*) or the eighth (*achtel*). Don't expect anything too special. *Heuriger* wine tends to be quite rough stuff. The main reason to go is for the fun and the atmosphere. When the Schrammel musicians (*see p. 117*) get out their violins and double-necked guitars and set to work on a repertoire of old evergreens, elderly ladies in tarnished pearls and vivid lipstick can frequently be seen dabbing their eyes.

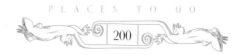
A GOOD DAY TRIP

*This trip takes you to Nussdorf with its vineyards-in-the-suburbs, and the wine taverns of
Grinzing, along lanes where Beethoven loved to ramble, and with two famous examples of
Viennese 20th-century architecture thrown in for good measure.*

*NB: If you want to visit a Heuriger in Grinzing, time your trip to arrive in the afternoon, as
the Heurigen are only open after 3pm.*

Take Tram D from the Ring (Burgring,
Karl Renner-Ring, Karl Lueger-Ring or
Schottenring), right to the last stop.
On the way, after passing the Franz
Josefs-Bahnhof, look out on your right
for the Fernwärme, the Spittelau

municipal incinerator built by
Hundertwasser (*picture on p. 89*). Two
stops after that, also on your right, the
Karl Marx-Hof begins, a vast workers'
housing development built between
1927 and 1930 (*see pp. 83-4*). Getting

Detail of the geometric façade of the Karl Marx-Hof.

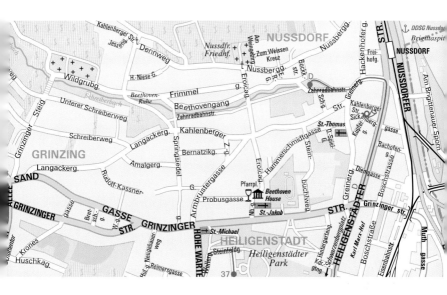

off the tram, you will find yourself directly outside a café and restaurant, Zur Zahnradbahn, once the terminus of a cogwheel railway. If you feel in need of fortification before you start, the plane-tree shade of its terrace is a pleasant place to sit. Nussdorf sits right on the edge of Vienna's wine district, and on the very eastern tip of the Vienna Woods, a great belt of green which stretches from here round to the north and west. During the Congress of Vienna in 1814 (*see p. 125*), hunting parties in the woods were laid on as part of the entertainment, with strict orders of precedence maintained. First shot at the game was taken by emperors. Then came kings, and princes and dukes followed after. In the 19th century the woods and

wine gardens became favourite destinations for family outings, and the woods were designated a green belt by the popular - and populist - mayor Karl Lueger. In the winter of 1919, when Vienna was at her lowest ebb after the First World War, and when the coal trucks from Poland had stopped coming, the desperate, freezing people came to the Vienna Woods to chop down trees for fuel. Contemporary photographs show nothing but a forest of stumps, with not a tree left standing.

To start the walk, retrace your steps to where you got off the tram, walk briefly uphill from the tram stop, then turn right up Bockkellerstrasse, and at the top of that left into Nussberggasse, a residential street

Column invoking divine protection of Grinzing's vines and vineyards. Suburban housing crowds behind.

the keyhole whenever he sat down to practise the piano. Infuriated, he thundered that he'd never touch the keyboard again unless the Grillparzers moved out. By no means the first touchy genius to fail to appreciate an admiring public, or to accept that they were in fact his main hope of a livelihood. Frau Grillparzer's life ended in suicide, but there is no evidence to suggest that Beethoven's hostile attitude drove her to it. Beethoven also lived in a house south of here, on the Pfarrplatz (No. 2). It is now the Mayer am Pfarrplatz restaurant and winery.

Continuing straight ahead up Dennweg, the vineyards begin to encroach more and more closely on the suburb. Turning steeply left down Kahlenberggasse (the turning as marked by another wayside cross), you come out on the Beethovengang, a path that follows the course of a little brook, the Schreiberbach. When Beethoven felt in need of inspiration, he would go for walks around here. The landscape is said to have inspired his *Pastoral Symphony*.

Turn right along the Wildgrubgasse, past the cemetery with its vines clambering up the hillsides behind it, and the Schreiberbach trickling along

shaded by young walnut trees. This leads gently uphill, passing a tall white column decorated with a crucifixion scene, and with an inscription invoking God's protection of the vines. Further on, at the junction of Eroicagasse, you begin to see vineyards above you to the right. The Beethoven connection with this part of town is a strong one. Beethoven lived in this part of Vienna in 1808, sharing accommodation a few streets away, on the Grinzingerstrasse, with the budding young playwright Grillparzer (*see p. 112*) and Grillparzer's mother. The mother drove Beethoven mad by listening at on your left. When you reach the steps of the Grinzingersteige, you have a choice. Turning right takes you up a narrow, rural lane, which snakes up to the Kahlenberg (Bald Mountain), allegedly so called because after the Siege of Vienna of 1683 the mountainside was littered with the heads of decapitated Turks (Ottoman soldiers in those days were shaven-headed). The Christian armies had pushed the Ottomans back from the city, and final victory came amid the oak forests here: difficult, steep terrain which the exhausted, harried janissaries could barely negotiate. Turning left takes you into the village-suburb of Grinzing. Once there, you can taste wine at one of the *Heurigen*. The Reinprecht, at Cobenzlgasse 22 (*open from 3.30pm*), usually has a good sprinkling of locals as well as tourists. If you are too early for the *Heurigen*, try the Brandl restaurant, a picturesque shingle-roofed tavern, serving Austrian fare in a homely Austrian interior of scrubbed wood and knickerbocker lampshades. In summer there is a sun-trap outdoor terrace, with shade under the vine trellis. *Cobenzlgasse 17. Open Tues-Sun 11am-10.30pm. Tel: 320 71 96.*

View of Grinzing's vines from Wildgrubgasse.

PART V

PRACTICALITIES

p. 205    FOOD & RESTAURANTS

p. 211 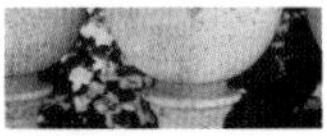   WINE

p. 216    HOTELS & PENSIONS

p. 220    PRACTICAL TIPS

A Wiener Würstl sausage stall at lunchtime.

FOOD & RESTAURANTS

Vienna has an abundance of restaurants, supported by a local population who regularly lunch and dine out. Styles range from the solid, not to say stolid, beer-and-deep-fried-breaded-meat to the ultra chic two-strands-of-designer-seaweed-on-a-large-white-plate, with probably the best food to be found somewhere in between. Perhaps surprisingly for a former imperial capital, Vienna's native cuisine is far from sophisticated, being more the kind of hearty fare to feed hungry peasants than languid aristocrats. The place to eat this sort of thing - frothing beer and platters of boiled meat, sausage and *sauerkraut* - is a *Beisl*, a simple, unpretentious tavern serving Viennese home cooking. Once upon a time they tended to be places of ill repute, haunted by highwaymen, hookers and hoodlums. Today they are a solid part of the bourgeois apparatus. Another type of Viennese inn is the *Heuriger*: a wine tavern with buffet food. Mainly a suburban phenomenon (*described in detail on p. 198*), a single centre-of-town example is listed here, for those who lack the time to go further afield. For typical Viennese fare on the hop, you need to visit a *Wiener Würstl* sausage stall (there is one tucked into Seilergasse opposite the

Stephansdom). Choose the kind of sausage you want from the list (*Scharfe Wurst* is excellent, spicy but not too much), and whether you want it with a roll (*Semmel*) or with a slice of bread (*Brot*). Mustard can be either mild (*süss*) or hot (*scharf*). The stallholder will cut up your sausage for you, and supply you with a toothpick to eat it with. Anything you don't want goes in the bin beside the stall. The plate goes back on the counter.

The list of restaurants below is subjective and not exhaustive. Of course the price of a meal will depend on what you eat and drink - nevertheless, restaurants are approximately ranked as expensive (€ € €), moderate (€ €) and cheaper (€).

TRADITIONAL

KÖNIGSBACHER € €
A genuine favourite with the Viennese, generally full and friendly, with tasty examples of all the staple dishes and a good wine selection. Excellent central location.

District 1, Walfischgasse 5. Tel: 513 12 10. mon-Fri 10am-midnight; Sat 10am-4pm. Closed Sun.

PLACHUTTA € €
Famous for its *Tafelspitz*, which is in turn famous for being Franz Joseph's favourite dish (*see p. 208*).
District 1, Wollzeile 38. Tel: 512 15 77. Reservations recommended. 11.30am-midnight every day.

FIGLMÜLLER €
Famous for its *Wiener Schnitzel*, tenderised breaded and deep-fried veal, which they promise will cover the plate - it does.
At two addresses. 1) District 1, Wollzeile 5 (entrance in the passageway). Tel: 512 61 77. 11am-1.30pm; 2) District 1, Bäckerstrasse 6. Tel: 512 17 60. Noon-midnight.

Sprucing up before a brisk day's trading at Plachutta.

Figlmüller's tiny Schnitzel restaurant is located in the narrow passage between Wollzeile and Bäckerstrasse.

GIGERL STADHEURIGER €

This rustic-looking restaurant is a *Heuriger* (see p. 198) in the centre of town - young white wines served loose, buffet food, pretty gingham tablecloths and Schrammel music (see p. 117).
Rauhensteingasse 3 (Entrance in Blumenstockgasse). Open from 3pm every day.

GRIECHENBEISL € €

Built right up against the former city walls, this ancient tavern is well on the beaten tourist path, but that doesn't stop it from being cosy, atmospheric and fun. During renovation work in the 60s, three Turkish cannon balls were found embedded in a wall. Purportedly the scene of Lieber Augustin's revels (see p. 178).
District 1, Fleischmarkt 11. Tel 533 1977. 11am to 1am every day (kitchen closes 11.30pm).

OSWALD & KALB € €

Diners with cropped hair and statement-making spectacles suggest that this is a favourite of the urban intelligentsia. In Vienna, though, they are more likely to be eating spinach strudel *au gratin* than seared yellowfin tuna. Another Viennese peculiarity - the lack of a generation gap - means that this is not purely the haunt of thirty-somethings
District 1, Bäckerstrasse 14. Tel: 512 13 71. 6pm-2am.

ZUM BASILISKEN € €

Close to the home of the Basilisk on the pretty Schönlaterngasse (see p. 177), with beautiful ornate dark-stained woodwork making for a cosy interior. They usually have good Croatian wines by the glass, and Austrian staples on the menu.
District 1, Schönlanterngasse 3-5. Tel. 513 31 23. Noon-2am every day.

TAFELSPITZ

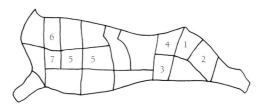

Boiled beef doesn't sound like a particularly glamorous food, but Emperor Franz Joseph loved it. He was a long way from being either a hedonist or an epicurean, preferring an iron bed to sleep on, and simple food to eat. Sisi, as Europe's proto-bulimic, wasn't interested in food either, and

1: *Tafelspitz* (Aitchbone)
2: *Tafelstück & Weisses Scherzel* (Topside & Silverside)
3: *Hüferschwanzel* (Top Rump)
4: *Hüferscherzel* (Rump)
5: *Beinfleisch* (Flat Rib & Top Rib)
6: *Kruspelspitz* (Chuck)
7: *Schulterscherzel* (Bladebone)

stories abound of depressed foreign ambassadors and attachés being taken to dine at the Hofburg, and leaving the table with their stomachs still rumbling after a frugal meal, or with their sense of personal dignity outraged at the humble fare they were served. Still, the emperor's love of good, plain home cooking has helped to make *Tafelspitz* one of Vienna's most enduring specialities. The word *Tafelspitz* in fact refers to a particular cut of beef (*see diagram*), though now it is used as a generic term to describe any suitable cut, boiled and sliced into thick, tender wedges, and served with sautéed potato, chive sauce, and puréed apple flavoured with horseradish.

ITALIAN

You may tell yourself you haven't travelled to Vienna to eat Italian food, but in its heyday the Austrian empire covered vast territories in modern-day Italy. Italian influence is present in much Viennese cooking, and *trattorias* in Vienna are an established tradition, not simply a passing fad:

NOVELLI € €

Good Italian cuisine in clean-lined, 90s-derivative surroundings. Good-value three-course lunch menu; delicious tomato bread. Also boasts two related restaurants, one in the courtyard of the Palais Kinsky (Freyung 4); the other in the courtyard of the Palais Esterházy (Wallnerstrasse 4). *District 1, Bräunerstrasse 11. Tel: 513 42 00. 11am-1am every day.*

SANTO SPIRITO €

In essence a gay restaurant, but everyone is welcome and the atmosphere is relaxed and friendly. Spanish tapas, Italian-inspired main dishes, simple pasta meals after midnight.
District 1, Kumpfgasse 7. Tel: 512 99 98 (after 5pm). Mon-Thur 6pm-2am; Fri 6pm-3am; Sat 11am-3am; Sun 10am-2am.

INTERNATIONAL

DO & CO STEPHANSPLATZ € € €

At the top of the Haas Haus, the mirror-glass faced edifice on the corner opposite the Stephansdom. *Sushi, teppan yaki*, Thai and Austrian cuisine for jaded urban palates among good-looking people in good looking surroundings (including a terrace with views down the Kärntnerstrasse and across to the Stephansdom). Its success has spawned a chain of restaurants, an event caterers business and an airline catering company.
District 1, Stephansplatz 12. Tel: 535 39 69. Noon-3pm; 6pm-midnight.

INDOCHINE 21 € € €

French-Indochinese cooking in chic zen surroundings for when the *Tafelspitz* gets all too much.
District 1, Stubenring 18. Tel: 513 76 60. Noon-3pm; 6pm-11.30pm.

Lots of traditional Central European dark wood panelling in Zum Basilisken on Schönlaterngasse.

MAK CAFÉ € €

Café and restaurant attached to the Museum of Applied Arts. A garden operates in summer. Lofty, well-lit restaurant space inside with clean white Thonet chairs and original Historicist ceiling. The menu is a blend of global standards like salmon carpaccio with Austrian-style fare such as spinach gnocchi.
District 1, Stubenring 5. Tel: 714 01 21. Tues-Sun 10am-2am. Closed Mon.

MÖRWALD IN THE AMBASSADOR HOTEL € € €

Excellent food with Austrian roots tending to the designer end of the spectrum but not excessively so - lobster with white cabbage (*lobster à la hongroise*), saddle of fawn with braised hearts of lettuce. *Chef de cuisine* is Christian Domschitz, winner of a Michelin star
District 1, Kärntnerstrasse 22/Neuer Markt 5. Tel: 961 610. Mon-Sat Noon-midnight.

PALMENHAUS € €

Mixture of Vienna specialities like *Tafelspitz* and standard modern stuff like rucola with parmesan shavings. Selection of gateaux. In graceful former imperial palm house, built for Franz Joseph in the Burggarten.
District 1, Burggarten. Tel: 533 1033. 10am-2am.

Outside and inside the Palmenhaus in the Burggarten.

WINE

Austria has a long wine tradition, going back at least as far as the Romans, and probably further, to the Celts who occupied the region before them. Short, hot summers, long, cold winters and a lingering balmy autumn make Austria ideal white wine country: wines are either dry and crisply acidic, or made in a variety of sweet, late-harvest styles (*see glossary below*). Reds are produced too, but at present make up only about a quarter of the country's total output. Most are simple, easy-drinking vintages from indigenous grape varieties, designed to be enjoyed relatively soon after bottling. Austrian whites, in contrast to the reds, have excellent ageing potential, although few are put to the test. The quality wine revolution in Austria is relatively recent, and stocks of wine are as yet too small for producers and consumers to be able to allow themselves the luxury of cellaring for the future.

NB: For information about Grinzing and Vienna's famous Heurigen, see p. 198.

MAJOR WINE REGIONS

Austria has a total of 10 wine regions, mainly in the east of the country where summers are sunnier. The main regions and selected producers are given below.

Burgenland

On the Hungarian border and lapped by the shores of the Neusiedlersee, Burgenland is known for two things: its sweet, sometimes botrytised wines, notably *Ausbruch* (*see glossary below*) from the town of Rust, and its reds, dominated by the *Blaufränkisch* grape. Producers: Feiler, Kracher, Lang, Opitz, Umathum.

Styria (Steiermark)

The pretty, rolling countryside of Styria is home to white wines made largely from the noble grape varieties Sauvignon Blanc and Chardonnay (known locally as *Morillon*).

Vienna (Wien)

Not strictly speaking a major wine region - it only comprises around 600 hectares - the Vienna district is unique in being so close to the city. What other major metropolis cultivates vineyards within its city limits? Vienna's wine production is concentrated in the north-eastern tip of the city, in Grinzing, Nussdorf, Neustift and Kahlenbergerdorf, little enclaves that are part-suburb part-village, and famous for their wine taverns, the *Heurigen* (*see p. 198*). The wines are often distinctly rustic, though some are of genuine quality. Almost all are white, made largely from *Grüner Veltliner*. The traditional *Wiener Wein* - which still exists - is a haphazard blend of whatever grapes are going, known as *Gemischter Satz*. Producers: Mayer, Wieninger.

Wachau & Kamptal

The dramatically beautiful Wachau region, where vineyards clamber up steep hillsides along the banks of the Danube, 100 or so kilometres west of Vienna, is Austria's most famous wine region. Together with the Kamptal, the valley of the river Kamp, 20 kilometres further to the east, both regions are known for their dry white wines, mainly Riesling and *Grüner Veltliner*. Producers: Bründlmayer, Freie Weingärtner Wachau (FWW), Hirtzberger, Knoll, Pichler, Prager.

Weinviertel

Stretching between Vienna and the Czech border, the flat, dry, fertile Weinviertel is Austria's largest wine region, and to some extent its workhorse region, producing mainly simple white table wines for everyday drinking.

THE MAIN NATIVE GRAPE TYPES

Austrians still respect and enjoy their ancient, indigenous grape varieties, and vineyards have not been grubbed up and turned over to large-scale plantings of Cabernet and Chardonnay, which has happened in so many other countries gripped by wine revolution. The native grape types which do best as single-variety wines, and which you are most likely to encounter, are given below.

WHITE WINE

Grüner Veltliner - Lean and miner[-]aly, with distinct aromas of white pepper, lemon and pineapple. Long regarded as a dull grape, it is now coming into its own: a good *Grüner Veltliner* can be rich and complex, with good acid-fruit balance, and a taste that is refreshingly different.

Welschriesling - No relation of true Rhine Riesling, the distinguished grape of premium Wachau wines, a good *Welschriesling* is nevertheless pleasant drinking. Bone dry, crisp and acidic, it should not be drunk too chilled: cold temperatures tone down fruit flavours and make it too austere.

RED WINE

Blauburgunder - The Austrian name for Pinot Noir.

Blauer Portugieser - Early-ripening, low-acid variety yielding soft, easy-drinking wines, excellent served slightly chilled on a summer's day.

Blaufränkisch - Makes a light to medium-bodied wine, always with a bracing peppery spice to it.

Zweigelt - A cross between *Blaufränkisch* and another indigenous variety, *St Laurent*. Produces a deep-coloured wine, fuller bodied than plain *Blaufränkisch*.

The leaves seen through the stone balustrade are vines, remnants of one of the city's oldest vineyards, on Schwarzenbergplatz. They are maintained by the Mayer am Pfarrplatz winery in Heiligenstadt (see p. 202).

GLOSSARY OF WINE TERMS

Ausbruch: A sweet wine from Burgenland, similar in style to Hungarian Tokaj.

Auslese, Beerenauslese (BA) and Trockenbeerenauslese (TBA): Three categories of rich, sweet wine made from specially selected super-ripe grapes - the riper the better. Some of the grapes, winemakers hope, will have been infected with noble rot (*botrytis*). The three categories listed are in ascending order of sweetness/quality.

Eiswein: Non-botrytised sweet wine made from grapes that have been left to freeze on the vine. Crushing when still frozen yields sweet grape must and very little water (because the water content freezes while the grape must does not), resulting in a highly concentrated wine.

Federspiel: (see *Smaragd*)

Kabinett: Very light-bodied wine, low in alcohol. A dry *Kabinett*, if well chilled, can make a lovely aperitif. Some are semi-sweet and rather insipid, though. Check the label carefully.

Schilfwein: Literally "reed wine". This is sweet wine made in Burgenland, from grapes dried to a raisin-like state on a bed of reeds from the Neusiedlersee. Drying in this way concentrates the sugars.

Smaragd: Taken as a marker of premium quality for Wachau wine (*Federspiel* and *Steinfeder* are quality labels two and three respectively), though seeing the terms as quality markers can be misleading. In fact what the names really denote is power and alcoholic potency. If you like your wine strong and punch-packing, *Smaragd* is for you (minimum alcohol content 12.5%). *Federspiel* (max. 12.5%) and *Steinfeder* (around 11%) are gentler and often more subtle.

Spätlese: Late-harvest wine, sweet or semi-sweet.

Steinfeder: (see *Smaragd*).

Where to Taste & Buy Wine

Meinl's Weinbar
This basement establishment serves mainly Austrian wines, by the glass or bottle, with snack food in abundance to prevent it all going to your head. *District 1, Graben 19 (entrance in Naglergasse). Open Mon-Sat 11am-midnight.*

Vinothek St Stephan
Classic wine merchants right in the heart of town. English-speaking staff will help you make up your mind. *District 1, Stephansplatz 6. Open Mon-Fri 9.30am-6.30pm; Sat 9.30am-5pm.*

Wein & Co.
Half wine shop, half wine bar, you will find examples of most major Austrian wines here, plus plenty of vintages from around the world. *District 1, Jasomirgottgasse 3-5. Bar open Mon-Sat 10am-2am; Sun 11am-midnight.*

Opposite: Enjoying the early spring sunshine and a viertel of Grüner Veltliner at the Brandl restaurant in Grinzing.

HOTELS & PENSIONS

Vienna has an enormous number of hotels and pensions - 330 registered with the Tourist Board at the last count - many privately-owned and family-run. In the list below the focus is on the better first-district hotels in their category. Chain-owned hotels, which can be found through their head office websites or switchboards, are excluded (with the exception of the Imperial). (The first district is the area on and inside the Ring.)

The "pensions" are often as good as medium-rate hotels. The difference is that hotels tend to be a building in their own right while pensions are frequently part of a residential building.

Prices, unless otherwise stated, are approximate for double occupancy of standard double rooms per night. This list is updated on the publisher's website - www.visiblecities.net - where readers' comments are welcomed and special offers may be recommended. Telephone numbers are the Viennese numbers - preceded by 00 43 1 from outside Austria (Europe) or 011 43 1 (US) etc.

There are any number of websites offering Vienna hotel listings - the official (but not very informative) Tourist Board's site at www.info.wien.at has a comprehensive listing. (Also http://www.austria-tourism.at/index_e.html). To help you find what you are looking for it is useful to remember how the four-digit postal codes work: the first digit (1) indicates Vienna, the next two denote the district of the city, the last a sub-division of that district. Thus 1011 is in Vienna's first district.

HOTELS

IMPERIAL ✪✪✪✪✪

A magnificent hotel (with prices to match), the interior is as grand as one would expect from a building that was once the Prince of Württemberg's palace. Because of the proximity to the Musikverein, its coffee house was traditionally the haunt of musicians. Johann Strauss (the younger), Anton Bruckner and Gustav Mahler all came here. Minutes before the premiere of Lohengrin in 1875, Wagner was still sitting over a coffee making changes

Imperial suite in the Hotel Imperial on the Kärntnerring, one of the grandest places to stay in Europe.

to the score.

76 rooms and 62 suites. From € 510. District 1, Kärntner Ring 16. Tel 501 10-333.

www.luxurycollection.com

SACHER ✪✪✪✪✪

An intimate and historic luxury hotel, home of the *Sachertorte*, a famous chocolate cake (*see p. 111*) as well as of owner Frau Gurtler's collection of oil paintings. Fight your way through the queues outside waiting to taste the former for more discreet enjoyment of the latter. Frau Gurtler is also organiser of the celebrity Opera Ball at the Opera House opposite every February.

105 rooms. From € 300. District 1, Philharmonikerstrasse 4. Tel: 514 560.

www.sacher.com

KÖNIG VON UNGARN ✪✪✪✪

Probably the nicest hotel in Vienna, perfectly located behind the Stephansdom. Rooms of different shapes and sizes, each individually decorated, are grouped around the covered courtyard of an old town house. Originally the rooms were town apartments rented annually by visiting nobles, often from Hungary - hence the name (King of Hungary) and the prevalence throughout the hotel of the image of the Apostolic Crown, the crown with which Hungarian kings have been crowned since 1000 AD. Reservations generally necessary several months in advance.

33 rooms, € 180.
District 1, Schulerstrasse 10. Tel: 515 84-0.
www.kvu.at

DAS TRIEST ✪✪✪✪

A self-consciously "hip" hotel designed by English style guru Sir Terence Conran in 1995 in a former coaching inn. Clean lines and minimalist articulation are a far cry - and for some no doubt a relief - from Vienna's traditional cluttered Biedermeier - Alfred Loos (*see p. 87*) would probably approve. Bring your

Silver Bar in the Hotel Triest.

Hotel König von Ungarn.

black clothing and don't be seen in the lobby without your pop band instruments in their travelling cases, preferably stickered from your latest Japanese tour. The Silver Bar (*see picture*) is well worth a visit for a cocktail.

72 rooms, € 190 and all the way up.
District 4, Wiedner Hauptstrasse 12.
Tel: 589 180.
www.designhotels.com

KÄRNTNERHOF ✪✪✪

Excellent central location on a cul-de-sac with a gateway through to the tranquil Heiligenkreuzerhof (*see p. 177*). Pleasant, slightly scruffy rooms. No minibar, room service or restaurant, but a friendly restaurant opposite.

43 rooms € 120-140. Singles € 90.
District 1, Grashofgasse 4. Tel: 512 1923.
www.karntnerhof.com

WANDL ✪✪✪

Central and quiet. A hotel since 1851, taking its name from its 1854 proprietor who installed one of Vienna's first elevators. Rooms of varying quality (and priced accordingly).

138 rooms, € 125-170. Singles from € 60.

District 1, Petersplatz 9, tel 534 550.

www.hotel-wandl.com

PENSIONS

PENSION PERTSCHY

Comfortable, very central pension cluttered with faux-Biedermeier fittings. Rooms around the central courtyard of the Palais Cavriani, the standard layout for all of the late 19th-century apartment blocks built for the capital's prosperous bourgeoisie.

50 rooms, € 95-135.

District 1, Palais Cavriani. Habsburgergasse 5. Tel: 534 49-0.

www.pertschy.at

PENSION NOSSEK

Right in the centre of town.

120 Rooms of which 22 are 3-star, from € 96.

District 1, Graben 17.

Tel: 535 7041 0; Fax: 535 3646.

Pension Pertschy.

PRACTICAL TIPS

PUBLIC TRANSPORT

Public transport in Vienna is swift, efficient, frequent and clean. The system - the *Wiener Linien* - incorporates trams, buses and the Underground. You buy tickets either in advance, or from a machine on the tram or bus (not from the driver). You can either buy per trip, or get strips of 2 or 4 tickets, or, if you're going to be hopping on and off public transport for most of the day, buy a 24-hour Vienna Rover card. The city also operates Viennabike, a hop-on-drop-off system based on the notoriously disastrous Amsterdam model (all the public cycles were pitched into the canals within weeks of the scheme being launched). Now it's Vienna's turn to try and prove that human nature does respect public property after all.

PUBLIC HOLIDAYS & FESTIVALS

Austria celebrates its national day on October 26th. May 1st, Labour Day, is also a public holiday. Other holidays tend to be feast days of the Catholic Church: Corpus Christi (in June), Ascension Day (40 days after Easter), the Assumption of the Virgin (August 15th). Christmas and Easter are major festivals. Christmas festivities begin in Advent. Hotels, shops and restaurants across town hang up Advent wreaths decorated with four candles, successively lit on each of the four Sundays leading up to Christmas. The origins of this ritual of the coming of the light are probably much more ancient than Christianity, going back to the old superstitions of St Lucy's Day (December 13th, the shortest day of the old calender, after which the earth began its long climb out of winter darkness). The name Lucy derives from the Latin word for light, and her symbols in traditional iconography are two eyes. You will also notice chalk inscriptions appearing over doorways: the numbers of the year flanking the letters C, M and B, the initials of the three Magi. Concerts of Christmas and Advent music are held all over the city, and Christmas markets spring up too, most famous of all being the *Christkindlmarkt* in front of the Rathaus.

Easter is celebrated with a festival of music called the *Osterklang*. On the night of Easter Saturday an Easter bonfire is lit in the courtyard of the Archbishop's Palace on the

Stephansplatz. Everyone present receives a candle to light at the fire, the bishop intones solemn words (Christ is the one true light), and the crowds process to the Stephansdom for the Easter vigil. Hotels put Easter baskets full of eggs and chocolate bunnies in all their guestrooms.

CONCERT TICKETS

Opera - Tickets for the opera are available from the central ticket office at Hanuschgasse 3. Tel: 514 44 7880; 514 44 ext. 2959 or 2960 (information); 531 15 31 (credit card reservations). *Open Mon-Fri 8am-6pm; Sat-Sun 9am-midday.* There is also a box office in the opera house foyer. *Open Mon-Fri from 9am until two hours before the performance; Sat 9am-midday.*

Musikverein - Box office at the venue itself, District 1, Bösendorfer str. 12. Tel: 505 86 90. *Open Mon-Fri 9am-7.30pm; and Sat 9am-5pm.* *www.musikverein.at*

Spanish Riding School - Tickets for the Saturday morning rehearsals are given on a first-come-first-serve basis, from 9am at the Riding School itself. Tickets to the actual performances are notoriously difficult to get, as events are sold out well in advance. Applications must be made

in writing to Spanish Riding School, Michaelerplatz 1, 1010 Vienna, or by fax to (43 1) 533 90 32 40, or by e-mail to tickets@srs.at

TOURIST INFORMATION

The bilingual *Wien Magazin* contains monthly listings of concerts, exhibitions and shows. You can pick up a copy in hotel lobbies and kiosks, or visit their website at www.wien-magazin.at

The Vienna Tourist Board has an office at District 1, Albertinaplatz/Maysedergasse. *Open 9am-7pm every day.* They also maintain a website with events information at www.info.wien.at

GUIDED TOURS

The Vienna Tourist Board offers a variety of city tours in German and English. Subjects include a *Third Man* tour, tours of Jewish Vienna, tours of Mozart, Beethoven and Schubert's homes, mediaeval Vienna, Jugendstil Vienna, the Hofburg, the Belvedere - and many more. For more detailed information, contact the companies who organise the tours:

Wiener Spaziergänge (Vienna Walks). Tel: 894 53 63; www.wienguide.at

Verliebt in Wien (In Love with Vienna). Tel: 889 28 06; website www.verliebtinwien.at

INDEX

Numbers in italics refer to illustrations. Numbers in bold are major references.

A

Adriatic 18
Adler, Alfred **139**
Aix-la-Chapelle 34
Albert, Prince of Saxe Teschen 52-3, 188, 192
Albertina (see Museums)
Albrecht V 129, 147, 161
Alsace 14, 26
Alt, Rudolf von *38*, 98, 156
Alt Wien, Café (see Coffee Houses)
Altenberg, Peter 106
Altes Rathaus 162
Am Hof *29*, 159-60, *159*
America (see also New World) 46, 57, 124, 181
American Bar 88, 146
Amerling, Friedrich von 58, *58*, 176, 193
Andersen, Hans Christian 145
Anker Clock 81-2, *81*, *160*, 162
Anschluss 30, 31
Armenian 105, 127, 170
Art Nouveau (see Jugendstil)
Aspern, Battle of 66, 191
Athens 69, 179
Attlee, Clement 110
Augustin N, piper 178-9
Augustinerkirche (*see Churches*)
Austerlitz, Battle of 18

B

Babenbergs 11, 12, 81, 129, 154, 164
Bach, Johann Sebastian 124
Ballhausplatz 29, 47, 48
Ballgasse 171
Barbarossa, Frederick 11
Baroque 9, 16, 25, 43, 44, 46, 54, 73, **75-77**, 85, 134, 136, 161, 165, 171, 184
Basiliskenhaus 177, *180*
Batthyány, Palais 152, 154
Batthyány family 155
Batthyány, Lajos 155
Baumann, Ludwig 68-9
Bavaria 34
Bäckerstrasse 176
Beethoven, Ludwig van 95, 114, 115, **121-2**, *121*, 125, 147, 154, 172, 189, 202, 221
Beethovens Wohnung (see Museums)
Beethoven Frieze **95-6**, *96*
Bellotto, Bernardo *8*, 92, *187*
Belvedere 15, 32, **53ff**, *53*, *55*, 77, 123, 146, 221
Benedictines 154
Berlin 31, 80, 103, 181
Bermuda Triangle 163
Bernard, St 177-8

Biedermeier 20-21, **99-102**, 122, 153

Bismarck, Otto von 22, *22*, 23, 68

Blenheim, Battle of 16, 166

Blutgasse 170

Bohemia 11, 13, 51, 55, 113, 124, 127, 128, 129, 147, 191, 195

Bonaparte, Napoleon (see Napoleon)

Bonfini, Antonio 7

Borromeo, Carlo, St 136

Bosch, Hieronymus 98

Bosnia, Bosnian 23, 57

Bourbons 16, 190

Bösendorfer 101

Brahms, Johannes 113-4, 114, 116, **123**, *123*

Brandl (see Restaurants)

Brazil 112

Brazil, Emperor of 193

Bruckner, Anton 72, 113, **122-3**, 216

Brueghel 91, *93*

Brunelleschi 115

Buda 13, 105, 166

Budapest 105, 152

Burgenland 37, 211

Burggarten 68, 210

Burgkapelle (see Churches)

Burgtheater 62, **70-1**, *71*, 109

Burgundy 13

Byron, George Gordon, Lord 118

C

Canova 92, 134

Capuchin church (see Churches)

Carl, Archduke 66

Carlone, Carlo 57

Carlos II 16

Casanova 148

Casanova Revue Theatre 148, 181

Catholics, Catholic Church 13, 18, 34, 75, 112, 127, 128, 129, 130, 133, 134, 135, 138, 177, 179

Cellini, Benvenuto 93

Central (see Coffee Houses)

Charlemagne 11, 34, 56, 81

Charles of Lorraine 14, 15, 38, 166

Charlotte of Belgium 46

Chotek, Sophie 23

Churches: Am Hof 160, 161;
Augustinerkirche **134-5**, 146, 191;
Burgkapelle **51**, 160;
Capuchin 146, *147*;
Franciscan 136, 171;
Greek Orthodox 133, *175*, 178, **179-80**;
Jesuit 76, *76*, *126*, **135-6**;
Karlskirche 55, 76-7, 85, 118, *129*, **136-8**, *137*;
Lutheran 133, 148;
Maria am Gestade 74, *74*, 164;
Minoritenkirche **138**, *138*;
Ruprechtskirche 163, 164;
Schottenkirche 154;
Votivkirche **72**

Cistercians 177-8

Clemenceau, Georges 28

Coffee Houses: *see p. 105 ff.*
Alt Wien 109, 176-7;

Museum 88, **110-1**, *110*, 112;
Central **106-7**, 112, 156;
Demel **107**, *107*, 111;
Diglas **108**, *108*;
Frauenhuber *170*, 172;
Griensteidl **108-9**, 112, 156;
Hawelka **109**, *109*, 148;
Kleines Café *169*, 171;
Landtmann **109-10**;
Sacher **111**;
Communism, Communists 28, 30, 32, 139
Congress of Vienna 20, 33, 47, 118, 121, **125**, 151, 201
Cooper, Gary 110
Counter Reformation 13, 127, 128, 135
Crimean War 22
Croatia, Croats 21, 23, 166

D

Danube 7, 11, 15, 74, 118, 129, 146, 152, 164, 212
Danube Canal 130, 163, 178
Deodatus, Johannes 105
Demel (*see Coffee Houses*)
Diglas (*see Coffee Houses*)
Dollfuss, Engelbert **28-9**, 30, 48, 72
Domgasse 169
Donner fountain 146
Donner, Georg Raphael 146, 162, *163*
Dorotheum 148

Dual Alliance 22
Dumba, Nikolaus 59, 65
Dürnstein 15, 144

E

Edict of Tolerance 9, 130, 131, **132-3**, 148
Edison, Thomas Alva 186
Eichmann, Adolf 32
Elisabeth, Empress **25**, *25*, 26, 44, 45, *45*, 47, 59, 71, 134, 146, 172, 184, 185, 186-7, 188, 195, 197, 208
Elizabeth of Hungary, St 137-8
England 16, 25, 61, 112, 125, 127, 139 (*see also Great Britain*)
Equitable Palais 145
Esterházy, Miklós (Il Magnifico) 153
Esterházy, Miklós (the Ostentatious) 119
Esterházy, Paul 152
Esterházy, Palais 152
Eugene, Prince of Savoy 9, 16, 39, 53, 54-5, 56-7, 66, 73, 82, 85, 86, **166**, 172

F

Fascism, Fascists 28, 61, 139
Ferdinand, Emperor of Austria 21, 47, 193
Ferdinand I 13
Ferdinand II 51, 91, 128, 130, 135, 138
Ferdinand III 91, 128

Ferdinand of Aragon 127
Ferdinand, Duke of Modena 188-9
Fernwärme (*see Spittelau*)
Figarohaus 121, 169
Figlmüller (*see Restaurants*)
Fischer von Erlach the younger 43, 44, 46, 52, 77, 86, 136
Fischer von Erlach, Johann Bernhard 9, 52, 76, 77, 78, **85-6**, 136, 137, *137*, 144, *144*, 160, 161, 165, 172, 183, 184, 195
Fleischmarkt 178-9
Förster, Emil 68-9
France, French 9, 14, 18, 23, 30, 34, 46, 57, 71, 95, 120, 133, 153, 166, 188, 190
Franciscan Monastery *169*, 171
Frankfurt 34, 196
Franks 11, 34, 50, 56
Franz Ferdinand **23**, 57, 61
Franz I of Austria 9, 18, 21, 34, *34*, 47, *47*, 49, 66, 125, 131, 188, 192
Franz Joseph 9, 21, **21-2**, 23, 25, *25*, 26, 44, 45, 46, 59, 64, 65, 68, 69, 71, 72, 84, 110, 114, 123, 134, 155, 183, 184, 185, 186, 187, 188, 193, 197, 208, 210
Franz Stephan 16, 17, 34, 190, 191, 192, 195-6
Franziskaner-Platz 171
Frauenhuber, Café (*see Coffee Houses*)
Frederick the Great 17, 166, 195
Freud, Sigmund 112, **139**
Freyung *149*, 153

Freyung, passage 151, *151*, 154
Freyung fountain 153
Friedrich III 34, 37, 40-1, 176
Friedrich the Handsome 165
Friedrich the Quarrelsome 129
Fröhlich, Kathi 153, 171
Furtwängler, Wilhelm 116

G
Geymüller, Johann 153
Geymüller Schlössel (*see Museums*)
Germany, Germans (pre WW2) 7, 22, 23, 25, 28, 34, 56, 66, 124, 127
Germany, Germans (WW2, *see also Nazis*) 30, 31, 32, 33, 85
Gerstl, Richard 97
Gestapo 30
Glacis 15, 63, 64, 65
Golden Fleece, Order of 49, *152*, **154-5**, 192
Gothic 37, 39, 51, **74**, 134, 138, 161, 178
Graben 143, 144, 148
Gran, Daniel 52, *73*, 137
Grand Alliance 16
Great Britain 23, 25, 30, 57
Greek Orthodox church (*see Churches*)
Greeks 127, 178, 179
Greene, Graham 181
Griechenbeisl (*see Restaurants*)
Griechengasse *173*, 178
Griensteidl (*see Coffee Houses*)
Grillparzer, Franz **112**, 153, 170-1,

202

Grinzing **198ff**, 203, 212, 214

Gustavus Adolphus, King 13

H

Haas Haus *141*, 145

Habsburgs, general 11, **12-14**, 15, 16, 17, 25, 28, 33, 34, 43, 44, 77, 85, 91, 113, 127, 129, 135, 146, 155, 162, 165, 195

Haimo, Otto 164-5

Hamilton, Johann Georg 191

Hamilton, Sir William 188

Hamilton, Lady Emma 119

Hansen, Theophil 69, 115, 179

Hasenauer, Karl von 68, 70-1, 92

Haydn, Franz Joseph 82, 113, **119-20**, 147, 162, 189

Haus der Musik Wien 116

Hawelka (*see Coffee Houses*)

Heiligenkreuz 26, 177

Heiligenkreuzerhof 177

Heine, Heinrich 25, 187

Heinrich II 11, 33, 154

Heldenplatz 31, 65, **66**, *68*, 69, 104

Herrengasse 101, 156

Herzegovina 23

Heurigen 117, **198-9**, *198*, 203, 207

Hildebrandt, Johann Lukas von 46, 47, 54, 77, *77*, **86**, 154, 170, 172

Himmelpfortgasse 172

Hindemith, Paul 116

Historicism 62, 65, 73, **78-9**, 82, 86, 87, 92, 95, 210

Hitler, Adolf 26, 28, 30, 31-2, 33, 34, 65, 69, 79, 124

Hofburg 25, 34, *35*, *42*, **43ff**, 66, 68, 74, 75, 84, 85, 86, 121, 186, 191, 193, 195, 196, 221

Hoffmann, Josef 98, 103

Hofmannsthal, Hugo von, **112**, 116

Hohenberg, Johann Fedinand von 134, 138, 195

Hoher Markt 162

Holland (see Netherlands)

Holocaust Memorial 130, *131*, 161

Holy Alliance 20

Holy Roman Empire/Emperor 9, 11, 13, 16, 17, 18, 33, **34**, 38, 40, 41, 47, *47*, 49, 50, 56, 81, 91, 125, 129, 136, 187, 188, 191

Horthy, Miklós 26, 197

Hotels: (*see p. 216ff*)
　　　Imperial 65, *78*, 111, *217*

Hundertwasser, Friedensreich **88-90**, *89*, *90*, 145, 200

Hundertwasser House 89-90, *90*, 200

Hungary, Hungarians 7, 11, 13, 14, 15, 17, 21, 22, 23, 26, 33, 37, 41, 55, 72, 127 , 129, 146, 152, 155, 166, 187, 197, 218

Hus, Jan 127

Hussites 129

I

Imperial Chancellery 47

Innsbruck 16, 75

Ireland 25, 186

Isaac, Heinrich 124

Isabella of Castile 127

Isabella of Parma 190, 192

Istanbul 105
Italy, Italians 21, 26, 30, 34, 46, 138, 166, 189, 208

J

Jefferson, Thomas 18
Jesuit church (see Churches)
Jesuits 13, 127, 130, 135
Jews, Jewry 9, 18, 30, 32, 112, 124, 127, 128, **129-32**, 133, 147, 161, 179, 221
Jordan, Johann 161
Jordangasse 161-2
Joseph I 16
Joseph II 9, **17-18**, 34, 46, 55, 74, 92, 113, 120, 130, 131, **132-3**, 138, 143, 148, 153, 154, 160, 166, 171, 179, 180, 185, 187, 188, *189*, 190, 192, 195, 196, 199
Josefsplatz 52, 181
Judenplatz *131*, 161, 165
Judenplatz Museum (see Museums)
Jugendstil 9, 62, 73, **79-82**, 83, 86, 87, **95-6**, 145, 162, 221
Jüdisches Museum (see Museums)

K

Kahlenberg 14, 15, 198, 203
Kaisergruft 26, 133, **146**
Karajan, Herbert von, 116
Kara Mustapha 15
Karl I 26, 28, 33, 70, 183, 191
Karl Marx-Hof *83*, 84, 200, *200*
Karl V 13, 91, 127
Karl VI 16, 44, 52, 77, 91, 136, 191

Karlskirche (see Churches)
Kaspar, Mitzi 26
Karlsplatz 123, 136
Kaunitz, Chancellor 17, 47, 125, 133, **166**, 187, 190
Kärntnerstrasse 102, 146
Kinsky family154
Kinsky, Palais *77*, 86, 154
Kirche am Hof (see Churches)
Kleines Café (see Coffee Houses)
Klemperer, Otto 116
Klimt, Ernst 62, 92
Klimt, Gustav 61, **62-3**, *62*, 65, 71, 79, 81, 92, **95-6**, *96*, 103, 110, 162
Klinger, Max 95
Knize 88, *143*, 144-5
Kokoschka, Oskar **60-1**, *60*, 102, 110
Kohlmarkt 102, 119, 151
Kolin, Battle of 195
Kolschitzky, Franz 169-70
Konzerthaus 114
Königgrätz, Battle of 22, 186
Kornhäusel, Josef 131, 154, 163
Kornhäuselturm 163
Kossuth, Lajos 21, 156
Kunstforum 99, 153
KunstHausWien 90, 99
Kurrentgasse 161
Kursalon 65-6, 114

L

Lamarr, Hedy **181**
Leipzig, Battle of 125
Leopold I 15, 16, 39, 46, 105, 113, **128-9**, 130, 144, *144*

Leopold II 166, 188, *189*, 191, 192

Leopoldsberg 15

Leopoldstadt 118, 119, 125, 130, 164

Leuthen, Battle of 195

Liebenberg, Andreas von 15, 81, 161, 162

Lippizaner horses 44

Liotard, Jean Etienne 188

Lobkowitz family 147

Lobkowitz, Palais 104, 147

Lobkowitz, Prince Joseph 147

Lobmeyr **101-2**

Lombardy 22, 46

London 105, 119, 137, 178

Loos Haus **84-5**, *84*, 88

Loos, Adolf 9, 61, 83, 84-5, *84*, 86, **87-8**, 98, 103, 106, 110, 111, *143*, 145

Lorraine 16

Louis XIV 16, 166, 183

Louis XVI 57, 133

Loyola, St Ignatius 13, 135

Ludwig of Bavaria 134

Lueger, Karl 201

Luther, Martin 127

Lutheran Church (*see Churches*)

Lutherans 128, 148, 177

M

Mackintosh, Charles Rennie, 103

Madeira 26, 197

Magyars (*see Hungary*)

Mahler, Gustav 113, 115, 116, **124**, 216

MAK (*see Museums*)

Makart, Hans **59-60**, *60*, 62, 65, *66*, 92, 101, *101*

Marcus Aurelius 7, 81, 162

Mann, Thomas 112

Maria am Gestade (*see Churches*)

Maria Amalia 188

Maria Anna 187-8

Maria Elisabeth 188

Maria Josepha of Bavaria 187, 188

Maria Karoline 188

Maria Ludovica of Spain 120, 191

Maria Theresa **16-17**, *17*, 18, 34, 46, 47, 51, 52, 53, 57, 78, 82, 91-2, 117, 118, 120, 121, 132, 133, 134, 146, 148, 153, 166, 172, 183, 184, 187, *189*, 190, 191, 192, 193, 195, 196

Maria Valerie 188

Marie Antoinette 18, 57, 133, 153, 188, *190*

Marie Christine 53, 134, 166, 188, 192

Marie Leopoldine 193

Marie Louise 9, *10*, 20, 49, 71, 118, 125, 134-5, 191, 193

Marlborough, Duke of 16, 166

Matsch, Franz 81, 92, 162

Matthias Corvinus 7, 13, 33, 37, 41, 48, 193

Matthias, Emperor 193

Maulbertsch, Franz Anton 52, **55**, 134, *135*

Max Franz 121, 189

Maximilian I **13**, 16, 41, 52, 74, 81, 113, 155

Maximilian II 128, 183, 193

Maximilian, Emperor of Mexico **45-6**, 72, 186
Mayerling 26
Mehmed IV 15
Metternich, Count, later Prince 18, 20, 48, 102, 111, **125**, *125* 191
Mexico 30, 46
Meytens, Martin van *17*, 190
Middleton, Bay 186
Milan 47, 92, 136, 138
Mill, John Stuart 65
Miller, Henry 109
Minoritenkirche (*see Churches*)
Minoriten-Platz 155
Mongols 11, 129
Montagu, Lady Mary Wortley 63, 162
Montenuovo, Prince 71
Morris, William 103
Moser, Kolo 97, 98, 103
Mozart, Wolfgang Amadeus 113, 114, **120-1**, *120*, 121, 143, 169, 171, 172, 184, 189, 191, 221
MUMOK (*see Museums: Modern Art*)
Munich 134, 153
Munkácsy, Mihály 92
Museums: Albertina 52-3, 192;
　　　Applied Arts (*see MAK, below*);
　　　Beethoven 122;
　　　Clock 104;
　　　Ethnographic 104;
　　　Figarohaus 121 169;
　　　Folklore 104;
　　　Geymüller Schlössel 101, 153;

　　　Haydn 120;
　　　Jewish (Jüdisches) 132
　　　Judenplatz 130-1;
　　　Kunsthistorisches 62, **91ff**, *92, 94*;
　　　Leopold **97-8**, 103, 111;
　　　MAK 100, 102, 103, 104, 210;
　　　Modern Art (MUMOK) 97, *98*;
　　　Mozart (*see Figarohaus*);
　　　Natural History, 92, 104;
　　　Schubert 122;
　　　Theatre 104;
　　　Treasury (*Schatzkammer*) **49-51**;
　　　Vienna History 104, 177;
　　　Wagenburg **196**
Museumsquartier **97-8**, *97, 98*, 103
Musikverein 65, 101, *113*, **115-6**, 123, 221
Musil, Robert **112**
Mussolini, Benito 30

N
Naples 188
Napoleon 9, **18**, *19*, 33, 34, 47, 48, 49, 50, 51, **56**, 66, 71, 74, 92, 118, 120, 121, 125, 134, 138, 147, 152, 183, 184, 189, 191, 193
Napoleon Franz (see Reichstadt)
Napoleon III 22, 46
National Library 13, **52**, 74, 85, *85*
Nazis 28, 29, 30, 31, 32, 37, 70, 72, 112, 130, 132, 139, 163, 181
Nelson, Horatio, Lord 119, 188

Netherlands 13, 16, 91
Neue Burg **68-9**, 104
Neuer Markt 146
Neupauer-Brauner, Palais 170
New World 13, 127
Nuremberg 34, 49, 51
Nussdorf 198, 201, 212
Nüll, Eduard van der 114

O
Olbrich, Josef 80
Opera House 59, 64, **114-5**, *116*,
122, 124, 221
Orthodox church (*see Churches*)
Ostmark 11
Otto the Great 11, 51
Otto von Habsburg 26
Ottokar, King of Bohemia 11
Ottomans (Turks) 13, 14, **15**, 33,
38, 39, 43, 46, 55, 56, 70, 73, 74,
75, 105, 128, 130, 138, 161, 164,
166, 169, 183, 198, 203
Ottoman siege (*see Siege of Vienna*)

P
Pacassi, Nikolaus 52, 78, 134, 184,
189
Paris 18, 28, 49, 62, 79, 105, 138,
166
Parkring 64, 65
Parliament **69**, *69*
Philip de Bourbon 16
Philip II of Spain 91
Pilgram, Anton 39, 40, *40*
Poland, Polish 14, 15, 28, 127, 181,
201

Popes, general 11, 26, 34
Popes: Leo III 34
          Leo X 165
          Pius VI 160, 166
Popper, Sir Karl **139**
Portugal 197
Postsparkasse 86-7, *86*
Pozzo, Andrea 76, 135, 136, 171
Pragmatic Sanction 16
Prague 13, 21, 49, 91, 128
Prater 130, 132, 181
Pre-March (*see Biedermeier*)
Princip, Gavrilo 23
Protestants, Protestantism 9, 13,
127, 128, 129, 130, 132, 133, 138,
148, 177
Providentia fountain 146
Prussia 17, 20, 22, 23, 48, 125, 195
Puchsbaum, Hans 37, 39, 81, 162

R
Radetzky, Field Marshal 21, 22, 66,
117
Rathaus **70**, *70*, 109, 220
Rauhensteingasse 171
Red Army (*see Russians*)
Reichstadt, Duke of 34, 49-50, **191-
2**, 197
Reinhardt, Max 110, 181
Reinprecht, *Heuriger 199*, 203
Rembrandt 91, 98
Renaissance 44, 48, 54, 59, **74-5**,
85, 114, 115, 164, 176
Renner, Karl 26, 28, 70
Restaurants (*see p. 206ff*)
          Brandl 203, *214*;

Figlmüller 176;
Griechenbeisl 178;
Trześniewski 148, *148*
Revolutions of 1848-9 **21**, 33, 63-4,
72, 100, 117, 125, 134, 152, 155,
156, 160, 162
Ribbentrop, Joachim von 30
Ricci, Sebastiano 137
Richard I, King of England 144
Rilke, Rainer Maria 112
Ringstrasse 59, 62, **63ff**, *64*, **79**, 80,
83, 87, 101, 114, 123
Rodin, Auguste 112, 115
Roman, Romans 7, 11, 34, 57, 81,
136, 144, 159, 162, 164, 176
Rome 34, 76, 85, 86, 135
Rome, King of (*see Reichstadt*)
Rosa, Joseph 189
Rosenkavalier, der 112, **116-7**
Rottmayr, Johann 55, 136
Rubens 91, 98
Rudolf II 47, 49, 91, 128
Rudolf the Founder 12
Rudolf von Habsburg 11, 33, 81
Rudolf, Crown Prince **26**, 65, 177,
197
Rupert, St 163, 164, *164*
Ruprechtskirche (*see Churches*)
Russia, Russian (pre-Soviet)20, 21,
22, 25, 48, 125, 155
Russia, Russian (Soviet) 32, *32*, 33,
54, 57, 106-7, 139
Russell, Bertrand 139

S
Sacher (*see Coffee Houses*)

Sacher, Anna 111
Sacher, Eduard 111
Sacher, Franz 111
Sachertorte **111**
Salvatorkapelle 164-5
Salzburg 55, 120, 143, 164
Sarajevo 23
Savoy 1
Saxony, Saxon 11, 34
Schatzkammer (*see Museums*)
Schiele, Egon **61-2**, *61*, 98, *99*, 103,
110
Schiller, Friedrich 95
Schindler, Emil Jakob, 98
Schmidt, Friedrich 70
Schnitzler, Arthur 106, **112**
Schoenberg, Arnold 97, 114, **124**
Schotten Abbey 154
Schottenkirche (*see Churches*)
Schönbrunn 18, 78, 81, 85, 110,
118, 120, **183ff**, *187*, *194*, *196*
Schönlaterngasse 177
Schrammel **117**, *117*, 199
Schratt, Katharina 45, 71-2
Schubert, Franz 59, 100, 113, **122**,
124, 162, 170, 171, 221
Schuschnigg, Kurt 26, **30**, 31
Schwarzenberg, Palais 53
Schwarzenberg, Prince Felix 21, 22
Schwarzenbergplatz 198
Schwind, Moritz von **58-9**, *59*, 115
Secession Building **80-1**, *80*, 95
Secession Movement 62, 79, 80, 95,
98, 102
Seitz, Karl 114
Semper, Gottfried 68, 71, 92

Serbia, Serbs 21, 23, 25
Sicardsburg, August Sicard von, 114
Sicily 50
Siege of Vienna **15**, 81, 82, 161, 166, 203
Silesia 17
Singerstrasse 170
Sisi (see Elisabeth)
Slavs 7, 23, 30
Sobieski, Jan **14**, 15, *15*, 38
Solferino, Battle of 22, 46
Soviets (*see Russians, Soviet*)
Spain, Spanish 13, 16, 33, 44, 77, 127, 155
Spanish Riding School 16, **43-44**, 75, 191, 221
Spittelau incinerator 89, *89*, 200
St Germain, Treaty of 28, 33
Stadtpark **65-6**, 114
Stadttempel **131-2**, *132*, 133, 163
Starhemberg, Count Ernst Rüdiger von **15**, 38, 81-2, 154, 156
Starhemberg, Palais *155*, 156
Stephanie of Belgium 26
Stephansdom 12, **37ff**, *38*, *40*, 74, 80, 81, 119, 146, 169, 221
Stock-im-Eisen **145-6**
Strauss, Johann (the Elder) 66, 114, **117**, 154, 216
Strauss, Johann (the Younger) 113, 114, **117**, *118*, 154, 216
Strauss, Richard 112, 116
Strohmayer, Alois 117
Styria 118, 211

Sweden, Swedes 13, 51, 159-60
Switzerland, Swiss 13, 26, 48, 189, 197
Synagogue (*see Stadttempel*)

T
Tegetthoff, Admiral 130
Teutonic Knights 170
Third Man, the 148, **181**, 221
Thirty Years War 13, 14, 51, 159, 164
Thonet 90, 98, **102**, *102*, 108, 210
Titian 91, 98
Toleranzhaus *133*, 179, 180
Toscanini, Arturo 112, 116
Trafalgar, Battle of 189
Treasury (*see Museums*)
Trieste 26, 46
Trześniewski (*see Restaurants*)
Turkey, Turks (*see Ottomans*)
Tuscany 22, 188
Tyrol 118

U
United States (*see America*)

V
Velázquez 91
Versailles 183
Vetsera, Mary 26, 177
Vienna Boys' Choir 13, 51, 74, 113
Vienna History Museum (*see Museums*)
Vienna Woods 28, 125, 201
Vienna, Battle of 32

Vinci, Leonardo da 138
Vindobona 7, 11, 81
Vogelweide, Walther von der 81,
162
Volksgarten 68, 71
Vorlauf, Konrad 147

W

Wagenburg (*see Museums*)
Wagner, Otto 9, 80, 82, *82*, 84, **86-7**, *86*, *87*, 98, 103, 145
Wagner, Richard 95, 134, 216
Wagram, Battle of 66
Waldmüller, Ferdinand **58**, 98, *100*
Wallnerstrasse 152
Walter, Bruno 116
Waltz **118**
War of the Spanish Succession **16**
Waterloo, Battle of 20
Weber, Constanze 143
Webern, Anton von, **124**
Welles, Orson 181
Wellington, Duke of 151
White Mountain, Battle of 128
Wien, river 65, 136, 183
Wiener Neustadt 41, 78
Wiener Werkstätte 60, 98, **103**
Wilder, Billy 178, **181**
Wilhelm, Kaiser 26
Willendorf Venus 104
Windischgrätz, Prince Albert 21
Windsor, Duke of 110
Wine 37, 198, 199, **211ff**
Winter Palace 85, 86, 172
Wittgenstein, Ludwig 110, **139**

Wollzeile 175
World War I 9, 25, 26, 27, 57, 103,
186, 201
World War II 31, 32, 37, 39, 69,
80, 114, 115, 122, 134, 162, 163
Württemberg 34, 48

Z

Zauner, Franz Anton 195
Zita, Empress 26, 197
Zweig, Stefan 106, **112**

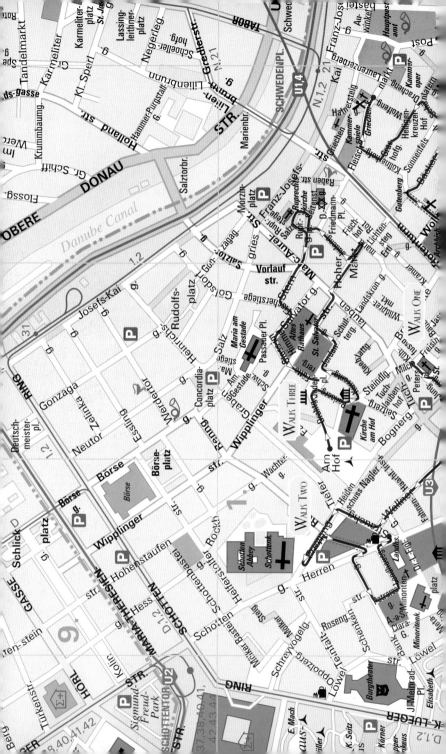

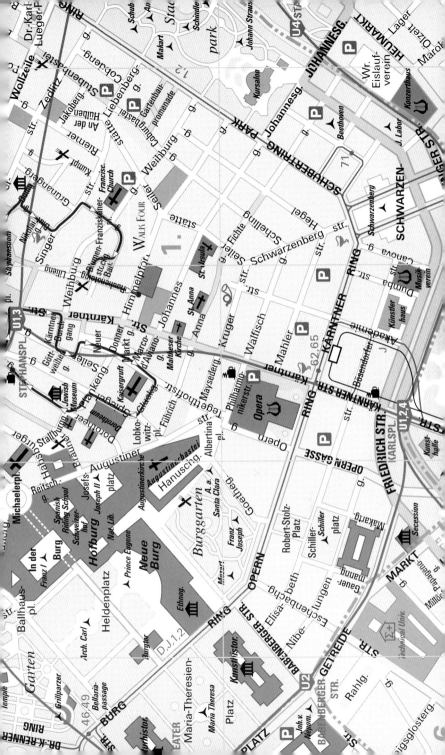

MAP REFERENCES FOR CENTRAL VIENNA MAP

NB: Most of the sights and places of interest mentioned in this guide are in central Vienna. Inevitably this is not always the case, and some are beyond the scope of this map.

HOTELS & PENSIONS

Imperial D3-4
Kärntnerhof B4
König von Ungarn C4
Nossek B/C3
Pertschy C3
Sacher D3
Triest E2
Wandl B3

CAFÉS & RESTAURANTS

American Bar C3
Central B2
Demel C2
Diglas C4
Do & Co C3
Figlmüller B4
Gigerl Stadtheuriger C3
Griechenbeisl B4
Griensteidl C2
Hawelka C3
Indochine C5
Königsbacher D3
Landtmann B1
MAK Café C5
Mörwald C3
Museum D1
Novelli C3
Oswald & Kalb B4
Palmenhaus C2
Plachutta C5
Sacher D3
Santo Spirito C4

Zum Basilisken B4

STREETS, SQUARES & QUARTERS

Albertinaplatz C3
Annagasse C3
Augustinerstrasse C2-3
Bäckerstrasse B4
Ballhausplatz C2
Berggasse A1-2
Blumenstockgasse C3-4
Bösendorferstrasse D3
Bräunerstrasse C3
Burggarten C/D2
Canovagasse D4
Domgasse C4
Dorotheergasse C3
Dorotheergasse C3
Dr Ignaz Seipel-Platz B4
Dr Karl Lueger-Ring B/C1
Freyung B2
Friedrichstrasse D2-3
Georg Coch-Platz B5
Graben B/C3
Grashofgasse B4
Grinzing (*see map on p. 201*)
Habsburgergasse C2-3
Hanuschgasse C2
Heiligenstädterstrasse - see map on p. ???
Heldenplatz C2
Herrengasse B2

Himmelpfortgasse C3-4
Hoher Markt B3-4
In der Burg C2
Jasomirgottgasse B3
Josefsplatz C2
Judenplatz B3
Karlsplatz D/E4
Kärntner Durchgang C3
Kärntnerring D3-4
Kärntnerstrasse C/D3
Kettenbrückenstrasse E1
Kohlmarkt C2-B3
Kumpfgasse C4
Kurrentgasse B3
Leopoldstadt A4-5
Linke Wienzeile E1-D2
Lobkowitz-Platz C3
Lothringerstrasse D4
Maria Theresien-Platz C/D1
Maysedergasse C3
Michaelerplatz C2
Minoritenplatz B2
Mölker Bastei B1-2
Museumsplatz C/D1
Naglergasse B2-3
Neuer Markt C3
Obere Donaustrasse A4
Opernring D2-3
Petersplatz B3
Philharmonikerstrasse D3
Rauhensteingasse C3
Rennweg E5
Satvatorgasse B3

Schillerplatz D2
Schönlaterngasse B4-5
Schulerstrasse C4
Schwarzenbergplatz D/E4
Schweizerhof C2
Seilerstätte C4
Seitenstettengasse B4
Spiegelgasse C3
Stadtpark C5-D4/5
Stubenring B/C5
Universitätsstrasse A1
Volksgarten B1-C2
Walfischgasse D3
Wallnerstrasse B2-3
Wiedner Hauptstrasse E2-D3
Wollzeile B4-C5

MUSEUMS, GALLERIES & CONCERT HALLS

Academy of Fine Art D2
Albertina C3
Beethovenhaus (*see map on p. 201*)
Beethovens Wohnung B1-2
Belvedere E5
Clock Museum B3
Ethnographic C2
Figarohaus C4
Freud House A2
Haus der Musik C4
Jewish Museum B3, C3
Konzerthaus D4
Kunstforum B2
Kunsthistorisches D1-2
Künstlerhaus D3

Kursalon D4
Leopold Museum D1
MAK C5
Museum of Modern Art D1
Museumsquartier D1
Musikverein D3
Natural History C1
Opera House D3
Palais Harrach B2
Schubert-Sterbewohnung E1
Secession D2
Theatre Museum C3
Vienna History Museum E3-4

SIGHTS & MONUMENTS

Anker Clock B4
Belvedere E5
Burgtheater B1
Chancellery B/C2
Hofburg C2
Kaisergruft C3
Karl Marx-Hof (*see map on p. 201*)
Loos Haus C2
National Library C2
Neue Hofburg C2
Palais Kinsky B2
Parliament C1
Postsparkasse B5
Rathaus B1
Spanish Riding School C2
Winter Palace C3

CHURCHES & SYNAGOGUES

Augustinerkirche C2
Burgkapelle C2
Capuchin Church C3
Greek Orthodox Church B4
Jesuit Church B4
Karlskirche E4
Maria am Gestade B3
Minoritenkirche B2
Schottenkirche B2
Stadttempel B4
Stephansdom C3-4
Votivkirche A1

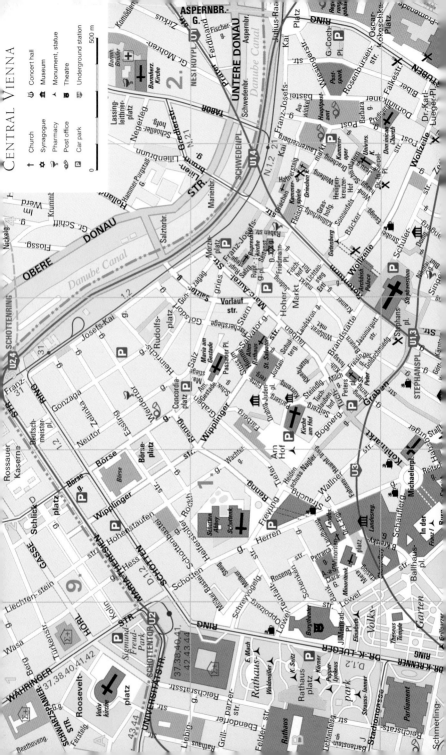

CENTRAL VIENNA

- ✝ Church
- ✡ Synagogue
- 💊 Pharmacy
- 〰 Post office
- 🅿 Car park
- ♫ Concert hall
- 🏛 Museum
- ⚓ Monument, statue
- 🎭 Theatre
- Ⓤ Underground station

0   500 m